Basic Linux Terminal Tips and Tricks

Learn to Work Quickly on the Command Line

Philip Kirkbride

Apress®

Basic Linux Terminal Tips and Tricks: Learn to Work Quickly on the Command Line

Philip Kirkbride
Montreal, QC, Canada

ISBN-13 (pbk): 978-1-4842-6034-0   ISBN-13 (electronic): 978-1-4842-6035-7
https://doi.org/10.1007/978-1-4842-6035-7

Managing Director, Apress LLC: Welmoed Spahr
Acquisitions Editor: Louise Corrigan
Development Editor: James Markham
Coordinating Editor: Nancy Chen

Cover designed by eStudioCalamar

Cover image designed by Freepik (www.freepik.com)

Distributed to the book trade worldwide by Springer Science+Business Media New York, 1 New York Plaza, New York, NY 10004. Phone 1-800-SPRINGER, fax (201) 348-4505, e-mail orders-ny@springer-sbm.com, or visit www.springeronline.com. Apress Media, LLC is a California LLC and the sole member (owner) is Springer Science + Business Media Finance Inc (SSBM Finance Inc). SSBM Finance Inc is a **Delaware** corporation.

For information on translations, please e-mail rights@apress.com, or visit http://www.apress.com/rights-permissions.

Apress titles may be purchased in bulk for academic, corporate, or promotional use. eBook versions and licenses are also available for most titles. For more information, reference our Print and eBook Bulk Sales web page at http://www.apress.com/bulk-sales.

Any source code or other supplementary material referenced by the author in this book is available to readers on GitHub via the book's product page, located at www.apress.com/9781484260340. For more detailed information, please visit http://www.apress.com/source-code.

Printed on acid-free paper

Dedicated to the open source community.

Table of Contents

About the Author

Philip Kirkbride has been developing software for over 10 years. After college he worked as a contractor developing websites and mobile apps in Southern Ontario, Canada. He has since worked at several software and hardware startups and contributed to open source projects. He is currently a research assistant on Dr. Fuhua (Oscar) Lin's Adaptive Cyberlearning research team, creating educational software used in COMP 272 *Data Structures and Algorithms and COMP 372 Design and Analysis of Algorithms* at Athabasca University. He is also a mentor for Manning's short course *Use Machine Learning to Detect Phishing Websites* and co-author of 2 books on JavaScript, Professional JavaScript (Packt, 2019), and *The JavaScript Workshop* (Packt, 2019). When he is not working or learning new things, he enjoys spending time outdoors. He can be reached at kirkins@gmail.com.

About the Technical Reviewer

 **David Both** is an Open Source Software and GNU/Linux advocate, trainer, writer, and speaker. He has been working with Linux and Open Source Software for more than 20 years and has been working with computers for over 45 years. He is a strong proponent of and evangelist for the "Linux Philosophy for System Administrators." David has been in the IT industry for over 40 years. He is the author of *The Linux Philosophy for SysAdmins* (Apress, 2018) and the three-volume set, *Using and Administering Linux* (Apress, 2019).

Acknowledgments

I'd like to thank the open source community and the developers of utilities explored in this book. Most of the ideas and techniques shared here have been learned with the help of the many developers online always willing to help with small and large problems. A number of people have contributed feedback and suggestions including Jason, Omm, and various users from the Unix SE and Telegram. I'd also like to acknowledge my grandfather Douglas Kirkbride for encouraging my early interest in computers, my parents, family, friends Colin, Matt, my thesis advisor Dr. Fuhua (Oscar) Lin, and the tech community in Waterloo, Ontario (Communitech, BlackBerry, ect.) where I was able to meet many talented people like Taylor Brynes who introduced me to SSH and Qbo who increased my expectations of what a quality user experience is. As well as Jasmine Samaras whose antics kept me entertained during the process of writing this book.

I'd also like to thank the editors at Apress – Louise Corrigan, Nancy Chen, and James Markham – for helping to mold the idea into a book as well as the technical reviewer David Both who has provided great feedback and adjustments.

Introduction

Despite graphics being more advanced than ever, the Linux terminal, or command line, continues to be one of the most useful tools for software developers, system admins, and IT professionals to know. From the terminal, complex tasks can be launched in a few words, when the equivalent action would take several steps in a GUI. In other cases, things which can be done from the command line are simply not possible from the GUI of an operating system.

In a world where many devices are embracing mobile-style interfaces which limit users, the power of the Linux terminal can feel freeing. It gives you fine-grained control of your system and the tasks you run. The only requirement is that you learn the magic words that will manifest what you want to happen. This book is for those who want to learn about the Linux terminal, bash, and terminal-based utilities.

Much of what you'll read here is applicable in many places due to the ubiquity of Linux. Whether it be your desktop OS, a remote server running a website, or physical hardware, if it's running Linux, you can access the command line.

CHAPTER 1

Linux Primer

Most people growing up today are introduced to computers through a graphical interface, whether it be through a video game console, a laptop, or an iPad. For most people's interactions with computers are done through a graphical interface of some sort. Despite the popularity of graphical interfaces, most serious programming and system administration are still done at the command-line level.

Graphics keep getting better. Innovations like voice-activated computing, wearables, and IoT are introducing even more ways to interact with computers. New versions of popular operating systems on both desktop and mobile are constantly changing. Yet it seems underneath most of these new systems from IoT to Android, there is a command-line world that exists in a stable state while everything built on top changes.

The persistence of the Linux operating system and the terminal command line as a method of input speaks to its efficiency and usefulness. While the simple green text on a black background may appear outdated, it is actually a gateway to magic-like efficiency. Each command is like a spell. With a few keystrokes, we can perform tasks and tricks that would take an eternity using a mouse and GUI. In some cases, we can even do things on the command line that would otherwise be impossible using a GUI.

This book is for the person who wants to explore Linux from a command-line perspective – whether you're completely new and learning from command line from square one or you know your way around a Linux machine but want to learn some new commands and utilities that could come in handy.

In this chapter, we'll look at what Linux is, review some popular distributions (*or distros*), and look at some basic commands for dealing with files and directories.

What Is Linux

Throughout this book, we'll be looking at different command-line applications, built-in commands, and techniques. Before we start, it's worth touching on "what is Linux." Some technical definitions will only include the Linux kernel (*the core part which works with the underlying hardware of a computer*).

1

© Philip Kirkbride 2020
P. Kirkbride, *Basic Linux Terminal Tips and Tricks*, https://doi.org/10.1007/978-1-4842-6035-7_1

Often such definitions will define the distributions as GNU/Linux. GNU is a recursive acronym which stands for "GNU is Not Linux." It refers to all (*or several*) open source applications which are popularly bundled with the Linux kernel. Some of these tools include `bash`, `coreutils`, `grep`, `groff`, `grub`, and `readline`, just to name a few. That said, not all the tools that commonly ship with the Linux kernel are created by the GNU organization.

In common language, Linux refers to an operating system which is built around the Linux kernel. This includes the kernel, the software that comes preinstalled, and everything in between. For simplicity and compatibility with common language use, we'll refer to Linux as the whole of an operating system, not just the kernel.

Unix vs. Linux

Linux is actually part of a larger group of operating systems which are known as "Unix-like" operating systems. These operating systems are all inspired by the original Unix operating system released in 1970. It includes several families of operating systems beyond just Linux:

- MacOS (since 2015)

- Android (built on modified Linux kernel)

- Linux

- Solaris

- BSD

- NetBSD

You might be surprised to see popular operating systems like MacOS and Android listed here. The impact of the original Unix operating system has been far reaching. The original Unix OS had key features still present today including

- Kernel between hardware and user space

- All data stored as files

- System for users and permissions

- Directory layout still used today (varies between OSs)

In Figure 1-1, a setup making use of PDP-11/20 (*the device furthest right below the experiment display system label*) is shown. This is an example of an early system which ran Unix in the 1970s.

Figure 1-1. *PDP 11/35, a microprogrammed successor to the PDP-11/20; the design team was led by Jim O'Loughlin*

The impact of the widespread adoption of Unix-based standards has been far reaching. Many of the core commands and utilities covered in this book will actually work on systems besides Linux. If you open a terminal session on a Mac or even Android, you'll find many of the commands here work just fine. Even Windows now includes an optional Linux subsystem, and various aliases on their own commandline system that direct Linux commands to their Windows equivilent, such as '`ls`' which is an alias for '`dir`' on Windows.

POSIX Standard

POSIX stands for Portable Operating System Interface. It defines standard syntax for scripts and a list of utilities that should be available. It's used to guarantee compatibility among Unix-like systems. If a program or operating system is POSIX compliant, you can expect bash scripts to run on it.

POSIX also guarantees that you will have access to a list of utilities including, among others, `cat`, `awk`, `cut`, `grep`, and `kill`, just to name a few. It also defines how the specified utilities should behave. In previous times, some utilities had competing implementations which created problems for portability.

Choosing a Distro

The first major decision that most people face when switching to Linux is what distribution *(commonly refered to as distro)* to use. Often people end up using what a friend or colleagues at work are using or simply the first one we hear about. There are dozens of popular distributions, each with strengths, weaknesses, and specific use cases it excels at.

Throughout this book, I'll be making use of `apt-get`, the package manager which comes installed on Ubuntu and other Debian-based operating systems. That said, almost all of which is presented will work just as well on any Linux distribution; it's just a matter of finding the package in question for your distribution and installing it via the provided package manager, manually installing it, or even building it from source.

There is an argument to be made for many popular Linux distributions. My personal choice in using Ubuntu mainly comes down to the aspect of compatibility. Ubuntu is the most widely used Linux distribution for desktop users. If you're working at a company that makes use of Linux, you may find it useful to use the distro which is used there. Despite the portability of bash and other aspects of Linux, there are differences between distros and bugs which may exist in one but not another. So if you're using Linux Mint but everyone else is using Fedora, you may be introducing unnecessary friction.

In my experience developing GUI-based applications for Linux, I found if I used a distro different from the end-user during development, there would often be visual differences which effected the design significantly or in some cases bugs present in only a single distro. For instance the system font-family or font-size might differ between end-user system and development system. Though in most cases the core functionality works across most Linux systems. The high variability between Linux distros is one reason much of the gaming industry is still yet to offer full support for Linux based operating systems.

Another benefit to starting with a popular distro is that when reading online tutorials and project documentation, you'll often see instructions for more popular Linux distributions like Ubuntu but nothing for less popular ones. In addition, if you do have issues and you want to submit a bug, the project may not provide support for less used distros.

With that said, there can be major benefits of running less used distros. As a young hobbyist, I found that running minimal distros like Arch Linux forced me to learn concepts about what components made up a Linux distro and how to navigate and fix my system using the command line. Often this learning process manifests itself in experimenting, breaking a system, fixing it, and in some cases having to reinstall everything and start from scratch.

If that exploring distributions and the inner workings of Linux excites you, I encourage you to explore Linux distros which are less used and may be more difficult to set up. Gentoo even requires the user to compile from code all the programs used. Getting up and running on a distro like Gentoo or Arch Linux can be an accomplishment and a learning process within itself.

Aside from the factors of convenience and learning process, it's also important to consider where one distro may excel over another. For example, Arch Linux is particularly useful for compiling custom operating systems for embedded or low-end machines. Kali Linux is notorious for its use in penetration testing. Red Hat–based distros are commonly used for enterprise servers. If penetration testing interests you, Kali becomes the obvious choice; if you want to be a system admin at an enterprise company, you may want to become comfortable with Fedora.

Branches of OSs

In the following sections, we're going to look at some of the more popular Linux distributions. I've included a tree showing the family branches of operating systems, to give you an idea of the relationship between different popular operating systems. Keep in mind that the relationship between parent/child OSs may vary significantly (see Figure 1-2).

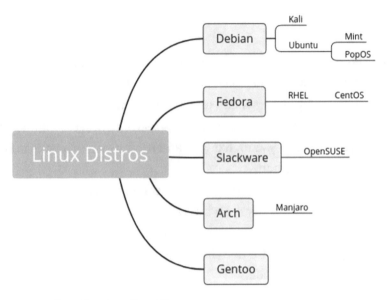

Figure 1-2. *Linux distribution families*

Debian

First released in 1993, Debian is the backbone of several popular Linux distributions including Ubuntu, Kali, and Linux Mint. It's known for having a very good packaging system apt, short for Advanced Package Tool. We'll be using apt throughout this book, and it is available on all the Debian-based operating systems listed later, though the packages which are available through the manager will differ between OSs.

To install packages with apt, simply run the following command, substituting <package> for the package you're looking to install:

```
sudo apt-get install <package>
```

Note   sudo in the preceding command is a keyword that lets a nonroot user make changes to files or aspects of the system which may affect other users. When using sudo, you'll be prompted to enter your password before being able to execute a command as a root. If you run a command and get back the message "Permission denied," you can simply prepend the command with sudo and it should work. That said, make sure you understand the command in question before using sudo as root permissions allow you to modify system files which are critical for the running of the operating system.

Ubuntu

Ubuntu is the most popular Linux distribution for desktop use, though it is commonly used for servers as well. It builds upon Debian and adds support for several nonfree software binaries and codecs that improve user experience for things like watching videos online and gaming.

It has many of the advantages that Debian has like the strong package manager apt and stability but is also designed to provide a good desktop experience. At present, the latest version of Ubuntu uses the GNOME interface (i.e., the GUI desktop of the operating system, which sits on top of lower-level software).

There are several variations of Ubuntu that usc other desktop user interfaces that may be preferable for lower-end hardware such as Xubuntu which uses xfce and Lubuntu which uses lxqt. These distributions generally just switch out the interface without changing much else. If you look at Figure 1-3 which shows the stack of Linux OS, the difference between Xubuntu/Lubuntu would for the most part simply be switching out the interface level, as well as swaping some of the preinstalled applications.

A comparison is how web applications like Facebook often have different interfaces to access the same core functionality. When using my phone, I can access Facebook using their website, their app, or even a lightweight version called Facebook Lite. All of these interfaces look different and may have enhancements or limitations, but ultimately all the functions (posting, viewing, liking, etc.) access the same core functionality.

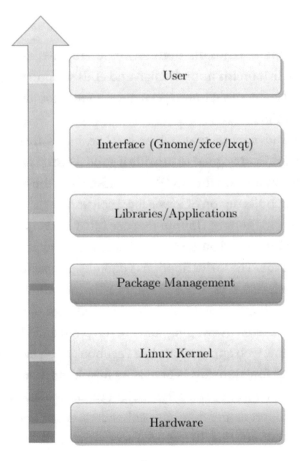

Figure 1-3. *Linux operating system stack*

Kali

Kali is a Debian-based distribution which is primarily focused on offensive security tools. It includes several preinstalled tools for digital forensics, penetration testing, and reverse engineering. It comes with over 600 preinstalled tools including Wireshark, Aircrack-ng, and Burp Suite. This makes it particularly useful for penetration testers. That said, it isn't recommended for everyday use.

It's also worth noting that these tools can be installed on other systems either via package manager or downloading them directly. The process is fairly straightforward for package managers, but when downloading directly, the process can vary between tools. For example, some packages might be installed via Python's package manager Pip, while others require you compile a binary or download a precompiled binary and put it in a folder where your system finds executables, for example, /usr/bin.

Another benefit of using Kali is that versions of tools on package managers on other distros may be older versions. Since these packages are just one of many which require maintainers to package, review, and update, they can fall behind, whereas on Kali, Linux security–related tools are the focus, and thus more effort is put into keeping them up to date.

Mint

Mint is another distribution that is based on Ubuntu which has become relatively popular. Linux Mint is based on Ubuntu but has an alternative interface which makes use of the Cinnamon desktop environment. It has the same repositories as Ubuntu so any of the `apt-get install` commands throughout this book should provide the same results as Ubuntu.

PopOS

PopOS is another Ubuntu-based distribution that has gained traction. It provides an alternative desktop experience to Ubuntu with the same packages, plus some additional packages provided via PPAs (Personal Package Archives). These extra packages include Nvidia graphics drivers, Steam, and other popular programs like Spotify. The operating system is maintained by System76, a computer manufacturer based in Colorado which focuses on producing quality hardware and values open source software.

Fedora

Fedora is the community-driven OS supported by Red Hat Linux. Fedora serves as a testing ground for many features which are eventually pulled into RHEL (Red Hat Enterprise Linux), Red Hat's primary product. For Fedora, RHEL, and CentOS, packages are installed using the command

```
dnf install <package>
```

In some cases, you may be able to simply swap `apt-get` for `dnf` if you're on a Fedora/ RHEL system. In other cases, the package may be named slightly different, or it may not be available as a package.

RHEL (Red Hat Enterprise Linux)

While Ubuntu may be the most popular distro used on desktops, RHEL is likely the most used on enterprise servers. It is both open source and a paid product, which includes enterprise-level support. If you plan to work as a system admin in a corporate environment, it's likely you'll work with RHEL.

The focus is security, stability, and speed. For this reason, there may be less packages available compared to Ubuntu or the more open version supported by Red Hat, Fedora.

CentOS

While Fedora is a more experimental and open free version of RHEL, CentOS is essentially the same OS as RHEL but completely free. When a license for RHEL is bought, it comes with support which is not included with CentOS. CentOS provides a great operating system for learning RHEL or simply using it without the need for external support.

Slackware

Slackware is a Linux distribution that dates back to 1993. It has a small dedicated group of fans but has not had a release in over 3 years, when it previously had a release at least once a year.

OpenSUSE

OpenSUSE was originally derived from Slackware, but it has grown its own set of legs and today has very little connection. While Slackware has been lacking in updates, OpenSUSE is still very active and has large corporate backing similar to what is seen with RHEL.

Arch

Arch Linux is a branch of Linux which is highly customizable and focuses on a rolling release package manager. The rolling release package manager means that packages provided are the most up to date possible. There are no major releases as is the case with most operating systems. This is achieved by removing package maintainers who review and confirm any changes before a major release on other distributions. A rolling release means it is possible to get the most up-to-date versions of applications, but on the downside less effort is put into reviews which can potentially lead to stability and security issues.

Packages are installed using the pacman package manager:

```
sudo pacman -S <package>
```

Another notable aspect of Arch Linux is the fact that by default it doesn't ship with the software required to run a desktop experience. Instead it is left up to the user to choose the specific programs for things like sound, window manager, and graphical interface.

Manjaro

Manjaro is a version of Arch Linux which addresses the difficulty of getting started by shipping with a preconfigured desktop experience. There are several variations as is the case with Ubuntu having variations like Xubuntu and Kubuntu.

Gentoo

Gentoo is a highly customizable version of Linux, which allows customization down to the kernel level. Instead of downloading precompiled applications, Gentoo actually compiles from source code on the local computer. It is particularly useful when a highly customized experience is needed.

Alpine Linux

Alpine Linux is a distro which essentially no one uses as their primary distro for desktop or servers, yet it is extremely popular as a base image for Docker containers. If you use or modify Docker containers, you'll likely run into Alpine Linux. It's extremely small and by default comes with nearly no applications though it does have its own package manager apk.

If you have an application or process you want to containerize with Docker, look into Alpine Linux. Many of the programs and scripts here are compatible, though if any programs are used, you'll have to install them first using apk.

Common Commands

In the following subsections, we'll look at common commands, most of which are installed on most Linux systems by default.

Reading the Manual with the man Command

I'll mention many programs throughout this book. For most of them, I'll only go into about 5–10% of their usage at best. If you want to explore these programs deeper, it's important you learn the man command which can be found on almost all Linux operating systems.

man is short for manual. It is used by running the command and passing in the name of another Linux command-line program. For example, if we wanted to get more information on the command ls, we would run the following:

```
man ls
```

This returns a description of the program and how to use it, as shown in Figure 1-4.

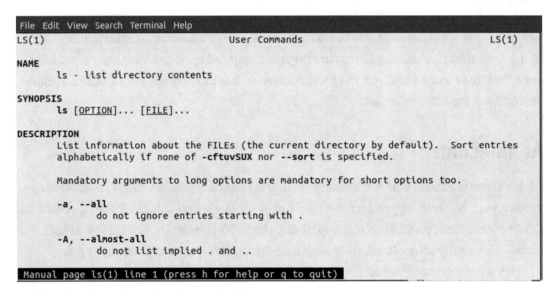

Figure 1-4. *Example of a man page*

I encourage you to make regular use of man as you explore the Linux operating system, as it can often save you the time of doing lengthy Internet searches. You can navigate the man page by using the arrow keys and the page up or page down buttons.

If you need to search through a man page to find some specific keyword, there is a built-in search function. To search, press / and then type in your term and press enter. You'll be taken to the first occurrence if one exists. To go to the next occurrence, tap n; each tap of n will bring you to the next instance. If you want to go back an instance, press capital N, as with n each press goes back an instance.

Numbered man Pages

In some cases, there may be multiple man pages for a single program. For example, with the program stat, we can run

```
man 1 stat
```

Or we can run

```
man 2 stat
```

These commands will bring us to different man pages which concern different aspects of the program. See Table 1-1 for a list of the different page numbers and what information they include. Not all programs contain a page for each type. For example, printf has a page 3 with information on C library functions but no page 2.

Table 1-1. *Description of information found in numbered man pages*

Page Number	Description
1	User commands
2	System calls
3	C library functions
4	Devices and special files
5	File formats and conventions
6	Games
7	Miscellaneous
8	System admin tools and daemons

In most cases, we'll be interested in a program from a user command perspective so we can just run man without a number which will default to 1 or the lowest numbered page found.

```
man man
man -s 6 --regex -k '.*'
```

If you want to see the list shown in Table 1-1 on your own system you can run "man man". You might be wondering is their really a page number dedicated to games? The answer is yes. The games section has been included since at least Unix System V in the 1980s. It is very seldomly used, but if you run the following command you'll get back a list of packages that use it on your system man -s 6 --regex -k '.*'. You might find some interesting easter egg programs such as "espdiff" a joke program installed on many machines which claims to read the user's mind.

Useful Commands for Navigating

Some commands you'll want to get familiar with for navigating and creating new folders are listed in Table 1-2.

Table 1-2. *Commands for navigating and working with files/directories*

Command	Description
ls	List directory contents
cd	Change directory
pwd	Print working directory
mkdir	Make directory
rmdir	Remove directory (*only works if empty*)

Navigating the Filesystem with ls and cd

The first commands most users learn when introduced to the filesystem are ls, short for "list directory contents," and cd, short for "change directory."

Knowing only these two commands allows you to navigate the filesystem – first by running `ls` to see which files and folders are in your current directory and then using `cd` with one of the folder names to navigate into it.

One thing to keep in mind when using `cd`. At any time you can run `cd` without any folder name to return to your home directory. If you go into a directory with `cd` and want to return to the directory containing the one you're in, you can use `..`, for example:

```
cd ..
```

Or if you wanted to return two folders up:

```
cd ../..
```

Some common things you might want to do with `ls` are list additional details beyond just the names of the files and folders; this can be done with the `-l` flag:

```
ls -l
```

If you want to sort by time last modified, you can use the `-t` flag, which is best combined with `-l`:

```
ls -lt
```

If you want to reverse the results so the oldest files are at the top, add the `-r` flag for reverse:

```
ls -ltr
```

You should get back output similar to that shown in Figure 1-5.

```
philip@philip-ThinkPad-T420:~/tmp/solar$ ls -ltr
total 36
drwxr-xr-x 2 philip philip  4096 Nov  7 08:26 libs
drwxr-xr-x 2 philip philip  4096 Nov 17 01:27 imgs
-rw-r--r-- 1 philip philip  8969 Nov 17 01:28 README.md
drwxrwxr-x 2 philip philip  4096 Dec  3 21:09 main
-rw-r--r-- 1 philip philip 12268 Dec 16 20:35 main.ino
philip@philip-ThinkPad-T420:~/tmp/solar$ █
```

Figure 1-5. *Result from running ls -ltr, l for additional information, t to sort by time modified, and r to show results in reverse order*

Invisible Files (dot files)

It's important to know that files which start with a **.** in Linux will not normally appear when using `ls` or a graphical file explorer. These files are meant for configuration and are hidden for convenience. Often we'll want to edit or look at these files so it's important to know about the `-a` flag for `ls`. The `-a` stands for all and will show all files including hidden ones.

```
ls -a
```

Get Current Directory with pwd

With all this navigating, it's easy to forget exactly where you are on the filesystem. If this happens, there is an easy solution to figuring out exactly where you are. Simply run `pwd` which will return the full path of your current location.

```
pwd
```

Make a Directory

Part of navigating the filesystem is creating new directories to put your files and subfolders in. This is relatively easy with the `mkdir` command which takes the folder name and will create the directory based on your current location. For example, if we run the following command in our home directory:

```
mkdir music
```

we'll end up with a folder called music. There is no limit to how many you can create at once. Say we want to create two additional subfolders, we could run

```
mkdir music/rock music/classical
```

It's also possible to use a full path instead of a relative one. For example, if I'm in my home directory and I want to make a new folder in my `/tmp` folder:

```
mkdir /tmp/test
```

This isn't unique to `mkdir`; essentially all programs where you can use a relative path also allow you to make use of a full path; it only requires starting the path with a "/".

Recursively Make Directories

Often when creating a folder, you already have a structure which is multiple directories deep in mind. For example, say we want to create a new folder called movies, with a subfolder for horror and another subfolder for 2012. If we run

```
mkdir movies/horror/2012
```

We'll get back an error saying "No such file or directory". The -p tag provides a way around this. -p stands for create parent directories, meaning if the parent directories of the directory we want to create don't exist, they will be created. Running the following command works as expected, leaving us with three new folders:

```
mkdir -p movies/horror/2012
```

Delete a Directory

After creating a directory, you may decide that you want to delete it. One way of doing this is with the rmdir command which is used similarly to mkdir; simply pass it the name of the directory you want to remove:

```
rmdir music/classical
```

Unfortunately, rmdir has a major limitation in that it can only delete a completely empty directory. Trying to use rmdir on any directory which contains a file or subdirectory will return "Directory not empty". Thus, in practice many people instead always use the command

```
rm -r music
```

The -r in this command stands for recursive. This command is practical as it will work on both files and directories regardless of whether the directory contains any content.

Working with Files

Once you can navigate directories, the next thing you'll want to do is work with files – doing things like creating files, deleting, and copying, as well as reading files and comparing their contents.

Editing Files

We briefly mentioned nano in the last section; it's a straightforward text editor similar to ones most people are familiar with like notepad. You simply open a text file by passing the file location as a command argument:

```
nano /tmp/myFile.txt
```

The file will open or one will be created if it doesn't exist. You can enter text as you would expect on most text editors, press backspace to delete text, and navigate using the arrow keys. At the bottom of the screen, a list of actions that can be performed is shown, for example ctrl+x to exit.

In later chapters, we'll look at more powerful editors Vim and Emacs, but if you find them difficult and getting in the way of you learning or doing what you want to do, you can always fall back on nano or a GUI based text-editor.

Commands for Working with Files

Some of the most useful and basic commands for using Linux are listed in Table 1-3. These commands come in handy for working with files. Most are used by providing a file name as an argument. You can use man <command> on any listed command to get additional information. We'll look at the details of how these commands work and are used as follows.

Table 1-3. *Commands for working with files*

Command	Description
touch	Creates a file or updates the timestamp on an existing file
cat	Outputs the full contents of a file
head	Returns the first X lines of a file starting at the top
tail	Returns the first X lines of a file starting at the bottom
cp	Copies a file or directory
rm	Removes a file or directory
mv	Moves a file or folder
less	Displays contents of file while allowing easy scrolling up and down
diff	Compares two files for differences
cmp	Checks if two files are identical on a byte-by-byte level
file	Gets information on file type

Create Files or Update Timestamps with the touch Utility

Sometimes you want to create a blank file, either as a placeholder that you plan to edit later or possibly as an indicator, for example, with a lock file. The touch command allows you to quickly create a blank file or multiple blank files. Simply run the command and use the desired file name or names as the argument, for example:

```
touch notes.txt
```

Or for multiple:

```
touch file1 file2 file3
```

Another thing the touch command can be used for is updating the timestamp on a file. After running a script, you may want to update a file with touch that was otherwise unused so you can leave some trace of when the script finished. For example, you might update a log file's timestamp despite not adding any new logs so others *(people or programs)* can infer that the script ran and no logs were produced. This is done in exactly the same way as creating a file except instead of providing the path to a file you want to create, you provide the path to an existing file:

```
touch log.txt
```

After executing touch on an existing file, you can use ls -l in the directory of that file to confirm that the timestamp has been updated. It's important to note that touch will never modify the contents of an existing file so don't worry about overwriting any existing contents with a blank file.

Get File Contents with Cat

When using the command line, cat is one of the most useful commands to know. cat simply takes the contents of a file and outputs them to the command line. This allows you to either visually see contents of that file (*without opening and closing a program*) or to use the contents of that file as the input for some other program, using a pipe (*an aspect of bash shell that we'll look at more later in the book*).

As an example of using cat, you can run the following which will output the contents of a file on your system:

```
cat /etc/passwd
```

This file lists the users on your system and some related information, but understanding the content isn't important. What's important here is that you can use cat to take the contents of any file on your system and show it as terminal output.

Get Less Content with Head or Tail

If you understand what cat does, you'll just as easily be able to understand the head and tail commands. When you used cat, the full contents of a file were returned. With large files, this means you may get several pages of content at once and have all your previous work and commands pushed up the screen.

If you want to get a preview of a file but don't want the whole thing, you can use head which will return the first X lines of a file. By default, X is 10 so if you run

```
head /etc/passwd
```

you should get back the first ten lines of the file *(assuming the file has at least ten lines)*. The `tail` function works exactly the same way as `head`, but instead of getting the first X lines, it will get the last X lines. So if we run the following command, we'll get the last ten lines of our file:

```
tail /etc/passwd
```

If you want to modify how many lines are returned, you can specify the amount of lines returned with the -n flag – if we want the first five lines, for example:

```
head -n 5 /etc/passwd
```

Aside from not filling up your screen with lots of text, the `head` and `tail` commands can be useful during scripting, in cases where you know exactly how many lines from some file you need. For example, you might have a script that wants to look at the last 20 lines in a log file to parse the text for some specific error; in such a case, we could make use of `tail -n 20 filename` and pipe the output into your parsing script *(more on piping and scripts later)*.

Copying Files with cp

If you're doing system administration or software development, it's likely you'll end up using the `cp` command often. It's a very simple but very useful command which stands for copy. When using the command the first argument is the file you want to copy and the second argument is the location to copy to, for example copying `file1` to location `file2` would be done with:

```
cp file1 file2
```

Running the preceding command would result in a new file called `file2` which contained the same contents as `file1`.

In addition to copying files, `cp` can also be used to copy whole folders. To use `cp` with folders, you need to specify the -r flag, which stands for recursive *(similar to using the rm command with folders)*. So copying a folder would be much the same as copying a file, for example:

```
cp -r folder1 folder2
```

Removing Files with rm

We've already made use of `rm` due to the limitations of `rmdir` in the section on directories. Be aware that the `rm` command is primarily used for deleting files, and when doing so, there is no need to include the `-r` flag, for example:

```
rm file1
```

Moving Files with mv

Another very popular built-in command, `mv` allows you to move a file or directory to a new location. It's used very similarly to `cp` except you only end up with one file, for example, if we use

```
mv file1 file2
```

Our file called `file1` will now be named `file2` – similar to moving a file on graphical desktop OS like Mac or Windows. Also like many of the other commands we've looked at, you can use `mv` with directories, but with `mv` there is no need to use a special flag, you can simply use

```
mv folder1 folder2
```

Be aware that `mv` will overwrite a file without a warning if it already exists. For example, if I moved file1 to file2 but file2 already existed, my original file2 will be lost forever. If you're worried about that happening, there is a special flag `-i` which will prompt you before overwriting anything.

Interactively View File Contents with Less

We mentioned how using `cat` can become a headache because large file outputs end up crowding your shell. We mentioned `head` and `tail` which allow you to view a small portion, but in most cases, we want the option to view the whole file but scroll through it slowly. This is what `less` is for.

Instead of outputting the contents of a file, `less` opens an interactive viewer separate from your terminal where you can scroll through the contents at your own pace. As with `cat`, `tail`, and `head`, you simply run the command with the target file as your input:

```
less /etc/passwd
```

You'll start at the top of the file and have the ability to scroll down and back up using the arrow keys and page up/page down buttons. It's a lot like scrolling through a man page, you even have access to the same method of searching *(vim style search)*. That is by pressing "/", typing the search term, and hitting enter. You'll be brought to the first instance of the term, and from there you can press n to go to the next instance or N to go one instance back *(this method of searching is also used in Vim, a text editor we'll look at later in this book)*.

Note   As you explore different programs on Linux, you may come across more and assume it's like less but different; after all that's the case with commands head and tail. more is actually an older program which less is based on. more has fewer features and is not as usable, for example, you can scroll down but not back up. It's likely you'll find more on your system, but we recommend using less in all situations where more could be considered.

Comparing Files

Comparing files is a task you may need to complete from time to time, certainly much less common than something like mv or cat, but nonetheless it is file related and useful command for software development. There are several programs which can be used for comparing files.

By default cmp and comm are installed on most systems. However, in practice, diff is much easier to use and colordiff is even better *(same as diff but with color coding)*. For practical purposes, diff or colordiff is recommended. In later chapters, we'll look at how you can alias diff to use colordiff.

To demonstrate comparing files, let's move to the /tmp directory and create two identical files. To get started with this, run the following commands:

```
cd /tmp
cp /etc/passwd file1
cp file1 file2
```

Next open up file2 with nano or your preferred text editor and change a single letter; it can be a change as small as adding a single letter. With the change made, save and close the file.

Compare with Comm Command

Now that you have two almost identical files, we can test a few commands for comparing the differences. The first we'll try is comm which can be run by passing 2 file names as arguments *(preferably similiar files for demonstration purposes)*:

```
comm file1 file2
```

This will return the contents of the file overlaid on one another, with three layers of depth. The furthest right depth which will be used for most of the lines in the file are lines which are contained in both files. Then when you get to the line where there is a difference, you'll have two different indentations, one for file1 only lines and another for file2 only lines.

It's not pretty but it gets the job done and can be found on most systems. Though as mentioned we recommend installing diff or colordiff.

Compare with Cmp Command

While comm can be completely replaced by diff, the command cmp is actually slightly different. Instead of comparing the text of a file, it compares files on a byte-by-byte basis. We can test the program by passing the command 2 file names:

```
cmp file1 file2
```

With cmp you'll get back a single line which specifies the line and byte where the first difference between the files occurs. In scripts where you simply want to compare if files are identical, cmp can be the fastest option since it returns as soon as a single difference is found instead of parsing the full file.

Compare with Diff Command

The diff command is similar to comm, but it is more readable and has additional features and flags. It's not installed by default on most systems so you'll have to install it first:

```
sudo apt-get install diff
```

With `diff` installed, we're ready to compare our files, which can be done similarly to `comm` and `cmp`:

```
diff file1 file2
```

Instead of returning all the lines in the files, `diff` will only return the lines which differ. That means you'll have two copies of each line which differs. The line in the first file will be prepended with a < and the line from the second a >, allowing you to see which lines belong to which file. Before the lines, you'll also see an indicator for what line numbers are being compared. This allows you to hone in on the difference and quickly find it in a text editor.

ColorDiff Even Better Than Diff

The main advantage that `diff` has over `comm` is the usability due to how differences are shown. If your terminal supports color *(most desktop terminals do)*, you might want to install `colordiff` instead. `colordiff` is a wrapper for `diff` which enhances the experience further by color coding the differences so you can quickly see what lines belong to which files. Like `diff` it will need to be installed:

```
sudo apt-get install diff
```

With `colordiff` installed, compare the two files and observe the difference in output:

```
colordiff file1 file2
```

Get File Type

If you're coming from Windows, you may be used to the concept that the extension of a file determines the type and what program it's run with. On Linux, file extensions are often used, but this is simply for the benefit of the human reader. File extensions are not mandatory and in some cases not used.

You may find a text file or program which has a name but no extension. In this situation, you may find the `file` command to be useful. Given a file as input, it will return information on the file type. For example, if we run the file command on `file1` created in the last section, by passing the file location as an argument like below:

```
file file1
```

You should get back the type "ASCII text." If you have an image file handy on your computer, try running `file` on it. In addition to the image type like JPG, you'll also get additional metadata like the dimensions of the photo.

Command Information with type, which, whereis, or locate

Similar to getting information about a file with `file`, we can get information on a command using `type`, `which`, `whereis`, or `locate`. The first command `type` is built into bash itself and searches your path and gets information on the command when found, for example:

```
type ls
```

On my system, it returns an alias (*more aliases in a later chapter*), as shown in Figure 1-6.

```
ubuntu@ip-172-31-42-231:/tmp$ type ls
ls is aliased to `ls --color=auto'
ubuntu@ip-172-31-42-231:/tmp$ 
```

Figure 1-6. *Output from checking the type of* ls

Then with `which` we can find the location of the executable:

```
which ls
```

Similiarly we can use `whereis` and find the executable location, source location, and manual page files for the command. The `whereis` command should return multiple file locations, as shown in Figure 1-7.

```
whereis ls
```

```
ubuntu@ip-172-31-42-231:/tmp$ which grep
/bin/grep
ubuntu@ip-172-31-42-231:/tmp$ whereis grep
grep: /bin/grep /usr/share/man/man1/grep.1.gz /usr/share/info/grep.info.gz
ubuntu@ip-172-31-42-231:/tmp$ 
```

Figure 1-7. *Location of program shown using* which *and* whereis

In some cases, you may not remember the exact command so it doesn't come up when using which; in this case, you can also try locate which will search a database index of the filesystem:

```
locate samba
```

There are two issues with locate; the first is that it can return lots of results, finding every match for the text input for the complete path to every file on the system. Given a username, ubuntu, for example, locate ubuntu would return every single file in the home directory *(as each file contains the username in the filepath)*, among others. The second issue is that the database which powers locate (making it faster than a manual filesystem search with find) is only updated once a day via cron. If you want to update it manually, you can run sudo updatedb *(run time can take anywhere from seconds to minutes depending on system and size of the filesystem)*.

More on Sudo

Normally when logging in to your operating system, you'll be given a username, which has permissions for a specific folder. Often the folder location will be

```
/home/<username>/
```

Normally each user has a dedicated home directory for which they have full administrative privileges. Sometimes you'll need to make use of files and folders which are outside the home folder. If you attempt to do something which requires permissions beyond your user account, you'll get a message saying "Permission denied" or "are you root?".

In this case, you'll have to retry the command by first appending sudo which specifies you want to run the command as the root user. For example, the command

```
cat /etc/sudoers
```

instead becomes

```
sudo cat /etc/sudoers
```

When using sudo, you'll be prompted for your password. Of course the success of sudo is dependent on your main user account being enabled to use sudo. The policy for which users can make use of sudo is defined in /etc/sudoers. In my default install of Ubuntu, for example, there is the line

```
%sudo ALL=(ALL:ALL) ALL
```

This specifies that all users which are in the group sudo can use sudo. To see what groups a user is in, you can run

```
groups <username>
```

Replace <username> with the username of your account, and you'll get back a list of groups you're in.

If you need to run multiple commands in a row which all make use of sudo, you may instead want to switch to root. By doing this, you can run commands that would normally require sudo without it. To switch to root, run the following command and enter your password when prompted:

```
sudo -i
```

Now you're free to run any command you want. To exit back to your normal user, press ctrl+d.

Less Pipe

While we're talking about file type detection, it's worth mentioning less pipe, which is a file type preprocessor for the command less which comes preinstalled on many systems. Less pipe lets you view files in the terminal that normally wouldn't be accessible in the terminal, for example, PDF files.

To see if you have less pipe installed, run the following command:

```
echo $LESSOPEN
```

If you get back a pipe followed by the location of a file, for example, |/usr/local/bin/lesspipe.sh %s, then it is installed on your system. If you find that running the command returns an empty string, then your system does not have lesspipe. If that is the case, don't worry as we'll cover installing *(or updating)* less pipe in the next section.

Update/Install Less Pipe

Ubuntu and other operating systems will come with a version of lesspipe installed that is good enough. So if you don't want to change the defaults, feel free to skip this section.

To make full use of all the features listed here, you may need to update lesspipe. On my system Ubuntu 18.04, I found the version of lesspipe was slightly outdated and didn't give me in-depth details about photo metadata which is available on the latest version. The older version also might not support all the file formats listed in the next section, though it should work for common ones like PDF.

As a preliminary step, git and make need to be installed. Git is a version control program useful for programming and make is used for compling source code. We'll make use of git throughout this book as a means to download publicly available code from GitHub. You can install it by running:

```
sudo apt-get install git
```

As mentioned, we'll also make use of the make command. make is used for compiling programs often written in C (*though not limited to any language*). If you download a program and it contains a file called Makefile, that's a good sign that the program can be compiled with make. The make utility is often bundled with other tools like the gcc compiler for C and C++ and common libraries. To install make on Ubuntu, run:

```
sudo apt-get install build-essential
```

With git and make installed, we can start updating lesspipe; this process starts with downloading the project code, moving into the folder, compiling the code, and testing the setup:

```
git clone https://github.com/wofr06/lesspipe
cd lesspipe
make
make test
```

After running make test, observe the results and any programs which are missing. For example, in my case, shown in Figure 1-8, I got a variety of suggested programs to install. Without installing said programs, you may not be able to open the related file type. You can decide which you want to install and which you don't based on what file types you find yourself using.

```
less     testok/a\ b.tgz:testok/a\"doc.gz          ignored, needs antiword
less     testok/a\#rtf                             ignored, needs unrtf
less     testok/a\ b.tgz:testok/a\&pdf.gz          NOT ok
less     testok/a\ b.tgz:testok/a\;dvi.gz          ok
less     testok/a\ b.tgz:testok/a\(ps.gz           NOT ok
less     testok/a\ b.tgz:testok/a\)nroff.gz        NOT ok
less -f  testok/perlstorable.gz                    ignored, needs perlpackage
less     testok/iso.image:/ISO.TXT\;1              ok
less     testok/test.rpm:test.txt                  ignored, needs rpm2cpio
less     testok/cabinet.cab:a\ text.gz             ok
less     testok/test.deb:../test.txt               NOT ok
less     testok/test2.deb:../test.txt              NOT ok
less     testok/test3.deb:../test.txt              NOT ok
less     testok/a\ b.tgz:testok/a\#b.sxw           ignored, needs sxw2txt
less     testok/a\ b.tgz:testok/a\~b.odt           ignored, needs sxw2txt
```

Figure 1-8. *Output from running* make test *after compiling* lesspipe

Based on the feedback from the test script install the missing packages *(feedback from test script may differ based on your system)*:

```
sudo apt-get install antiword unrtf rpm2cpio
```

If you get back a message that a package isn't found, you'll have to omit it or search for the correct name on your OS package manager. For example, I found that sxw2txt could be installed using the name odt2txt.

Next, run

```
sudo make install
```

That will replace your old version of lesspipe or install it if you didn't have it. The final step is to open your ~/.bashrc file and add the following lines to the bottom:

```
LESSOPEN="|/usr/local/bin/lesspipe.sh %s"; export LESSOPEN
```

With these steps done, you'll get the full power of less pipe to work with as many file types as possible.

Note   The `.bashrc` file contains account-wide configurations and variables that can be accessed from the command line. For example, if we add a line saying `export FAVORITE_COLOR="Blue"` and then open a new terminal, we can access the variable. Running `echo $FAVORITE_COLOR`, for example, would print "Blue" to the screen. Some programs will allow you to change settings based on variables like this, for instance, a GUI-based program might look for $FAVORITE_COLOR to set the colors for the layout. This particular variable isn't commonly used but demonstrates how programs can be configured this way. We'll look at `.bashrc` more in a later chapter and how it can be used to improve your command-line experience.

Regular Use of Less

As mentioned previously, `less` is used for viewing file text data in a way that allows you to start at the top and slowly scroll your way down. Let's review using `less` normally once more before opening some other file types. First create a long file with several lines of text using the command seq, short for sequence. The seq command takes a starting number and an ending number as arguments and returns a sequence of numbers between them:

```
seq 1 999
```

This should output the numbers 1 to 999 (*seq can be useful for custom scripts or testing*). Now run the same command again but direct the output to a file using the special > character, which is used for directing text output into a file:

```
seq 1 999 > /tmp/numbers.txt
```

Note   When creating files for tests, I'll often make the location `/tmp`; this folder has the special property that everything in it will be deleted when you restart your computer. If you know you'll later delete a file as is the case with our `numbers.txt` file, you should create it in the `/tmp` folder. That way you don't have to worry about having junk files laying around if you forget to delete it. Just be careful not to leave anything important in your /tmp folder. Sometimes a script that starts out as a throw away can develop into something you want to save for later.

Now that we've created our file for testing purposes, open it using `less /tmp/numbers.txt`. This will open the file with `less` starting at the top, as shown in Figure 1-9. You can scroll down and up with the arrow keys or the page down and page up buttons. To quit press q.

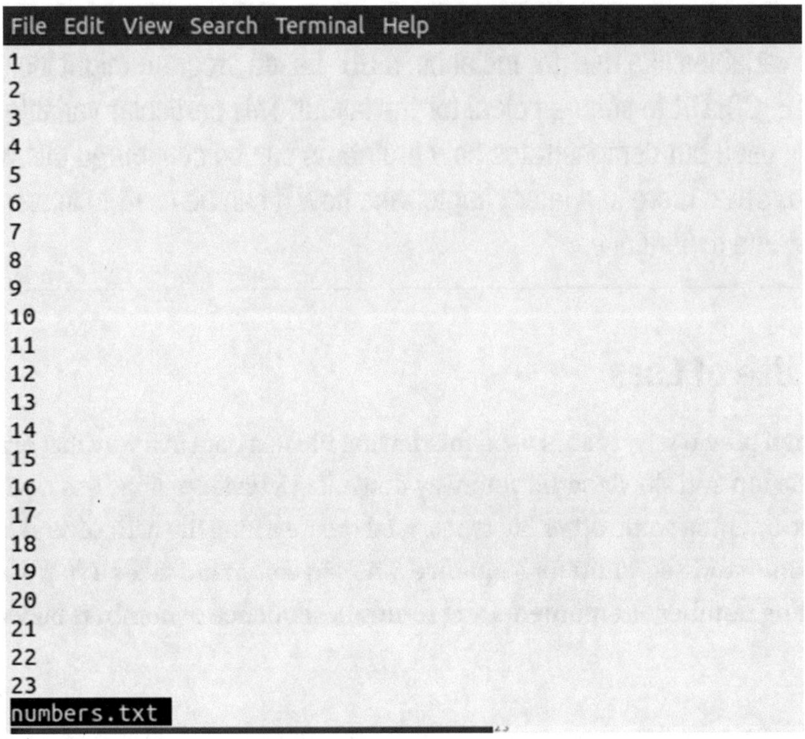

Figure 1-9. *Viewing a long file in* `less`

Opening PDFs with Less Pipe

Less pipe also makes `less` capable of opening and reading PDF files. Similar to an image, run `less <filename.pdf>` and you'll get a text version of the PDF in your terminal.

Opening Compressed Folder with Less Pipe

Compressed files and folders can be opened with `less` when you have less pipe installed. To demonstrate, create a folder with some files and compress them using tar *(a common utility for compressing and uncompressing files)*:

```
cd /tmp
mkdir folder
cd folder
touch file1 file2 file3
cd ..
tar -zcvf folder.tar.gz folder
```

After running these commands, you'll have a compressed folder which contains three empty files. Next let's try opening it with `less`. You should get a list of folders and files including the permissions of each file, as shown in Figure 1-10.

```
drwxr-xr-x philip/philip       0 2019-12-21 17:17 folder/
-rw-r--r-- philip/philip       0 2019-12-21 17:16 folder/file1
-rw-r--r-- philip/philip       0 2019-12-21 17:16 folder/file2
-rw-r--r-- philip/philip       0 2019-12-21 17:16 folder/file3
(END)
```

Figure 1-10. *Output created from opening compressed folder with* less

Image Metadata with Less Pipe

For the next example, you'll need to download an image or find an existing one on your system. Navigate to the folder containing the image and open it using `less`; if you've installed the latest version, you'll get back detailed metadata when opening an image with less, as shown in Figure 1-11.

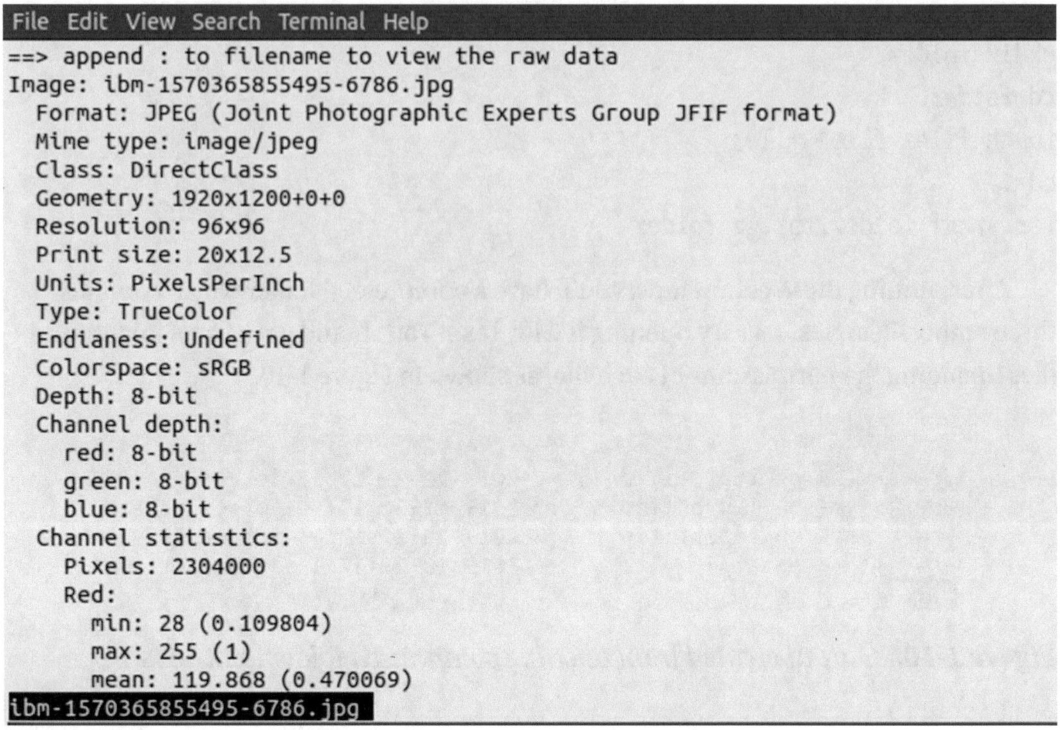

```
File Edit View Search Terminal Help
==> append : to filename to view the raw data
Image: ibm-1570365855495-6786.jpg
  Format: JPEG (Joint Photographic Experts Group JFIF format)
  Mime type: image/jpeg
  Class: DirectClass
  Geometry: 1920x1200+0+0
  Resolution: 96x96
  Print size: 20x12.5
  Units: PixelsPerInch
  Type: TrueColor
  Endianess: Undefined
  Colorspace: sRGB
  Depth: 8-bit
  Channel depth:
    red: 8-bit
    green: 8-bit
    blue: 8-bit
  Channel statistics:
    Pixels: 2304000
    Red:
      min: 28 (0.109804)
      max: 255 (1)
      mean: 119.868 (0.470069)
ibm-1570365855495-6786.jpg
```

Figure 1-11. *Viewing image data in less with lesspipe*

Other Files with Lesspipe

There are all kinds of files that can be opened and viewed with lesspipe. We won't go in depth on all of them, but here are a few others, so you know what is possible:

- All kinds of compressed folder including zip, gzip, 7-zip, and so on

- Java JAR files

- RAR files

- RPM (Red Hat Package Manager files)

- Microsoft Word, PowerPoint, and Excel

- ePub books

- HTML

- PDF

- MP4

For a complete and up-to-date list, as well as any other companion programs you might need to install for a file type, check out the official repository at `https://github.com/wofr06/lesspipe`.

Note   Some of the file types listed here depend on your system having some additional packages installed. If you find a package you want to read isn't working, refer back to the install step where `make test` was run. If the file type you open is tested and returns "ignored" and lists a package to install, you'll need to install the said program. If the file type says "Not Ok" or says "Ok" but still doesn't work, you'll need to visit the GitHub page listed earlier and check the issues tab for others having similar problems (*or opening your own issue if none are found*).

Scheduling Processes with Cron Jobs

Another important tool to know about is cron jobs. A cron job is a script or process that runs at a specific time or interval. This can be useful for things like cleaning out a log folder or backing up files at a set interval (*we'll look at this in the chapter 6*).

To get started, run crontab with the -e flag, short for "edit"

```
crontab -e
```

The first time you run it, you'll be asked to select an editor. If you're not comfortable with command-line editors (*we'll look at Vim and Emacs in later chapters*), you should choose nano as it's the easiest to use. If you later decide you want to change the editor used, you'll need to modify `~/.selected_editor` or delete it to bring back the prompt.

Once `crontab -e` brings you to a file, go to the very bottom and create the example job shown in Figure 1-12. Each of the five * symbols can be replaced with a number to signify when they should run. The * symbol signifies a wildcard meaning it matches any value. When all 5 values are wildcards is means the command will be run every minute, of every hour, of everyday ect. The command shown in Figure 1-12 will create or update the timestamp of the file `/tmp/hello` using touch every minute.

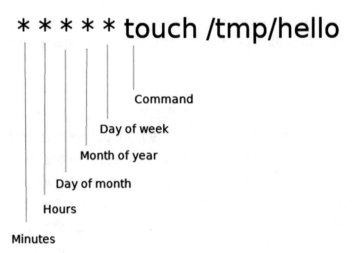

Figure 1-12. *Labels for each element of a cron job*

After adding the cron job, wait a minute or two and run `ls /tmp`; you should see a new file named `hello`. After confirming the cron job worked, be sure to delete the job to keep your system clean.

Table 1-4 contains examples of cron schedules which use the various columns including minutes, hours, weekdays, calendar days, and months.

Table 1-4. *Examples of time intervals in cron*

Cron Time	Description
* * * * *	Every minute
5 * * * *	The fifth minute of every hour
*/5 * * * *	Every 5 minutes
0 0 0 0 1	Every Monday at midnight
0 2 1 1 *	January 1st, at 2:00am

Summary

In this chapter, we looked at choosing a Linux distro, finding information about a program using man, common commands, creating scripts, and file permissions. We've only touched on these topics briefly to get started. As we continue, we'll go more in depth especially on several of the topics listed.

CHAPTER 2

File/Folder Navigation

No matter what you're doing in the terminal, you'll want to be aware of where you are in the file structure of your system. You'll also want to know how to navigate to other folders which have files you may need to work with. In this chapter, we'll reiterate the basics and look at other tools and methods for navigating the filesystem.

Basics

The most basic commands that anyone on terminal should be aware of are ls to list structure and cd for change directory. Entering ls will return a list of files and folders in your current directory, and then you can move into directories with cd followed by the directory name. Table 2-1 lists some useful options that can be used with -ls.

Table 2-1. *Options for ls*

Command	Description
-a	Show hidden files and directories
--color	Color highlighted output
-F	Symbol at the end of file name to indicate type
-i	Show file index number (*inode number*)
-l	Long format with details
-t	Sort by date time
-S	Sort by file size
-r	Reverse order
-R	Recursively list current folder and subfolders

© Philip Kirkbride 2020
P. Kirkbride, *Basic Linux Terminal Tips and Tricks*, https://doi.org/10.1007/978-1-4842-6035-7_2

While `ls` has several commonly used options, `cd` is almost never used with options though it does have two, `-P` to not follow symbolic links and `-L` to force follow symbolic links. While you won't need options while working with `cd`, there are a few symbols you should know.

When navigating, there are some global symbols which can be used as part of your path shown in Table 2-2.

Table 2-2. *Directory symbol*

Command	Description
.	Represents the current working directory
..	Represents the folder containing the working directory
~	Represents the home folder for the current user

These short forms are handy when using `ls` or `cd`; we can be anywhere in the filesystem, and if we want to return to our home folder, we can simply run

```
cd ~
```

inodes

We mentioned that `ls -i` will return a file index number or inode number, but what exactly is an inode? Every time a file is created on a Linux system, it is assigned an inode in the background. Each inode points to a place in memory where the file is located and metadata related to the file including file size, file owner, and last time accessed.

All the inodes on your system are stored on a table which is preallocated a set amount of memory. An interesting side effect of this is that you can run out of file space without running out of disk space. To do this, you'd need to create enough tiny (*or empty*) files to fill up the inode table, which nearly never happens. To get an idea of how many inodes you could possibly store, run

```
df -i
```

You'll get back a list with a column called `IFree` for each drive on your system; this represents the amount of free inodes on the drive. In my case, I have over 6.5 million free inodes; thus to hit the maximum number of inodes, I'd have to create over 6.5 million files.

Though unlikely, it is possible. If you're curious and you'd like to simulate running out of free inodes, here is a one liner that will use up all your inodes. Before using it, make sure you're in the /tmp folder, so if you need to restart, all the files will be gone on the next boot.

```
cd /tmp
mkdir test
cd test
for i in $(seq 1 7000000) ; do touch $i ; done
```

You'll need to replace 7000000 with a number greater than the total amount of free inodes on your drive. This command is purely for educational purposes and could take hours to complete. Running out of inodes is extremely rare, but it can happen particularly on systems which run for extended periods of time and have limited memory.

Get Current Location

Whenever you open a new terminal, you'll likely be in the home directory for your user. So for user ubuntu, you'd be in /home/ubuntu/. This isn't always the case and sometimes you'll find yourself forgetting your location. You can find your current location by running

```
pwd
```

This will return the full path to your current location. It stands for "print working directory."

Symbolic Links

In some cases, a directory is not a folder itself but a shortcut to another directory. These are known as symbolic links, or soft links. You can create a symbolic link for an existing file by running

```
ln -s original_file link_file
```

This will create a file called link_file in your working directory which points to original_file. This new symbolic link file doesn't contain any data itself. The symbolic link only contains the filesystem address of the file it's an alias for. This means you'll have to be careful when moving or renaming the aliased file as the system link will still point to the original location.

When using the detailed version of the list structure command `ls -l`, you'll see an arrow pointing from `link_file` to the actual file location (Figure 2-1). The -l flag actually stands for "long" here.

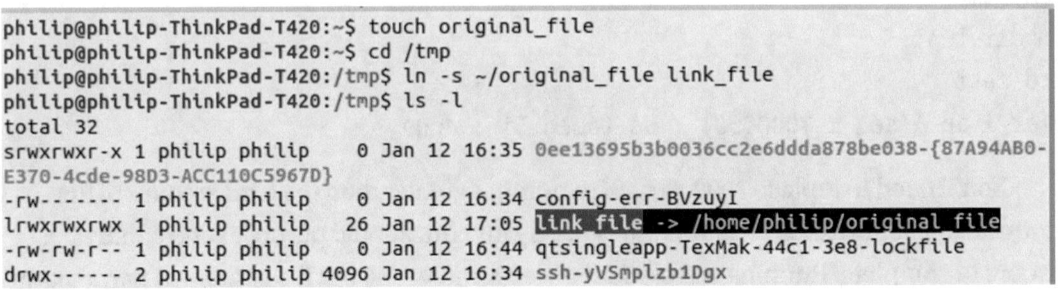

```
philip@philip-ThinkPad-T420:~$ touch original_file
philip@philip-ThinkPad-T420:~$ cd /tmp
philip@philip-ThinkPad-T420:/tmp$ ln -s ~/original_file link_file
philip@philip-ThinkPad-T420:/tmp$ ls -l
total 32
srwxrwxr-x 1 philip philip    0 Jan 12 16:35 0ee13695b3b0036cc2e6ddda878be038-{87A94AB0-
E370-4cde-98D3-ACC110C5967D}
-rw------- 1 philip philip    0 Jan 12 16:34 config-err-BVzuyI
lrwxrwxrwx 1 philip philip   26 Jan 12 17:05 link_file -> /home/philip/original_file
-rw-rw-r-- 1 philip philip    0 Jan 12 16:44 qtsingleapp-TexMak-44c1-3e8-lockfile
drwx------ 2 philip philip 4096 Jan 12 16:34 ssh-yVSmplzb1Dgx
```

Figure 2-1. *Details of a system link file*

Or if you use `ls -F`, you'll see an @ symbol at the end of files which are symbolic links, as shown in Figure 2-2.

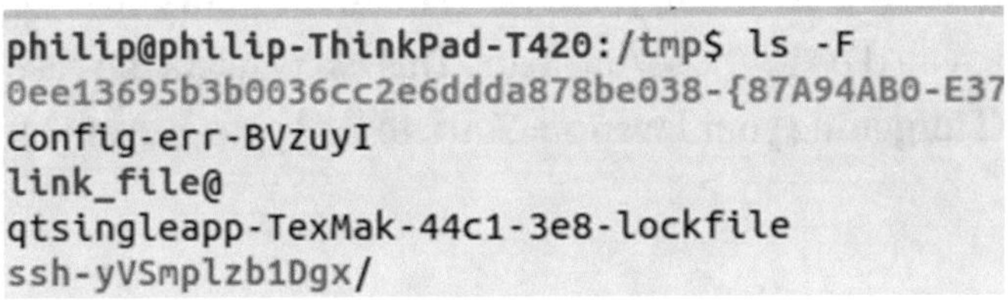

```
philip@philip-ThinkPad-T420:/tmp$ ls -F
0ee13695b3b0036cc2e6ddda878be038-{87A94AB0-E37
config-err-BVzuyI
link_file@
qtsingleapp-TexMak-44c1-3e8-lockfile
ssh-yVSmplzb1Dgx/
```

Figure 2-2. *Symbol @ specifying a system link*

Symbolic links can also be applied to folders, making one folder which is a shortcut to another.

Hard Links

Besides symbolic links, there are also hard links. A hard link is a clone of a file that points to the inode for a file. Deleting the hard link (directory entry) for a file that has only a single one also deletes the file. Multiple hard links can point to the same inode so long as they are all in the same filesystem. Deleting one or more hard links to an inode does not delete the inode or the file it points to until all of the hard links are deleted. A symbolic link on the other hand is only a shortcut pointing to the original file. Unlike symbolic links, a hard link cannot be applied to a folder, only to a file.

Creating a hard link is similar to creating a symbolic link but without the -s flag:

```
ln original_file link_file
```

Using ls -l or ls -F, you will not be able to identify the hard link as being a special type of file. Essentially, it is just as much a normal file on equal footing with the original file; changing one will change the other. This is because both files point to the same inode which in turn points to a single instance of the file. This means unlike soft links you can move the location of either file without effecting the link.

As mentioned previously, every file on a Linux system has an associated inode. By using ls -i, we can see the inode of each file in our current directory. Figure 2-3 shows an example of using ls -i on a hard link and the original file; notice that the inode is the same.

```
philip@philip-ThinkPad-T420:/tmp/test$ ls -i
8156940 link_file  8156940 original_file
philip@philip-ThinkPad-T420:/tmp/test$ █
```

Figure 2-3. *Output from 'ls -i' showing 2 files with the same inode number*

Even when you move a file, the inode stays the same. The directory entry that points to the inode moves from one directory to another. The inode remains unchanged, and the locations of both the inode and the data belonging to the file are unchanged.

Navigation Stack with pushd and popd

cd and ls are fairly well known, but there are a few more commands that can come in handy once you get familiar with navigating file directories. The first of these is pushd. pushd acts like cd but it creates a stack of directories so you can easily return to your current directory later. For example, say you're in directory /tmp/ and you use pushd ~, this moves you into the home directory just like 'cd' would,next do pushd /usr/local/bin. This again changes your location like 'cd', but noice that a list of locations we've visited is returned in Figure 2-4.

```
philip@philip-ThinkPad-T420:~$ cd /tmp
philip@philip-ThinkPad-T420:/tmp$ pushd ~
~ /tmp
philip@philip-ThinkPad-T420:~$ pushd /usr/local/bin
/usr/local/bin ~ /tmp
philip@philip-ThinkPad-T420:/usr/local/bin$ █
```

Figure 2-4. *List of folder locations shown in pushd stack*

The current directory is shown on the left, and the furthest down the stack directory on the right (*in our case* /tmp). Now if we run popd, we'll pop our current directory from the stack and move one to the right, in this case ~; then running it again we'll return to /tmp. This can be a useful alternative to cd when you want to keep track of a set of directories to return to.

Another related command is simply running cd -. When you use the minus sign after cd, you'll actually navigate into whatever directory you were in previously; you can repeat this several times backtracking through all the directories you've visited.

Ranger

Another one of my most used Linux command-line programs is Ranger. Ranger is a command-line program which makes file and directory exploration quick and easy, especially on servers or devices which have no GUI-based directory explorer.

Install ranger by running

```
sudo apt-get install ranger
```

Once installed you can start it by simply running the command in the directory you want to start in:

```
ranger
```

You'll get a three-pane view like shown in Figure 2-5. Pressing up and down will change your selection on the middle pane. Press right to go deeper into the directory displayed on the right, and left to explore the parent directory.

```
philip@philip-ThinkPad-T420 /home/philip/Arduino
 philip    Arduino                    2   libraries
           Desktop                    2   sketch_jun06a
           Documents                111
           Downloads                282
           ebooks                     1
           Music                      0
           packt                      8
           Pictures                 627
           Public                     0
           research                   5
           sketchbook                 1
           snap                       2
           Templates                  0
           tmp                       11
           Videos                     0
           VirtualBox VMs             1
           vyper-venv                 4
           VyperContractGUI           2
           examples.desktop      8.77 K
           texput.log             725 B

drwxrwxr-x 4 philip philip 2 2019-06-06 16:43     200K sum, 64.9G free  1/20  All
```

Figure 2-5. *Navigation with Ranger*

Navigating this way will quickly become second nature. Ranger also comes with several keyboard shortcuts, inspired by the bindings in Vim. Some of my favorites include

> S – Typing capital S will open the directory selected in the far left pane to be opened in a bash session. From that point, if you press ctrl+d or manually run exit, you'll return to Ranger.

> s – Typing lowercase s will open a small text box in the bottom left of your screen where a shell command can be input. For example, navigate to /tmp and after press s, enter the command mkdir hello, and press enter. You'll see a new directory called hello appear in /tmp.

> Q – Typing capital Q will quit Ranger and return you to the command line.

> @ – Typing the @ symbol will allow you to enter a bash command without leaving Ranger, for example, you enter touch hi and press enter, and you'd see the current directory you're in add an empty file of that name.

~ – Typing the ~ symbol will switch between the three levels of directory view and a view that focuses on just the current one; press it again to go back. The larger view is great when you're dealing with long folder names or don't want to get distracted.

o – Typing lowercase o will display a list of possible ways to sort the files in the current directory, for example, by time changed or alphabetically.

File Structure Visualization with Tree

Besides ls, ranger is my most used program for viewing file structure. However, another worth a mention is tree, which will need to be installed on most distros. 'tree' is also very lightweight, instead of opening up a full program like ranger to explore the file structure, 'tree' can be used to immediately create a visualization of your file structure – for example, if I navigate into a project and run the following command

```
tree -L 2
```

Note   Two here signifies how many levels (or directories) deep show; to go deeper, simply increase the number.

---

the command will produce the visualization of file structure with a depth of two folders down like shown in Figure 2-6.

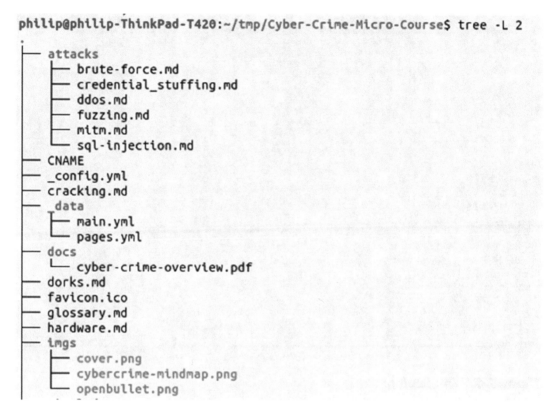

```
philip@philip-ThinkPad-T420:~/tmp/Cyber-Crime-Micro-Course$ tree -L 2
├── attacks
│   ├── brute-force.md
│   ├── credential_stuffing.md
│   ├── ddos.md
│   ├── fuzzing.md
│   ├── mitm.md
│   └── sql-injection.md
├── CNAME
├── _config.yml
├── cracking.md
├── data
│   ├── main.yml
│   └── pages.yml
├── docs
│   └── cyber-crime-overview.pdf
├── dorks.md
├── favicon.ico
├── glossary.md
├── hardware.md
├── imgs
│   ├── cover.png
│   ├── cybercrime-mindmap.png
│   └── openbullet.png
```

Figure 2-6. *Filesystem tree displayed using tree*

Navigate Filesystem with Vim

We'll have a dedicated chapter for editing with Vim, but it also has a built-in file/folder explorer. With Vim open in normal mode, run the following command:

`:Ex`

This is short for `:Explore` which also works. Running the command will open a file explorer within Vim, as shown in Figure 2-7, similar to Ranger but without a preview.

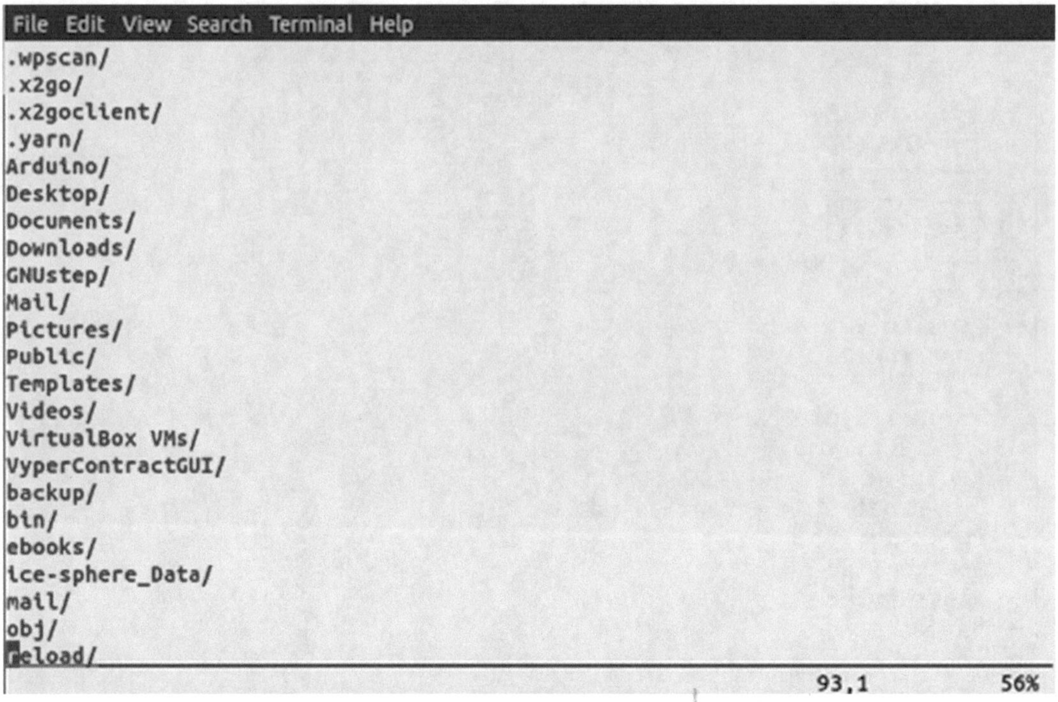

File Edit View Search Terminal Help
```
.wpscan/
.x2go/
.x2goclient/
.yarn/
Arduino/
Desktop/
Documents/
Downloads/
GNUstep/
Mail/
Pictures/
Public/
Templates/
Videos/
VirtualBox VMs/
VyperContractGUI/
backup/
bin/
ebooks/
ice-sphere_Data/
mail/
obj/
reload/
                                                 93,1              56%
```

Figure 2-7.   Vim Explore

Optionally you can pass an argument of the folder you want to open with explore in Vim, for example:

`:Ex /home`

This will cause explore mode to open in the home folder instead of your current working directory. You'll be able to navigate using normal Vim keybindings j for down and k for up or using the arrow keys. You can press enter on a folder or file to open it.

Summary

In this chapter, we explored commands related to navigating the file directory. We also looked at file attributes such as system links, hidden files, and metadata like time last modified. We saw how inodes play a key role in how the underlying filesystem works by associating file names to metadata and the underlying data in disk space.

In addition to looking at attributes of the filesystem, we introduced tools that make exploring the filesystem easier. Ranger and Vim Explore both allow us to quickly navigate files. While the additional flag options on ls allow us to see file attributes which are normally hidden.

CHAPTER 3

History and Shortcuts

In this chapter, we're going to look at using shell history, built-in keyboard shortcuts for bash terminal, and file globbing. These techniques will help you move faster as you enter new commands, repeat past ones, or modify partially written ones.

History

It's great having lots of useful commands at your fingertips, but with so many it's easy to lose track. That's where the history command comes in handy. The history command should come preinstalled on most Linux systems. Running the command returns a list of your last run commands.

By default most systems will only retain about 2000 commands before deleting old history. I recommend increasing that number. You can do so by modifying your ~/.bashrc; search for the lines containing HISTSIZE and HISTFILESIZE:

```
# see HISTSIZE and HISTFILESIZE in bash(1)
HISTSIZE=10000
HISTFILESIZE=10000
```

It's also possible to set your history to unlimited; simply declare an empty value:

```
HISTSIZE=
HISTFILESIZE=
```

To cut down on space when saving a larger number of commands, I like to turn on ignoreboth and erasedups. ignoreboth is a shorthand that combines both ignoredups and ignorespace. The ignoredups option causes commands run more than once in a row to only be recorded once. The ignorespace option causes commands that start with a space not to be saved to history. So, if for any reason you don't want a command to be saved, just prepend it with a space. The erasedups option will actually go through your whole history

© Philip Kirkbride 2020
P. Kirkbride, *Basic Linux Terminal Tips and Tricks*, https://doi.org/10.1007/978-1-4842-6035-7_3

each time you run a command and remove any other instances of it. One potential downside of erasedups is that if you get history, and then run multiple commands, the deleting of a command can shift the numbers, in which case you'd have to run history again to update the correct numbers, or accidentally run the wrong command.

```
HISTFILESIZE=10000
# don't save duplicate lines or lines starting with space
# See bash(1) for more options
HISTCONTROL=ignoreboth:erasedups
```

Another history option worth turning on is histappend to help with keeping track of history when you're using multiple terminal sessions. By default, when a terminal instance is closed, the history file is overwritten instead of appended. This causes only the history of the last closed session to be saved. You can turn histappend on with

```
# append to the history file, don't overwrite it
shopt -s histappend
```

Scrolling 10,000 lines can take a long time; that's where grep comes in handy. Say you remember using ffmpeg for cutting a video, but you don't remember the exact flags and inputs. Simply run

```
history | grep ffmpeg
```

Once you see the command you're looking for you can use the number on the left handside to quickly run it again. Another example of history output is shown in Figure 3-1.

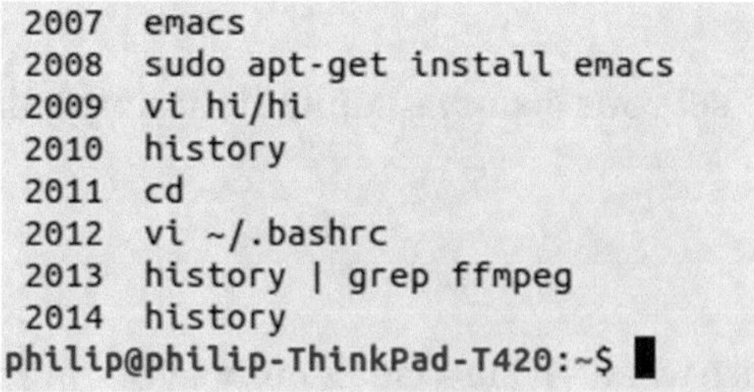

```
2007  emacs
2008  sudo apt-get install emacs
2009  vi hi/hi
2010  history
2011  cd
2012  vi ~/.bashrc
2013  history | grep ffmpeg
2014  history
philip@philip-ThinkPad-T420:~$ █
```

Figure 3-1. *Command history*

Given the history output shown in Figure 3-1, we could run Emacs by entering

```
!2007
```

This workflow will speed up the rate at which you can enter commands significantly. In some situations, you can combine these two steps into a single one by using !? instead of just !. For example, if we wanted to run command 2012 from Figure 3-1 we could run

```
!?vi
```

What this does is search for the most recent command in your history that contains vi. It doesn't have to reference the start of the command either, as long as the string is within the command. So the following would also result in command 2012 being run:

```
!?bash
```

Using the preceding methods of working with history can greatly increase the speed with which you enter commands. However, you have to be careful since if the text is found in a command other than the one you intended, it will automatically run.

Bash Shortcuts

Keyboard shortcuts come in handy on most programs, and this is true with bash. You should be aware that a large amount of keyboard shortcuts for bash shell exist. Personally, I only use a few of these commands, but the ones I do use have been extremely useful.

When you first start, you may find you only use one or two. It's likely you'll slowly and gradually learn commands, and once comfortable you may decide to add more to your regular workflow. Start with a few useful commands listed here, and as you become used to them, come back and try to incorporate more.

The most basic shortcut while using bash is the tab key. The tab key when double tapped activates autocomplete, as shown in Figure 3-2. To demonstrate, try writing the ls command followed by a space, and before pressing enter, tap tab twice.

```
philip@philip-ThinkPad-T420:/$ ls
bin/            lib/            opt/            sys/
boot/           lib32/          proc/           tmp/
cdrom/          lib64/          root/           usr/
dev/            libx32/         run/            var/
etc/            lost+found/     sbin/           vmlinuz
home/           media/          snap/           vmlinuz.old
initrd.img      mnt/            srv/
initrd.img.old  nix/            swapfile
philip@philip-ThinkPad-T420:/$ ls █
```

Figure 3-2. *Double tapping folders available for autocomplete*

You should see all the files in your working directory like in Figure 3-2. Tab can be used in this way with nearly any command which takes a file as an input.

Note   Keyboard shortcuts that make use of `ctrl` plus a letter are based on the default keybindings for most distros. If you find that these shortcuts aren't working on your machine, you'll want to see the next section "Emacs vs. Vim Keyboard Bindings". As it's possible the default mode differs on your system or has been changed. It's also possible these shortcuts might not work if your distro has assigned some global behaviour to the binding. For example, when using Xubuntu I found that some of my most used bash keyboard shortcuts didn't work. I ended up doing some research and found a settings panel specific to the distro where I could remove some of the global keyboard shortcuts which caused the application specific shortcuts to be active again.

Next to tab, my most used keyboard shortcuts are `ctrl+b` and `ctrl+a`.

ctrl+a = moves text cursor to the start of the command

ctrl+b = moves text cursor to the end of the command

So if you've written a long command and notice a typo before pressing enter, you can use `ctrl+a` to quickly move back and fix it, then return to where you were with `ctrl+b`.

I often find myself using this in combination with &&. This tells bash to run the command after && only after the first command runs successfully. Alternatively, you can use a single & if you want the second command to run regardless of whether the first command is successful (e.g., if `tmp.txt` doesn't exist, with && the `git add *` won't run, whereas with & it will).

Say, for instance, you've entered the command `git add *`, but you realize you had a file you wanted to delete first. Simply press `ctrl+a` to move your cursor to the first charachter of the terminal input and change the command to

```
rm tmp.txt && git add *
```

Instead of deleting what you've written and having to enter it again later, simply write the prerequisite command at the start and chain it using &&. There is something satisfying about chaining several commands together and having them all run successfully. I might think that because the moment after entering a chain of commands can be the perfect time to pour a cup of coffee while waiting for them to process.

The other two commands I use are `ctrl+c` and `ctrl+d`.

ctrl+c = cancels the current command

ctrl+d = closes the current terminal

Pressing `ctrl+d` simply closes your current terminal instance, producing the same result as running the command `exit`. The obvious use is quickly closing a terminal window when you're finishing it, but you can also use it to close other programs like tmux or end an ssh session.

Have you ever written a long command and realize you want to do something completely different? When this happens, our instinct is to hold down the backspace button, for what can seem like forever. Next time try `ctrl+c`, short for clear input, instead. It'll give you a fresh input to write on without executing the command.

If you often find yourself running the command `clear`, you'll want to take note of `ctrl+l`.

ctrl+l = clears the screen of all text and leaves you with a new command line at the top of the terminal session

A list of all the Emacs keyboard shortcuts (default mode on most systems) is shown in Table 3-1.

Table 3-1. *List of default (Emacs style) bash keyboard shortcuts*

Sequence	Description
ctrl+a	Go to the beginning of the line
ctrl+e	Go to the end of the line
alt+b	Move cursor one word back
ctrl+b	Move cursor one character back
alt+f	Move cursor one word forward
ctrl+f	Move cursor one character forward
alt+t	Swap last two words
ctrl+t	Swap last two characters
alt+r	If you've modified command from history, reset changes
ctrl+k	Delete all after cursor
ctrl+u	Delete all before cursor
ctrl+w	Delete last word
ctrl+y	Paste deleted words (works as undo for ctrl+w)
ctrl+l	Clear past terminal output (same as `clear` command)
ctrl+z	Background running process

Emacs vs. Vim Keyboard Bindings

An interesting fact is the bash keyboard shortcuts are actually based on the keybindings in Emacs, a popular open source text editor. Many of the keybindings that work in bash will also work in Emacs. However, it is possible to enable Vim-like keybindings in bash. To do so, run the following command:

```
set -o vi
```

Running `set -o vi` will set Vim keybindings for your current session only; to enable it permanently, you should add it to your `.bashrc` file. You can set bash and even more programs to use Vim bindings at once by adding the following line to your `.inputrc` file:

```
set editing-mode vi
```

Alternatively, if you want to explicitly specify Emacs-style bindings, you can instead add

```
set editing-mode emacs
```

The `.inputrc` file affects the input of all programs which use the GNU readline library, a popular library used by several utilities including bash, and other operating systems like OpenBSD. Some of the programs that use GNU readline library include but not limited to

> *Abiword, Amanda, Atari800, Bacula, Bareos, GNU bc, BlueZ, Cdecl, ConnMan, Freeciv, FreeRADIUS, GNU ftp, NetKit ftp, FVWM, GDB, GPG, Guile, Hatari, Hunspell, Lftp, NetworkManager, nftables, Parted, the rc shell, Samba, SQLite, GNU Units, VICE, Wesnoth, WPA Supplicant, Lua REPL, Python REPL, Ruby REPL …*

Hence, any setting which is changed in `.inputrc` will affect them all. The `.inputrc` file doesn't exist by default but if added will affect the way bash receives input. Aside from changing between the default emacs mode and vi mode, other behaviors of the terminal can be modified. We'll look at `.inputrc` in depth in a later chapter.

The `vi`-style keybindings don't have an equivalent set of shortcuts but rather mimic the idea of having separate modes for typing and running commands. If you are using `vi` mode and press `esc`, you'll switch to command mode where you can use some (but not all) `vi` commands like `0` to go to the start of the line, `$` to go to the end, `w` to go forward a word, and `b` to go back a word.

If you're not familiar with Vim or `vi` and the various commands, we recommend sticking with the default Emacs keybindings, though Vim is definitely worth learning and there will be a chapter dedicated to Vim further in the book. After reading it and getting comfortable with using Vim, you may wish to return to your bash settings and experiment with `vi`-style shortcuts. I use Vim as an editor but still prefer the Emacs style keybindings on bash as they're simple and the common default.

Reverse Search

Another shortcut that we didn't discuss in the last section is `ctrl+r` for reverse search. I prefer to use the `history` command, but many people prefer using the interactive reverse search.

After pressing `ctrl+r`, you'll go into an interactive mode where if you start typing a previously written command, it will show in the autocomplete as shown in Figure 3-3.

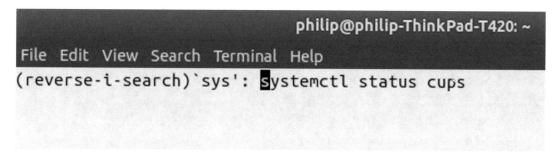

Figure 3-3. *Reverse search in terminal*

Once you see the command you want to run, you can press enter to run it. Or you can press tab to return to normal shell mode with the command ready to be run or modified. For example, given the preceding command, I might press tab and then `ctrl+e` to go to the end of the line, delete `cups`, and then write a different service to fetch status on.

If you've started writing a command in reverse search and autocomplete isn't the one you want, you can press `ctrl+r` to go one further back. So in the example shown, pressing `ctrl+r` would show the next match in history which starts with `sys`.

File Globbing or Wildcards

File globbing is a feature in Linux which allows multiple files to be represented through the use of wildcard characters. The most well-known wildcard character is * which represents one or more of any character. For example, run

echo *

This will run the command echo on all files in your current directory. The wildcard can also be used in combination with other characters, for example:

```
ls /dev/sd*
```

It will not return all files in /dev/ but only files within the folder which start with "sd".

The * isn't the only character that can be used, though it is by far the most common. Another possible wildcard for globbing is ?. The ? character is similar to the * in that it can represent any character, but it is only a single character rather than any amount. If we modify our previous command to be

```
ls /dev/sd?
```

instead of getting back all files that start with "sd", we now only get back files that start with "sd" and have one additional character. Notice the difference in output between the two in Figure 3-4.

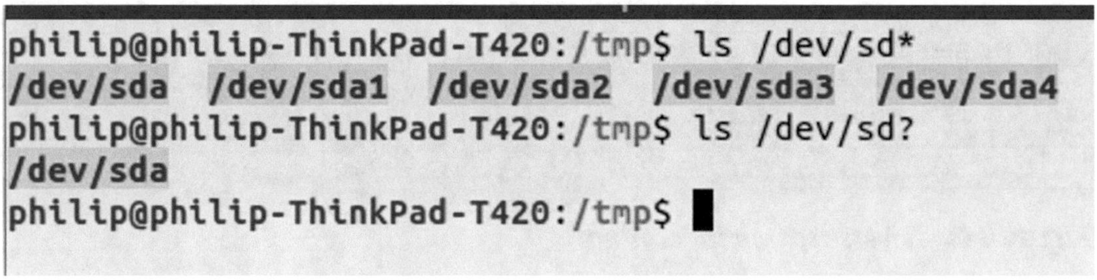

```
philip@philip-ThinkPad-T420:/tmp$ ls /dev/sd*
/dev/sda  /dev/sda1  /dev/sda2  /dev/sda3  /dev/sda4
philip@philip-ThinkPad-T420:/tmp$ ls /dev/sd?
/dev/sda
philip@philip-ThinkPad-T420:/tmp$ █
```

Figure 3-4. *Comparing the * and ? wildcard characters*

The last character that can be used, or rather character combination, is the square bracket [ ], known as a set often used with characters inside. For example, if we wanted to repeat our preceding command that used ? but also include other drives like sdb and sdc (*if they exist*), we can do

```
ls /dev/sd[abc]
```

This will match a single character as long as it is one specified inside the brackets, in this case, a, b, or c.

Summary

In this chapter, we looked at using bash history, shortcuts, and file globbing. By making use of these techniques, you'll significantly speed up your workflow by having to write less as you enter commands.

CHAPTER 4

Scripts and Pipes

Creating Scripts

Once you get familiar with working with files and using various commands, you'll soon find you want to combine several commands, sometimes creating long sequences that can be somewhat time consuming. We'll go more in detail later on, but for now it's good to know this is possible. Creating a list of commands to run one after the other is as easy as writing a grocery list of things you need to buy (*once you know the basic steps*).

You simply open a text file using any editor (*nano was mentioned earlier, but you can even use a desktop text editor if that's easier*). On the first line of the text file, you write or paste in a special line called a "shebang" which indicates that the file is a script (*more details in the next section*). Then you start listing off commands to be run line by line.

Creating scripts for commonly run sequences of commands can come in handy. You can save the commands as a text file and then run the sequence as a single step. The steps required for creating a script from a bird's eye view are as follows:

1. Create a text file containing the commands.

2. Make the top line of the file a shebang (explained later).

3. Save file.

4. Make the file executable using permissions (explained later).

5. Run the command ./myScript.sh.

Below is an example of a simple script called name.sh:

```
#!/usr/bin/env bash

echo First name: $1
echo Last name: $2
```

© Philip Kirkbride 2020
P. Kirkbride, *Basic Linux Terminal Tips and Tricks*, https://doi.org/10.1007/978-1-4842-6035-7_4

This script takes two arguments, one for first name and one for last. These arguments are represented in the code with $1 and $2. It would be executed by running

```
./name.sh Philip Kirkbride
```

When run two lines will output, the first line being "First name: Philip" and the second line "Last name: Kirkbride". Unless of course you swap the input for your own name in which case the names will be swapped out.

We'll look more at steps 2 and 4 in the preceding list which are needed before actually running the script in the following sections.

Shebang

A shebang refers to the first line in a script, when that line begins with #!. The word comes from the musical notation term for # sharp and the ! sometimes being called "bang"; combining these two becomes "sharp-bang" or shebang for short.

The shebang when used as the first line of a file specifies the program which will be used to interpret the script. The most popular one relevant to writing Linux scripts is

```
#!/bin/bash
```

The same thing can be expressed using /usr/bin/env which increases portability by using whatever version of bash is found in the user's path.

```
#!/usr/bin/env bash
```

The shebang is not limited to bash scripts. It should also be the first line when writing scripts in other scripting languages such as python, ruby, or perl.

```
#!/usr/bin/env python
```

File Permissions

As mentioned previously, the fourth step in making an executable script is changing the permissions on the file to allow execution. The short and simple way of doing this is to run

```
chmod +x name.sh
```

This simply adds the execution permission to the file for our current user. After running the command, you'll be able to make use of it simply by running the following (assuming you're in the same directory as the file):

```
./name.sh
```

It's worth understanding the concept of permissions on Linux as it's a crucial aspect of the operating system. Every file has three different types of permissions:

- Read

- Write

- Execute

Each of these three permissions can be set separately for three groups:

- User

- Group

- Others

When using ls -l, you can see the set permissions for each file expressed on the left-hand side, as shown in Figure 4-1.

```
srwxrwxr-x 1 philip philip
-rw------- 1 philip philip
drwxr-xr-x 2 philip philip
-rw-r--r-- 1 philip philip
drwxr-xr-x 2 root   root
```

Figure 4-1. *Permissions for files shown in the first column when running ls -l*

Note   The first letter in this ten-letter sequence is used to indicate special file types. The possible values are d=directory, c=character device, s=symlink, p=named pipe, s=socket, b=block device, and D=door. We don't have to deal with these special types, but it's worth knowing what the first letter is.

After the first letter which indicates special file types, there are nine more letters. We can break these nine letters into three sets of three, as shown in Figure 4-2 – the first being file permissions for file owner, the second for user group, and the third for all other users.

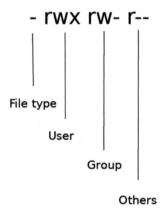

Figure 4-2. *Components of file permissions*

For the three sections, we have three different letters which if present indicate that groups has said permission:

- r = read

- w = write

- x = execute

In the example given, we have a file with all permissions for the owner, read and write for the user group, and only the ability to read for all others who can access the file.

Permission data can also be displayed as a set of three numeric symbols where a single number represents the combination of the permissions. Each of the permission types is given a numeric value:

- 4 = read

- 2 = write

- 1 = execute

For any group we add up the permissions to get a number representing allowed permissions. For example, read and write would be 6 (2 + 4), write and execute would be 3 (1 + 2), and no permissions would be 0.

Using this notation, we would express rxw rw- r-- as 764. Either of these notations can be used when changing permissions for a file. For example, we can run

```
chmod 777 numbers.sh
```

This gives all permissions to all users. Or if we want to use the notation with letter, we could run the following command to take away execution permission for all groups (*note the-; if we wanted to add, it would instead be +*):

```
chmod -x numbers.sh
```

If we want to use number notation for a specific column (user, group, or others), we can first specify the group, for example, add execution permission back but only for the owner:

```
chmod u+x numbers.sh
```

File Types

While we've defined our script using the file type .sh, this is not actually required in Linux. We can just as easily have named it name instead of name.sh, and it would work just the same.

Note   Some teams prefer scripts without the '.sh' extension, for example, the Google Shell Style Guide actually specifies the extension .sh should not be used. Despite this several public repositories managed by Google contain shell scripts which include the .sh. This just goes to show even at a company which states a preference you can't be sure if scripts will include the .sh extension.

A useful command for detecting file type is file. To experiment with this, first change the file name of name.sh to name. Next run the following:

```
file name
```

You should get back a message saying the file type is Bourne-Again shell script. Next try opening the file and editing the shebang to be the one for python, as listed in the shebang section.

```
#!/usr/bin/env python
```

After saving try running file again. Repeat this process trying different shebangs, including python, ruby, and perl. You should get results similar to those shown in Figure 4-3.

```
philip@philip-ThinkPad-T420:/tmp$ file name
name: Bourne-Again shell script, ASCII text executable
philip@philip-ThinkPad-T420:/tmp$ vi name
philip@philip-ThinkPad-T420:/tmp$ file name
name: Python script, ASCII text executable
philip@philip-ThinkPad-T420:/tmp$ vi name
philip@philip-ThinkPad-T420:/tmp$ file name
name: Ruby script, ASCII text executable
philip@philip-ThinkPad-T420:/tmp$ vi name
philip@philip-ThinkPad-T420:/tmp$ file name
name: Perl script text executable
philip@philip-ThinkPad-T420:/tmp$ █
```

Figure 4-3. *Results of changing file type by editing the shebang*

Pipes

Pipes are one of the most common features of basic syntax. If you're familiar with them, feel free to skip over this section. A pipe simply connects the output of one command as the input to another command. We'll use a fun example to demonstrate the concept.

To start install fortune and cowsay:

```
sudo apt-get install fortune-mod cowsay
```

Fortune is a full little command-line program with a long history dating all the way back to version 7 of Linux in the early 1990s. It simply generates a random quote, for example, running the command on my computer now returned

"You never know how many friends you have until you rent a house on the beach."

Try it yourself by running fortune a few times. Each time it's run, a random quote from a long list is output. Now for fun let's pipe the output into cowsay:

```
fortune | cowsay
```

Now we get back a random fortune inside a little piece of text art shown in Figure 4-4.

```
philip@philip-ThinkPad-T420:~$ fortune | cowsay
_____
/ I have never let my schooling interfere \
| with my education.                       |
|                                          |
\ -- Mark Twain                            /
 ------------------------------------------
        \    ^__^
         \  (oo)_____
            (__)\        )\/\
                ||----w |
                ||      ||
philip@philip-ThinkPad-T420:~$ ▮
```

Figure 4-4. *Piping fortune to cowsay*

As the fortune generated is from a random list, the one you see should be different from the one in Figure 4-4. What's happening here is that the output from the fortune code is being used as the input for the `cowsay` command. The receiving command is completely unaware of the process which generates said text.

We can, for instance, swap our `fortune` command with a simple `echo`:

```
echo hello world | cowsay
```

In this case, as you might expect, the cow says "hello world". There is no limit to how many pipes can be used. We can further process our text before sending it to cow say using another pipe in between the two commands:

```
echo hello world | rev | cowsay
```

In this case, our "hello world" text is reversed to "dlrow olleh" before it reaches the `cowsay` command. In the next section, we'll look more at using multiple pipes.

Multiple Pipelines

Throughout this book, we'll be writing bash scripts in addition to simply exploring command-line programs. As you start to write more bash scripts, you'll often find you need to use pipe, not just once but several times.

With complex scripts that string together command-line programs with pipes, you'll find your scripts start to look a little bit messy. One of the most useful formatting techniques is the multiline pipeline. This is simply when you separate a series of pipes into multiple lines by using \.

If your command pipeline fits nicely on a single line like the following, you don't need to worry about spreading it out on multiple lines:

```
# All fits on one line
command1 | command2
```

If however you're using multiple commands in a chain and it goes beyond a single line or looks hard to read, spread it out to multiple lines as shown in the following:

```
# Long commands
command1 \
  | command2 \
  | command3 \
  | command4 \
```

The preceding example came from the Google Shell Style Guide, a great resource for tips on making your shell scripts more readable. Some of the guidelines are related to internal preferences at the company (e.g., using two spaces instead of tab), while other tips are generally applicable to all shell scripts.

Once you become more comfortable writing shell scripts and find you're doing it often, you should take a look at the Google Style Guide for shell scripts. It'll help you consider factors that make your scripts more readable to other developers or system admins who might come across your scripts.

```
https://google.github.io/styleguide/shell.xml
```

Chain Commands with && and ||

In this section, we're going to talk about some logic syntax built into bash that can come in handy – specifically, && which can be used as AND and || which can be used as OR.

```
&& the operator for "and"
|| the operator for "or"
```

This is very useful when you need to use a long-running command followed by another command. For example, say you're connected to an IoT device with slow Internet connection, you need to update the system and, once that's done, install a new program. You could simply run

```
sudo apt-get update \
  && sudo apt-get install -y program-x
```

Note the -y flag used; this tells apt-get to answer yes when asked for confirmation.

This can be very useful in combination with tmux (a program for switching between terminal instances quickly, which we'll explore in depth in a later chapter). At a previous job, I often found myself on site having to SSH into five to ten different IoT devices. Stringing together multiple commands, I could give a device enough work to keep it busy for 15 minutes and then immediately switch to another tmux session already connected through SSH to another device and get to work immediately.

The or operator ‖ can be just as useful when you know you need to run a second command but only in the case that your first command fails. For example, say we have a common problem on our IoT device where if a command fails, we're likely out of disk space; in said case we want to remove all logs:

```
sudo apt-get install -y program-x \
  || sudo rm -rf /var/log/*
```

Exit Codes for && and ‖

It should be noted that whether the || or && are triggered depends on the exit code of the command that precedes it. It isn't sufficient just to have output on standard error. For example, let's write a file at /tmp/err.sh with the following:

```
#!/usr/bin/env bash
>&2 echo Error
```

Make the file executable with chmod +x /tmp/err.sh and then run the command with a || statement like the following:

```
/tmp/err.sh || echo error
```

Notice that you get back the standard error text, but the echo error command is never run. This is due to the fact that our program is still returning an exit code of 0. We can see the exit code by adding the following to the bottom of our script:

```
echo $?
```

Now when running the script, you should see an additional "0" output. If you'd like to change the exit command, you can use the exit command. At the bottom of our script, add

```
exit 1
```

Now if we run the script again with our || statement, we'll see the echo error command trigger. We aren't limited to exit code 1 here, numbers 0–255 are all valid exit codes. The exit code 0 specifies a successful execution, while codes 1–255 specify an error. Some of these exit codes are normally used for specific errors; others are left for program-specific errors. A list of standard error code numbers and their meanings are shown in Table 4-1.

Table 4-1. *Standard meanings for exit codes*

Code	
0	Default, command ran without issue
1	Catchall for all nonspecific errors
126	Command invoked is not executable
127	Command not found
128	Invalid argument to exit
128+n	Fatal error signal "n"
130	Script ended by ctrl+c
255*	Exit status out of range

As you can see, even with these reserved error ranges, there is plenty of room for you to define your own custom errors. This can be useful if there are multiple ways your script can fail and you want a way to programmatically detect those particular cases.

Using && with ||

You can also mix the operators together for more complex use cases. Say, for example, we want to check if a string is in a text file using grep, then pass the word "true" or "false" to the cowsay program. In that case, we need to introduce the use of brackets:

```
( grep -q dog /tmp/test && echo true || echo false ) \
 | cowsay
```

Similar to the use of brackets in math, the statement inside the brackets will be evaluated and passed through a pipe to cowsay, as shown in Figure 4-5. If the file /tmp/ test exists and contains the word dog, we should see something like:

```
philip@philip-ThinkPad-T420:~$ ( grep -q dog /tmp/test && echo true || echo false ) \
>   | cowsay
grep: /tmp/test: No such file or directory
 _____
< false >
 ---------
        \    ^__^
         \   (oo)_____
            (__)\        )\/\
                ||----w  |
                ||       ||
philip@philip-ThinkPad-T420:~$ █
```

Figure 4-5. *Cowsay saying true or false based on a condition*

Of course false is returned since the file /tmp/test doesn't exist. Try creating the file with some text that includes "dog". You can do that quickly with the command

echo dog > /tmp/test

Once you've run this command, running the previous command should instead return true. The > symbol used here is a redirect which we'll look at more closely in the next section.

Redirects

As we saw in the last section, we can use the > character to send text into a file rather than piping into another program. This can be done with the output from any program. When using the standard redirect, you should be aware that any existing content in that file will be overwritten. Running

echo dog > /tmp/test
echo cat > /tmp/test

will result in /tmp/test only containing the text "cat". If you want to append text to the file instead of replacing the content, you should instead use >>:

echo dog >> /tmp/test
echo cat >> /tmp/test

This will instead result in a file which contains two lines, one with "dog" and one with "cat".

The output in a redirect by default contains both the output and any errors. We can instead redirect errors to a separate location by adding

```
echo cat > /tmp/test 2> /tmp/error
```

However, with the preceding example, no errors are being created. To generate both standard output and standard error in a single command, use ls on an existing file and a nonexistent file:

```
ls /tmp/test /tmp/nope777 > /tmp/test 2> /tmp/error
```

After running the preceding command, you should have content in both the /tmp/test file and /tmp/error. As with a normal redirect, we can use >> to append instead of replace the text:

```
ls /tmp/test /tmp/nope777 >> /tmp/test 2>> /tmp/error
```

If you run the preceding command multiple times, you'll end up with lines in each file for each time it was run.

Redirect and Pipe at Once with tee

Redirecting output to a file and piping are both powerful tools, but what if you want to do them both at once? A popular utility called tee exists for exactly this purpose. It duplicates the input and sends it to both a file and the output as shown in Figure 4-6.

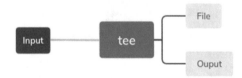

Figure 4-6. *Diagram of output from tee command*

The tee command takes output from standard output, saves it to a file of your choice, then passes that output to its own standard output. For example, say we have the following command using a redirect to write the output "hello" to a file called greeting:

```
echo hello > greeting
```

Running the preceding command, we'll end up with "hello" in our greeting file but will see nothing in our standard output. The same program modified to use tee would be

```
echo hello | tee greeting
```

With tee, we'll end up with "hello" in our greeting file, but we also see "hello" in the standard output. If you want tee to act like >> and append to a file rather than > which replaces the text, you can use the -a flag.

Another example of using tee, say we want to pass a math equation to the math utility bc for processing. We'll output the result to a file called math, but we also want to show the equation that led to the result. We could make use of tee for this using the following command:

```
echo "7 * 7" | tee math.txt | bc >> math.txt
```

This causes the file math.txt to be written to twice. Once using tee and the input, and a second time via '>>'. The file math.txt should contain:

```
7 * 7
49
```

xargs

While wildcards are good for file expansion when running commands on multiple files, sometimes you want to instead run a command on each line of output from another command. For this we can use xargs to demonstrate; we'll use a command that could just as easily be done with a wildcard:

```
ls | xargs cat
```

The preceding command has the same output as cat *; it outputs the contents of each file in your current directory. The difference is in how it is done. Rather than expanding the wildcard and passing each file into a single cat command, we instead take each line output from the ls command and use it as the input for a separate cat command for each line.

Using xargs allows you to do things which are not possible with a wildcard. For example, say I want to remove all files of a certain type. An example I'll use is .swp files; these are recovery files for the text editor Vim. In my case, they don't contain any useful data but were left behind by exiting the program abruptly (e.g., closing a terminal window without closing the editor). I can run a find and remove on my home directory by running

```
find ~/ -name "*.swp" | xargs rm
```

This will take each result which is returned by find and run rm on it. I ran find before and after the command to demonstrate all the .swp files are removed, as can be seen in Figure 4-7.

```
philip@philip-ThinkPad-T420:/tmp$ sudo find ~/ -name "*.swp"
/home/philip/tmp/serial/serial_comm/.test.js.swp
/home/philip/.cache/yarn/v4/npm-jshint-2.9.7-038a3fa5c328fa3ab03ddfd85df88d3d87bedcbd/n
ode_modules/jshint/src/.precedence.js.swp
/home/philip/.cache/yarn/v4/npm-colors-1.3.2-2df8ff573dfbf255af562f8ce7181d6b971a359b/n
ode_modules/colors/lib/.colors.js.swp
/home/philip/research/.eqn.ms.swp
/home/philip/research/event-generation-from-knowledge-structure-for-mobile-larp-game/so
urce/client/src/modules/.SettingsPage.js.swp
/home/philip/research/event-generation-from-knowledge-structure-for-mobile-larp-game/so
urce/server-interface/node_modules/jshint/src/.precedence.js.swp
/home/philip/research/event-generation/src/modules/.SettingsPage.js.swp
philip@philip-ThinkPad-T420:/tmp$ sudo find ~/ -name "*.swp" | xargs rm
philip@philip-ThinkPad-T420:/tmp$ sudo find ~/ -name "*.swp"
philip@philip-ThinkPad-T420:/tmp$ █
```

Figure 4-7. *Results from searching for swp files with find*

Conditional Expressions in Bash

As you start to combine several components of programs using && and || via the command line, you'll likely find it starts to get easier to write a dedicated script rather than manually enter a long string of commands from the command line. As you move from command line to writing a script, it'll be easier to use some of the more complicated syntax tools.

One of these tools is the if statement, which is more like a series of possible tests, each with their own specific option. For example, if we want to check if a file exists, we'd use the -e option. Create a script and add the following:

```
if [ -e /etc/passwd ]; then
  echo passwd exists
fi
```

When you run the script, you should get the output "passwd exists". Try changing /etc/passwd to a file that doesn't exist. Or if you'd like to test if the file doesn't exist, you can add a ! as shown in the following:

```
if [ ! -e /etc/passwd ]; then
```

As with other languages, we can add an else to our if statement:

```
if [ -e /etc/passwd ]; then
  echo passwd exists
else
  touch /etc/passwd
fi
```

The preceding syntax works for several different possible tests that can be run by substituting the -e. The list is quite long and can be found by running man bash and scrolling down to the conditional expression section. Some of the more commonly used flags are shown in Table 4-2.

Table 4-2. *Conditional expression options*

Code	
-d	True if exists and is a directory
-f	True if exists and is a regular file
-e	True if exists
-s	True if file exists and has a size greater than 0
-x	True if exists and is an executable

Is a Directory with -d

The -d flag can be used to confirm that a file exists and is a directory. This can be useful if you want to make use of a directory but aren't sure that it exists or if it does exist that it is a directory and not a file. An example of using -d is shown here:

```
mkdir /tmp/test
if [ -d /tmp/test ]; then
  rmdir /tmp/test
fi
```

Is a Normal File with -f

The flag -f is similar to -d but tells us if a file is a regular file, rather than a directory. Again this can be used before making use of a file to ensure that it exists and is the right type. An example of -e is shown here:

```
touch /tmp/test
if [ -f /tmp/test ]; then
  rm /tmp/test
fi
```

Check if File Exists with -e

The -e is a sort of combination of both -f and -d as it only tests that a file exists and does not consider whether what the type of the file is. An example of using -e is shown here:

```
touch /tmp/test
if [ -e /tmp/test ]; then
  rm -rf /tmp/test
fi
```

Check if Exists and Size Greater Than 0 with -s

If you're doing something with the contents of a file, you might also want to know if the file in question has anything in it. In this case, you can use -s which will only return true if the file exists and has a size greater than 0. An example of the use of -s is shown here:

```
touch /tmp/test
if [ -s /tmp/test ]; then
  echo "doesn't run"
fi
echo data > /tmp/test
if [ -s /tmp/test ]; then
  echo "does run"
fi
```

Check if Exists and is an Executable with -x

If your use of a file is actually executing it as a program, you may want to confirm that the file exists before doing so. This is where the -x comes in handy which checks the file permissions of a file to confirm that it is executable. Though keep in mind that this only checks the file permissions to confirm that a file is executable, it doesn't actually check that the file contains a script. In the following example, our executable file is actually just a blank file, yet after running chmod +x /tmp/executable, the -x flag recognizes it as an executable:

```
touch /tmp/executable
if [ -x /tmp/executable ]; then
  echo "doesn't run"
```

```
fi
chmod +x /tmp/executable
if [ -x /tmp/executable ]; then
  echo "does run"
  bash /tmp/executable
fi
```

It's also possible to compare strings using a similar syntax. A list of flags for comparing strings is shown in Table 4-3.

Table 4-3. *String compare conditions*

Code	
-z S1	True if S1 is a string with length 0
-n S1	True if S1 is a string with a length greater than 0
S1 == S2	True if S1 is the same string as S2
S1 != S2	True if S1 is not the same string as S2
S1 < S2	True if S1 sorts before S2
S1 > S2	True if S2 sorts before S1

Check Value Is a String of Length 0 with -z

When programming or writing scripts, often an unset or empty variable can throw a wrench into things. Bash provides a method for checking if a variable is empty using the -z flag. An example is shown here:

```
S1=""
if [ -z $S1 ]; then
  echo "is empty string"
  S1="something"
else
  echo "not empty"
fi
```

Check Value Is a Non-empty String with -n

If instead of checking for an empty value, you'd want to check that a value is not empty, you can use -n. It's essentially the opposite of -z and will return true for any non-empty string. An example is as follows, in which we use the variable $S1 only if it is not empty:

```
S1="something"
if [ -n $S1 ]; then
  echo $S1
else
  echo "variable is empty"
fi
```

Check That Strings Are Equal

Like many programming languages, bash also provides a way to check that strings are equal to one another. This can be done with the double equal sign ==. A simple example is as follows:

```
S1="something"
S2="something"
if [ $S1 == $S2 ]; then
  echo "same"
else
  echo "not the same"
fi
```

Check That Strings Are Not Equal

As you might expect, we can test that strings are not equal in a similar way by using !=. An example is as follows, which should return the text "same":

```
S1="something"
S2="something"
if [ $S1 != $S2 ]; then
  echo "not the same"
else
  echo "same"
fi
```

Check String Sort Order

When working with strings, we can also use the > and < symbols to compare. On first seeing these, you might expect that these compare mathematical values or which string is longer. In actuality, the greater than and less than symbols used with strings check for sort order.

By default this is alphabetically. To demonstrate sorting, we can run the following command; feel free to replace the letters with numbers or symbols:

```
letters='a y b v b c'
echo "$letters" | tr ' ' '\n' | sort | tr '\n' ' '
```

Running the preceding command should return "a b b c v y". You can ignore the `tr` commands which simply convert the spaces to newlines and after sorting replace newlines with spaces. You can experiment with the preceding command to get an idea of how things sort.

This sorting order is what is used for the > and < symbols. In the following, we have an example of using <:

```
S1="a"
S2="b"
if [ $S1 < $S2 ]; then
  echo $S1 sorts before $S2
else
  echo $S2 sorts before $S1
fi
```

In addition to testing files and strings, there is also support for testing integers. Table 4-4 outlines several methods for comparing integers. Note that in Table 4-4, N1 and N2 are variables which could contain any integer.

Table 4-4. *Arithmetic operators*

Code	
N1 -eq N2	True if N1 is equal to N2
N1 -ne N2	True if N1 is not equal to N2
N1 -lt N2	True if N1 is less than N2
N1 -le N2	True if N1 is less than or equal to N2
N1 -gt N2	True if N1 is greater than N2
N1 -ge N2	True if N1 is greater than or equal to N2

Check If Numbers Are Equal

When comparing numbers, there is a whole different set of flags that can be used. One of these is the -eq flag which checks that two numbers are equal. An example of the use of -eq is as follows; it should return "1 and 1 are equal":

```
N1=1
N2=1
if [ $S1 -eq $S2 ]; then
  echo $N1 and $N2 are equal
else
  echo $N1 and $N2 are not equal
fi
```

Check If Numbers Are Not Equal

For checking if numbers are not equal, use the -ne flag. This is essentially the same as -eq but opposite. An example of using -ne is as follows; it should return "1 and 2 are not equal":

```
N1=1
N2=2
if [ $S1 -ne $S2 ]; then
  echo $N1 and $N2 are not equal
else
  echo $N1 and $N2 are equal
fi
```

Check If a Number Is Less Than

We can also use a flag to check that a number is less than another number. An example of using -lt is as follows; it should return "1 is less than 2":

```
N1=1
N2=2
if [ $S1 -lt $S2 ]; then
```

```
  echo $N1 is less than $N2
else
  echo $N1 is not less than $N2
fi
```

Check If a Number Is Less Than or Equal

The flag -le is nearly identical to -lt with the sole exception that it also returns true if numbers are equal to each other. An example is shown in the following where equal numbers trigger true, though if $N1 was less than $S2, it would also trigger as true. Running the code should return "2 is less than or equal to 2":

```
N1=2
N2=2
if [ $S1 -le $S2 ]; then
  echo $N1 is less than or equal to $N2
else
  echo $N1 is not less than or equal to $N2
fi
```

Check If a Number Is Greater Than

Whenever you have the ability to check if a number is less than, you likely also have the ability to check if it is greater than. This is the case with bash where you can use the -gt flag to check if a number is greater than. The following is an example of the use of the -gt flag. The following should return "3 is greater than 2":

```
N1=3
N2=2
if [ $S1 -gt $S2 ]; then
  echo $N1 is greater than $N2
else
  echo $N1 is not greater than $N2
fi
```

Check If a Number Is Greater Than or Equal

If you'd prefer to match both greater than or equal, you can use -ge. An example of its use is as follows. Running the following code should return "3 is greater than or equal to 3":

```
N1=3
N2=3
if [ $S1 -ge $S2 ]; then
  echo $N1 is greater than or equal to $N2
else
  echo $N1 is not greater than or equal to $N2
fi
```

While the preceding code can be handy, there is also syntax dedicated to arithmetic expressions using double brackets which we'll look at in the next section.

Arithmetic with Double Parentheses

While comparing integers is possible using tests surrounded with square parentheses in bash, it is preferred to use double parentheses which allow syntax anyone who programs in another language would be comfortable with, for example:

```
if ((2 < 3)); then
  echo 3 is greater than 2
fi
```

In the preceding code, exactly ((2 < 3)) will evaluate to true. We're using hard numbers here, but in most cases, you'll be comparing variables which can be used in their place.

```
((N1 < N2))
```

If you want to use math to set a variable, you'll also need to make use of double parentheses, preceded by a dollar sign, for example:

```
N1=$((1+1))
if ((N1<3)); then
  echo 3 is greater than $N1
fi
```

The $ is required anytime you want to make use of the result, whether you're setting it to a variable or not – even if we just want to echo the result:

```
echo $((1+3))
```

Be aware that if you try to use arithmetic without the double parentheses, it will append as if the number is a string, for example:

```
N1=2
N1+=1
echo $N1
```

The preceding code returns "21", whereas

```
N1=2
((N1+=1))
echo $N1
```

will instead return 3.

Subshell with Parentheses

We've seen what double parentheses do, but what about single parentheses? When code is placed inside parentheses, it's run as a subshell. The current shell runtime is copied and a new one is created. The effect of this is that nothing that happens within the subshell affects the outer shell, for example:

```
S=Hi
(
  echo $S
  S=Hello
  echo $S
)
echo $S
```

In the preceding script, we create a variable S. Then we open a subshell and echo the value; notice that the subshell can see the value of the S variable that existed when it was created. Then we change the value of S within the subshell.

On the outside of the subshell, we echo the value again. The value will still be "Hi" rather than "Hello" since the change was made inside the subshell.

Subshells themselves can in turn spawn their own subshells, which act as child processes.

Expansion with Curly Brace

Another symbol which is built into bash is the curly braces {}. The curly braces can be used for shell expansion of lists. For example

```
echo {1..100}
```

will expand into all numbers between 1 and 100.

```
philip@philip-ThinkPad-T420:~$ echo {1..100}
1 2 3 4 5 6 7 8 9 10 11 12 13 14 15 16 17 18 19 20 21 22 23 24
25 26 27 28 29 30 31 32 33 34 35 36 37 38 39 40 41 42 43 44 45
46 47 48 49 50 51 52 53 54 55 56 57 58 59 60 61 62 63 64 65 66
67 68 69 70 71 72 73 74 75 76 77 78 79 80 81 82 83 84 85 86 87
88 89 90 91 92 93 94 95 96 97 98 99 100
philip@philip-ThinkPad-T420:~$
```

Figure 4-8. *Echoing 1 to 100 using expansion*

We can also specify the amount to increment by. For example, if we want to increment by 2 each time, we can instead do

```
echo {1..100..2}
```

Now we'll instead only get odd numbers (*1, 3, 5, etc.*). This same technique can be applied to letters as well as numbers.

```
echo {a..z..2}
```

The preceding code will return all odd letters (*a, c, e, etc.*).

We can even combine these two, say we want two versions of each letter:

```
echo {a..c}{1..2}
```

This returns a small set including (*a1 a2 b1 b2 c1 c2*) though we can make it as complex and long as we like. For example, say we wanted to print all combinations for binary numbers with a total of five digits:

```
echo {0..1}{0..1}{0..1}{0..1}{0..1}
```

Another example use case, say we wanted to create a list of files in /tmp:

```
touch /tmp/{file1,file2,file3}
```

Or even better:

```
touch /tmp/file{1..3}
```

Either of these commands will generate three files in the /tmp directory.

Loop in Bash

Like other languages, bash also provides a way to do loops over a set of items. For example, given a set of names, we can print "hello" for each:

```
for name in jesse james jen
do
  echo "Hello $name"
done
```

This can be useful with the expansion we looked at in the previous section, for example:

```
for i in {1..100}
do
  echo "Hello $i"
done
```

We can also do a traditional style loop with an i++ statement as you've likely seen in other languages:

```
for ((i=1;i<=100;i++));
do
  echo "Hello $i"
done
```

It's also possible to make an infinite loop:

```
for (( ; ; ))
```

```
do
  echo "Hello [CTRL+C to stop]"
done
```

In some cases, you may want to break out of a loop early.

```
for i in {1..100}
do
  if((i==10))
  then
    break
  fi
  echo "Hello $i"
done
```

In the preceding example cases, 1–9 run, but before 10 runs, we hit the break keyword which stops the loop early. Alternatively, we can use the continue keyword to end the current iteration without exiting the loop. As an example, we'll cause continue to trigger on all the even numbers. *Be careful in regard to the spaces on the if line as missing spaces can cause issues with the script running correctly.*

```
for i in {1..100}
do
  if [ $((i%2)) -eq 0 ];
  then
    continue
  fi
  echo "Hello $i"
done
```

The preceding script will run the loop for numbers 1 to 100, but any numbers which are found to be even will exit the loop early and make way for the next in line. This is because in iterations where i is even, the continue keyword is read causing the iteration to end early.

It's also possible to use an array as the data provider for a loop. Arrays are defined using bash as shown here:

```
array=( 1 39 47 )
```

Then to make use of the array, it needs to be expanded using curly braces:

```
for i in ${array[@]}
do
  echo "Hello $i"
done
```

While we've used integers here, you can just as easily use strings or another data type in your array.

While Loops

In some situations, you may be better off using a while loop rather than a for loop. Instead of having a set number of iterations, you might want to end the loop based on a value not related to iterations. For example, say we want to see how many times we can loop through some code in 7 seconds.

Note   For the following example, you'll need to put the code into a script file and run chmod +x to add execution permission. This is because of our use of the special variable $SECONDS. The $SECONDS variable contains the amount of seconds a terminal, or in our case, script, has been running.

```
#!/usr/bin/env bash

i=0
while [ $SECONDS -lt 7 ]; do
  i=$((i+1))
done

echo $i
```

Executing the script will return the amount of times the loop was able to run in 7 seconds. You might be surprised with how high the number is. In my case, the loop ran 927375 times.

The while loop allows us to limit the running of a code section without a specific number like the for loop. While we've used the example of time, you could also use some external value. For example, if a website is down, you may want to keep checking every few minutes until it is back up.

```
working=false
while [ $working == false ]; do
  curl google.com && working=true
  echo $working
  sleep 60
done
```

The preceding script will likely only run once as we're checking `www.google.com`. If you want to see how it would work when a website is down, try switching the website to one that doesn't exist (and thus will always fail).

The while loop also makes infinite loops particularly easy. To make a loop run forever, simply make the checked value `true` as shown as follows. The following is an example of a script that will say "hello" every minute until turned off:

```
while [ true ]; do
  echo "hello"
  sleep 60
done
```

Until Loops

An until loop is almost identical to a while loop except instead of checking that a value is true, we instead check that a value is false. Notice the following script is almost identical to our while loop, but instead of running while false, we're running until true:

```
working=false
until [ $working == true ]; do
  curl google.com && working=true
  echo $working
  sleep 60
done
```

Quotes in Bash

Quotes in bash can be used to prevent special characters from being interpreted and instead be interpreted as their literal value. For example, we `echo` the following symbols which would otherwise cause an error without the quotes:

```
echo '$ & * ; |.'
```

By surrounding these special charachters with quotes, we cause them to take on their literal meaning.

Double quotes are similar to single quotes but still allow for the processing of dollar signs, back quotes, and backslashes. In the following example, the variable in double quotes will be expanded while the one in single quotes will not be:

```
greeting=hello
```

```
echo '$greeting world'
echo "$greeting world"
```

Another example of this is how spaces are interpreted; consider the following two commands:

```
touch hello world
touch "hello world"
```

As the space is the default delimiter in bash, the first command will process the input as two separate arguments, whereas the one using quotes will treat the input a single file name.

Command Substitution Using Backtick

The backtick or back quote is completely different from both single and double quotes. Instead of preventing interpretation of special characters, the backtick causes the enclosed text to be interpreted before evaluation.

To demonstrate, we'll be making use of the following command which pipes an addition statement into bc to generate a number:

```
echo 5 + 5 | bc
```

The preceding code will output the number 10. Now let's say we want to make use of this command in a larger command. For example, we'll use the result of this command as the name of a file to create.

```
touch /tmp/`echo 5 + 5 | bc`
```

In the preceding example, the command enclosed in backticks will be interpreted before anything else. Once the backticks are interpreted, the command will be run as

```
touch /tmp/10
```

This can be useful when you have a dynamic process for generating a filename or some other aspect of your script.

Defining Functions

If you're writing a script, you may want to define a block of code as a reusable function. This is useful when you'll be using the same piece of code in multiple places throughout your script (programming concept DRY, short for don't repeat yourself). By wrapping some functionality as a named function, you can avoid rewriting the same code and also updating in multiple locations if you decide to change the code used.

Creating functions is fairly easy in bash. We'll create a very minimal example to stay with. To start we'll create a function called greet which takes a name as input and outputs "hello" plus the name.

```
greet() {
  echo hello $1
}
```

With the preceding code defined, we can now run

```
greet David
```

This will pass the input "David" to echo hello $1 within our greet function. Note that variables passed into functions are not named but rather specified by the order they're input. If we wanted to process a second argument, we'd add it as $2 and a third would be $3 and so on.

The lack of named parameters isn't the only missing feature in bash. Another thing people with experience in other languages expect to find while writing functions is the ability to return a value from a function. Unfortunately, there is no return keyword that can be used inside a function like you might expect. As a way around this, you can define a variable inside the function and use it outside the function. To demonstrate this, we'll create a random time generator which could be used as part of a testing script.

Note We'll use the shuf command for generating random numbers. You don't need to worry about installing it as it's GNU Coreutils and present on nearly all Linux systems.

```
random_time() {
  hour=$(shuf -i 0-12 -n 1)
  min=$(shuf -i 0-60 -n 1)

  hour=$(printf %02d $hour)
  min=$(printf %02d $min)
  r_time=$min:$hour
}
```

With our random time-generating function defined, let's run it and echo the results. We'll do this twice to make sure we get a different value each time.

```
random_time
echo $r_time
```

```
random_time
echo $r_time
```

Source Code from a File

If you're coming from another programming language, you're probably used to importing source code from external files. Importing is relatively simple. Let's say we've saved our random_time function from the previous section as random.sh. First take the random_time function from the previous section where we define and save it as a script file called random_time.sh. Be sure to include a shebang on the first line (example further down in this section for reference), and after saving run chmod +x on it.

Now that we have our random_time function saved as random_time.sh, we'll make use of it in another file in the same directory. To do this, create a new script file called sourcing.sh; include the code shown here:

```
#!/usr/bin/env bash
```

```
source random_time.sh
random_time
echo r_time
```

If you're not in the same directory as the random_time.sh file, make sure to use the full path. Once the file is imported, you can make use of any variables or functions which are defined in the file.

Summary

In this chapter, we started by looking at pipes and redirects which can be used for gluing different Unix utilities and commands together, either through processing outputs directly or saving to files.

Then we looked at various aspects of bash scripting syntax including conditional expressions, functions, quotes, and importing files.

CHAPTER 5

Using SSH

In this chapter, we'll look at SSH (Secure Shell). SSH is one of the most commonly used tools in system administration. It allows you to connect to a remote server or device through an encrypted connection. It's also the basis for other programs which are built on top of SSH, for example, X2Go which is a Linux equivalent to RDP (remote desktop protocol) clients like VNC.

SSH can also be used for file transfer in a way similar to FTP (File Transfer Protocol) by using the SFTP (Secure File Transfer Protocol) command (more on this in the next chapter).

In some cases, SSH is simply used as a means to proxy traffic to hide the location or IP address of a user or script. This can be done with SSH tunnels and SOCKS proxies.

History of SSH

While SSH only dates back to 1995, it actually builds on early programs like `telnet` dating back to 1969. This is hinted at by the fact that SSH by default listens on port 22, only one away from port 23 used by `telnet`. Historically, almost all Linux systems were used through a system of time sharing in which a central computer could be connected to via several different text-based terminals. These text-based terminals didn't include anything besides the software needed to remotely connect to the central computer.

This history has had a large influence on the Linux operating system. This is evident in the fact that text-based tools like SSH are still widely used, allowing multiple users to connect to a server to run jobs, access data, and manage systems.

The major flaw with earlier programs like `telnet`, short for teletype network, is that they lacked security. With `telnet` communications between the client and server are completely unencrypted clear text (including any passwords). Two-way encryption and more advanced security features allowed SSH to quickly overcome earlier tools like `telnet` in popularity.

© Philip Kirkbride 2020

P. Kirkbride, *Basic Linux Terminal Tips and Tricks*, https://doi.org/10.1007/978-1-4842-6035-7_5

While `telnet` has nearly been completely replaced by SSH, there are still some fun services which are online today including a recreation of *Star Wars* in ASCII, online text-based chess over telnet, and a service for checking weather over telnet.

```
telnet towel.blinkenlights.nl
```

```
telnet freechess.org 5000
```

```
telnet rainmaker.wunderground.com
```

Figure 5-1 shows an opening text-based animation from `towel.blinkenlights.nl`.

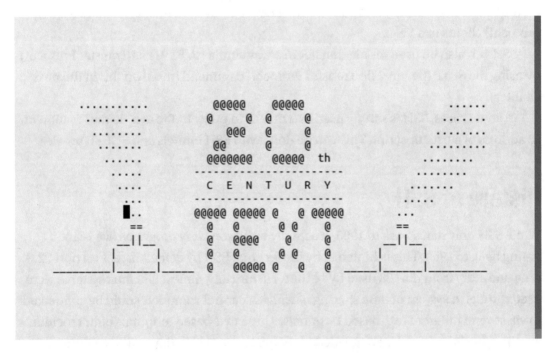

Figure 5-1. *Text-based recreation of Star Wars over telnet*

Basic SSH Use

The most important command you'll want to be familiar with for connecting to servers is SSH. SSH is the program used to remotely connect to servers, computers, and embedded devices. It provides a secure encrypted connection to a server or device and is widely used. When it comes to remotely managing servers, there is really no alternative to SSH, besides possibly vendor-specific management dashboards which are extremely limited.

To check if your system has SSH preinstalled, try running

```
which ssh
```

If you get back a file location for an ssh file, you're good to go. Otherwise go ahead and install it:

```
sudo apt-get install ssh
```

If you already have a server or device running which is opening for connections, it will be as simple as running

```
ssh <username>@<address>
```

After which you'll be prompted to enter your password.

Keypairs with ssh-keygen

If you've successfully logged in to a server or device using SSH and password, one of the first things you'll want to do is switch to using public key authentication. There are two major benefits:

- Keypairs are considered more secure than passwords.

- Keypairs are more convenient as they eliminate the need for passwords.

A keypair is a set of two parts – firstly the private key which will remain on your computer and should never be shared and secondly a public key which can be shared publicly and used to sign requests which anyone with the public key can verify came from you.

To get started creating a keypair, first run

```
ssh-keygen
```

You'll be prompted to choose a passphrase; this is optional. The passphrase is simply used to encrypt your private key locally. That way if someone gets access to your laptop and private key, they won't be able to read it, assuming you choose a strong passphrase.

If you've followed these instructions correctly, you should get some output which looks like that shown in Figure 5-2.

```
ubuntu@ip-172-31-58-133:~$ ssh-keygen -t RSA
Generating public/private RSA key pair.
Enter file in which to save the key (/home/ubuntu/.ssh/id_rsa):
Enter passphrase (empty for no passphrase):
Enter same passphrase again:
Your identification has been saved in /home/ubuntu/.ssh/id_rsa.
Your public key has been saved in /home/ubuntu/.ssh/id_rsa.pub.
The key fingerprint is:
SHA256:iMk3dMi0CL6iNVFHZz7rEf7+b5mwOe9J43V69WCRSRE ubuntu@ip-172-31-58-133
The key's randomart image is:
+---[RSA 2048]----+
|   . ..+ o     Eo |
| . o = *       .  |
|   o . = =     . o |
|   + + + +     + |
|. + + + S       . |
|.o . . o o   . o .|
|.         . . =o+=|
|         .  +o+=+|
|            ...*B. |
+----[SHA256]-----+
ubuntu@ip-172-31-58-133:~$ █
```

Figure 5-2. *Output from ssh-keygen*

Next we'll copy our new public key to our remote SSH server/device; SSH has a built-in command to make this easy:

```
ssh-copy-id <username>@<address>
```

You'll again be prompted for password to log in to the server. Once this command successfully runs, you'll be able to log in to the server automatically without using the server password. However, if you choose a passphrase to encrypt your private key, you will need to enter this before making use of the key.

PEM and Other Key Files

In some cases, servers may make use of PEM files, short for Privacy-Enhanced Mail. A popular example is Amazon EC2 servers. These keys are specified using the -i flag, for example:

```
ssh -i <pem-file-location> <username>@<address>
```

An alternative to using the -i flag is to add your key to the session with ssh-add, for example:

```
ssh-add <pem-file-location>
```

This will add the key file to the authentication agent. It will remain active until SSH is restarted, which mainly happens when the computer is restarted.

The preceding methods are not specific to PEM files but can be used with any key file which is required by an SSH server. Others include PPY, short for Putty Private Key, or .pub files, short for public key.

Disable Password Login on Server

We mentioned that one of the main benefits of using an ssh keypair is that it is more secure than password authentication. To gain the benefit of this added security, you'll have to disable password logins on the server. When you first add the keypair, the server will allow login with either of the two methods. As keypair is more secure, it is recommended that you turn off the ability to use passwords to avoid any type of brute-force attacks.

Firstly, connect to the server using SSH. Then you'll need to find the file /etc/ssh/sshd_config. Open sshd_config and modify the line which mentions ChallengeResponseAuthentication; you'll need to ensure it is set to no like the following:

```
ChallengeResponseAuthentication no
```

Secondly, in the same file, find the line mentioning PasswordAuthentication and set it to no:

```
PasswordAuthentication no
```

These two settings will ensure the passwords can't be used to log in to the server. For this reason, it is very important you ensure that public key authentication is working correctly before changing the values. Otherwise you may find yourself completely locked out of the server.

Finally, there is one last step which is to have the SSH server reload the settings which have been changed so they can take effect. To do that, run the command:

```
service sshd restart
```

This last step of restarting your SSH server is worth noting as it isn't specific to this setting. Whenever you make any change to your SSH configuration, you'll need to restart the service on the server for those changes to take effect.

Server Nicknames with SSH Config File

Another handy tip to make SSH a bit easier is to create a client-side SSH config file. You can use this to create default username, server IP, and authentication key file for each server you regularly log in to. This becomes particularly useful when you often have to switch between multiple servers or devices.

The first thing you need to do is create the SSH config file, which should be located at `~/.ssh/config`:

```
touch ~/.ssh/config
```

Next you'll need to make sure it has the correct permissions:

```
chmod 600 ~/.ssh/config
```

With this done, you can open up the config file and create an entry for each one of your servers. As an example, I'll use an AWS server I'm currently using:

```
Host aws
 Hostname ec2-35-174-116-189.compute-1.amazonaws.com
 User ubuntu
```

Now instead of specifying the whole hostname and user, I could do

```
ssh -i ~/.ssh/file.pem aws
```

You may not need the `-i ~/.ssh/file.pem`, depending on whether your server requires an identity file. Key file types `.pub` or `.ppk` can also be used with `-i`.

We can simplify this further by adding the identity file to our config:

```
Host aws
 Hostname ec2-35-174-116-189.compute-1.amazonaws.com
 User ubuntu
 IdentityFile ~/.ssh/file.pem
```

Now we can simply do

```
ssh aws
```

To add entries for multiple servers, simply add additional blocks below in the config file. This makes connecting to different servers a lot easier as you don't need to remember the server address for each.

> **Note**   The `IdentityFile` can also be used to specify the RSA key for public/private key login. Though by default the value will be `~/.ssh/id_rsa`. So if you're using the default location for your key, you don't need to add it.

Run a Command on Connection

Sometimes you just want to connect to a server to run a single command. Often this will be related to having to perform some fix on several similar devices or servers in a row. In one instance, a company I worked at had several devices which had a bug which broke our configuration management setup. The fix was to simply remove a lock file on each of these devices. We were able to quickly fix them all by creating a for loop that took the IP of each device, connected, and then run the needed command.

> **Note**   If you often find yourself having to connect to multiple systems to run the same command, modify a configuration, or update a program, you'll want to check out the program Ansible, a lightweight open source program for simultaneously making the same change on several machines. Ansible is built on top of SSH, so when you write a configuration to send to multiple devices, it's actually connecting over SSH and running commands under the hood. Other popular alternatives to Ansible include Puppet, Chef, and Salt.

To do this, all you have to do is supply a command in quotes at the end of your ssh command, for example:

```
ssh user@server.com "touch /tmp/testing123"
```

After connecting you'll almost immediately be disconnected and return to your local machines command line, as shown in Figure 5-3.

```
philip@philip-ThinkPad-T420:~$ ssh -t aws "touch /tmp/testing123"
Connection to ec2-35-174-116-189.compute-1.amazonaws.com closed.
philip@philip-ThinkPad-T420:~$ ▮
```

Figure 5-3. *Specifying a command to run on SSH connection*

If you want to run a command on connection but don't want to disconnect immediately, you can modify the command run on connection to start a bash session:

```
ssh user@server.com "touch /tmp/testing123; bash"
```

This will run the command and then put you in a bash session, without disconnecting.

Break a Hanging SSH Session

A common issue that can occur when using SSH is that you leave a session running in the background or another window, and when you return, it is completely frozen. Connection issues can also be a common cause of an SSH session hanging. When a client loses its connection to the server, it will hang until the server reconnects. You might think to try pressing ctrl+c, or ctrl+d, but even this won't end the frozen SSH session.

When this happens, the easiest way to escape the session is to press enter followed by ~ and then .. Doing so should exit the session and return a message like

```
Connection to yourServer.com closed.
```

This combination of keys is the most well known escape sequence, but it's not the only one. If you instead press enter, ~, then ?, you'll get back a list of all supported escape sequences which include the ones in Table 5-1.

Table 5-1. *List of escape sequences*

Sequence	Description
~.	Terminate connection (and any multiplexed sessions)
~B	Send a BREAK to the remote system
~C	Open a command line
~R	Request rekey
~V/v	Decrease/increase verbosity (LogLevel)
~^Z	Suspend ssh
~#	List forwarded connections
~&	Background ssh (when waiting for connections to terminate)
~?	List all sequences
~~	Send the escape character by typing it twice

In most cases, you'll mainly want to use the regular ~., unless of course you just entered a newline and you really did want to type the ~ character; in that case, just tap it a second time. Also note that the ~ will only be read as an escape sequence if it's the first character on a line; if you're already partway into a line, you'll need to press enter or clear the input first.

stty sane

Sometimes when you have to break connection, or if you ever have to connect to a device using a serial port with a program like minicom or sometimes even SSH, you'll have the terminal window glitch as shown in Figure 5-4. When this type of glitch happens, the characters you type may not appear as you expect. This can result in unexpected behavior, having chunks of the terminal screen unreadable or simply not looking right.

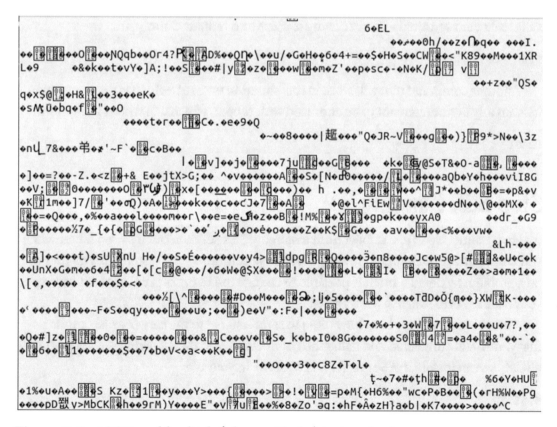

Figure 5-4. *ASCII garble glitch (aka mojibake) in terminal*

Or you might not be getting ASCII-type characters like in the figure, but your spacing is off and the terminal is generally not acting as expected; see Figure 5-5 for the type of strange spacing that can occur.

```
philip@philip-ThinkPad-T420:/$ ls
                              bin      etc                 lib       lost+found  opt
   sbin      sys   vmlinuz
                        boot     home               lib32    media          proc  snap
   tmp    vmlinuz.old
                    cdrom   initrd.img         lib64   mnt             root  srv          us
r
   dev    initrd.img.old  libx32  nix         run    swapfile  var
                                                             philip@philip-Thi
nkPad-T420:/$ █
```

Figure 5-5. *Visual spacing glitch*

If either of these glitches or anything visual in nature happens, you can use the `stty` sane to fix your terminal without having to close and reopen. Simply run

```
stty sane
```

Another command that will work in this situation is `reset`, which is run stand-alone without any arguments (not to be confused with reboot, which will restart the system).

```
reset
```

Stop SSH Hanging

It's great being able to disconnect from a hanging SSH session, but it's even better when you can avoid it from happening altogether. Depending on your system, this might not be a problem by default, but it is possible to change the `ServerAliveInterval` setting in your client's `/etc/ssh/ssh_config` file.

This setting tells the client how often to send a signal to the server which confirms that you're still connected and using the connection. Add the following lines if you don't already see an instance of `ServerAliveInterval` in your file:

```
Host *
ServerAliveInterval 100
```

You'll have to edit the same file, /etc/ssh/sshd_config, on the server you're having issues with:

```
ClientAliveInterval 60
TCPKeepAlive yes
ClientAliveCountMax 10000
```

This tells the server to send a keep alive message to the client every 60 seconds if nothing is received to keep the session alive. TCPKeepAlive ensures firewalls don't drop idle connections, and ClientAliveCountMax specifies how long the server will keep sending keep alive messages even without hearing anything from the client.

SSH Tunneling

SSH tunneling is the process of forwarding a port on one computer to a remote machine via SSH. There are several uses for SSH tunneling which we'll go over in the following sections.

Local SSH Tunnel

One of the simplest SSH tunnels is a local tunnel which binds a local port to an address on a remote machine. For example, we can bind our local port 8080 to a website which is accessed through a remote machine using the -L flag:

```
ssh -L 8080:textfiles.com:80 user@server.com
```

At the time of writing, this works great on the website textfiles.com (an interesting piece of Internet history. Check out Jason Scott's Defcon 17 talk for the story behind it). Unfortunately, depending on the website you want to tunnel, it may or may not work. Modern server software like nginx will actually check the hostname being used in your browser and not work due to the mismatch.

In some cases websites won't work over tunnel because they check what URL the browser is using and will malfunction when 'localhost' is used. This is the case for most popular web apps like Youtube. If you want to tunnel a website that doesn't work you can either map that URL to your own server's IP by updating /etc/hosts or you can send a false header which says your hostname is actually the intended website. You may need to install curl depending on your OS.

```
sudo apt-get install curl
```

Below is an example of using `curl` to manually set the host header with the -H flag:

```
curl -H "Host: youtube.com" -L localhost:8080
```

This should return the source code for YouTube. If you want a more practical way to use an SSH tunnel for web browsing, we provide a better solution in the next section on SOCKS proxy.

While this example shows us how a local SSH tunnel works, it doesn't exactly show why it might be used. For anything browsing related, the SOCKS proxy method shown in the next section would be preferred.

SSH tunneling comes in handy when you want to make a service that's running on a server accessible via SSH. This is a particularly secure way to serve a web service intended for a small group without having to worry about a lot of security issues. As the website is only available to those accessing it through SSH on port 22, there is no threat of attacks that might be able to target a publicly facing login page.

Create a SOCKS Proxy with SSH

SSH is great for connecting to remote servers and devices, but it can actually be used for all sorts of things. One of those things is to create a SOCKS proxy connection that can be used to direct traffic on a local computer, when using applications like web browsers.

SOCKS proxy has most of the benefits associated with using a VPN (virtual private network) including

- Anonymous web browsing

- Bypass geolocation blocking

- Bypass website blocking on local network or from ISP

- Faster than a VPN

Keep in mind the first benefit "anonymous web browsing" is only going to be partially true depending on who you plan to be anonymous from and the server you're using to proxy traffic through. If you're trying to hide your identity from the government and you're using a server which is registered under your name, this might not be effective.

However, from the perspective of a website that you're visiting, they'll only see the IP address of your end server. They may see, for example, that the traffic came from an AWS server located in eastern USA.

Another caveat to keep in mind when using your own server as a SOCKS proxy is that some server provider IPs may be tagged as such and limited by some services and websites. This is due to the fact that many automated scripts and malicious services originate from these types of servers. If you're using a server from a smaller hosting provider, you might bypass this type of issue.

To get started, simply run the following, substituting the username and host for your own:

```
ssh -D 8123 -f -C -q -N user@server.com
```

The flags included here are shown in Table 5-2.

Table 5-2. *Flags used*

Flag	Description
-D 8123	Bind connection to port 8123
-f	Fork process to background
-C	Compress data before sending
-q	Quiet mode
-N	Do not execute a remote command

If this runs without error, you should have SOCKS proxy listening on port 8123 (*feel free to substitute the port number with another*). We can double check using ps and grep:

```
ps aux | grep ssh
```

If running you should see the command you ran listed as a running process. Using the proxy will depend on the specific application you're using. As an example, we'll look at Firefox. In Firefox open preferences and then scroll down to "Network Settings." In network settings, shown in Figure 5-6, you can configure "manual proxy configuration" using "localhost" with your chosen port as SOCKS host.

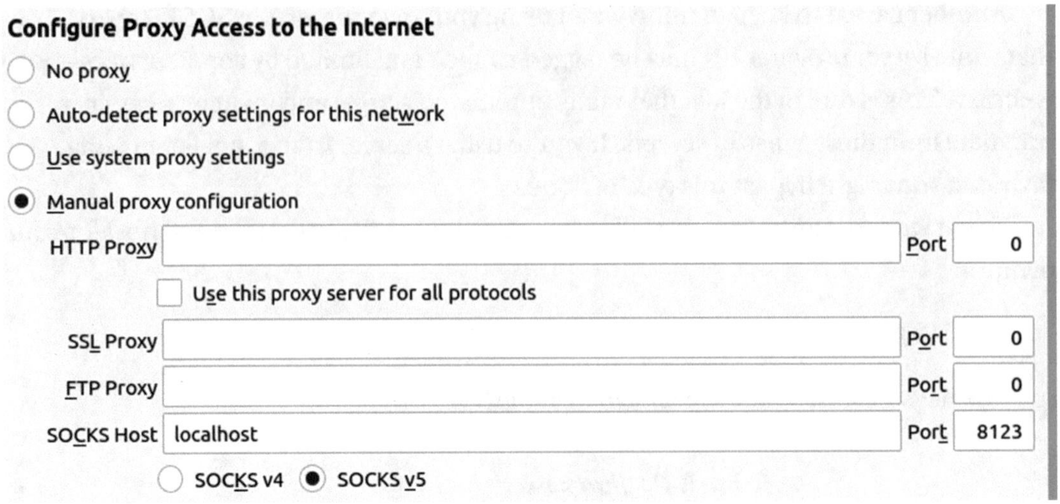

Configure Proxy Access to the Internet

○ No proxy

○ Auto-detect proxy settings for this network

○ Use system proxy settings

● Manual proxy configuration

HTTP Proxy		Port	0

☐ Use this proxy server for all protocols

SSL Proxy		Port	0
FTP Proxy		Port	0
SOCKS Host	localhost	Port	8123

○ SOCKS v4 ● SOCKS v5

Figure 5-6. *Setting up web browser to use SOCKS proxy*

After updating your proxy on Firefox and saving, you'll want to verify that it's working as expected. To do this, you'll want to find a website that checks your IP. My preferred method is going to www.duckduckgo.com (privacy-oriented search engine) and searching for "what is my ip." Doing this should show your IP address and location, as shown in Figure 5-7, without having to click through to any third-party website.

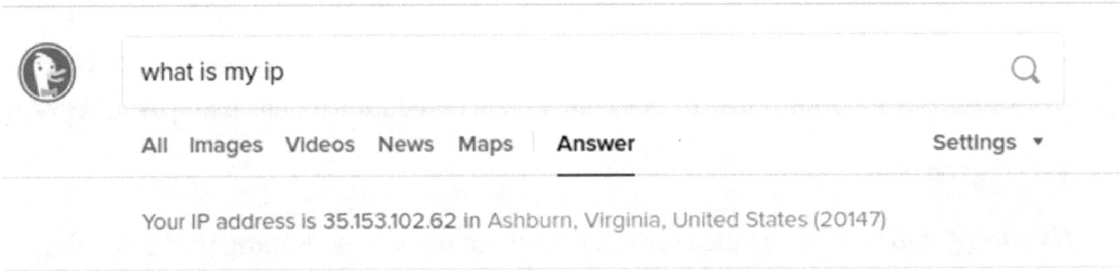

what is my ip	Q

All   Images   Videos   News   Maps   **Answer**   Settings ▾

Your IP address is 35.153.102.62 in Ashburn, Virginia, United States (20147)

Figure 5-7. *DuckDuckGo showing the IP of our remote SSH server*

Reverse SSH Tunnel

SSH is a great tool for connecting to remote servers and devices, but sometimes firewalls and routers can get in the way. For example, if you have a Raspberry Pi running a Linux server at home and want to SSH into it from outside your local network, you'll likely have trouble due to restrictions from both routers and Internet providers.

A great way around this is creating a reverse SSH tunnel. A reverse SSH tunnel relies on the device in question to maintain an active outgoing connection. For example, our Raspberry Pi would continually remain connected to our remote server. Since it's the Pi which has restrictions for incoming connections and not the other way around, there are no issues with the Pi making an outgoing connection.

When we're ready to SSH into the Pi, we actually create our connection within the tunnel which is the Pi's outgoing connection. Thus, the Pi receives an incoming connection within its own outgoing connection.

To set up a reverse SSH tunnel, first open a terminal session on the server in question; in this case, our Raspberry Pi behind a firewall. Run the following:

```
ssh -R 9876:localhost:22 user@server.com
```

The -R flag creates a smaller tunnel within the tunnel which is the main SSH connection; the -R standing for remote as tunnel entry point is on the remote machine; this is similar to the -L flag except the -L flag has the entry point on the local side.

Also note that we've selected port 9876 to be where the inner tunnel that enters on the remote end will end up on our local side. Feel free to swap port 9876 with any unused port on your device.

Once you're ready to connect to your device that's running the reverse proxy, just use SSH as you normally would but specify the port used in the previous step. So in our example, we'd use the following command:

```
ssh -p 9876 user@server.com
```

Serving a Website over Reverse Proxy

This type of SSH tunneling is the basis for the popular development tool ngrok. Ngrok allows developers to instantly publish a web application that's running on their local machine on a web URL for anyone to see. You can do the same thing using your own web server.

To demonstrate first we'll create a minimal site running on port 8080. If you're running a recent version of Ubuntu, you should have python3 installed by default; otherwise you'll need to install it.

```
cd /tmp
echo Hello World > index.html
python3 -m http.server 8080
```

After running these three lines, you will be able to go to localhost:8080 in your web browser and see the text "Hello World." With our small site running on port 8080, we can now run the following command:

```
ssh -R 8080:localhost:8080 user@myServer.com
```

This will mirror port 8080 on our local machine to port 8080 on the remote server, thus allowing us to make our localhost website available to demo on a live IP.

SSH Proxy Jump

Sometimes you don't want to connect to an SSH server directly. There are two main reasons you might want to use a jump box:

- Reduce security risks by only allowing connections to the final destination server from certain IPs or on a nonpublic network.

- You don't want the final destination server to log your actual IP address.

In the first scenario, your destination server might not be available on the public Internet. In this case, the jump box acts as a DMZ (*demilitarized zone*) from which you can connect. This means the protected box is completly hidden from port scanners or any kind of malicious scripts scanning the open Internet.

You can make use of a jump server using the -J flag like the following:

```
ssh -J user@server1.com user@server2.com
```

Making use of SSH config file will come in handy when using a jump server as you don't have the ability to specify an identity file to the jump server directly using the -i flag, but if you're using an SSH config file as described in this chapter, you can define the identity file there.

If your situation is more in line with trying to hide your origin, you might even want to use a series of jump servers. With multiple jump servers, even the jump server which connects to the destination server won't know your IP. You can use multiple jump servers by providing multiple separated by a comma:

```
ssh -J user@jump1.com,user@jump2.com user@server.com
```

Change Default Port on SSH Server

There are a few reasons you might want to change the default port for your SSH server – if you know you'll be connecting to the server from a network which restricts outgoing connections to anything other than port 80 or 443.

Or if you'll be using password authentication and you want to lower the chances of your server being found by crawlers who may attempt a brute-force attack, in this case, use an uncommon port like 79279. If you're unsure if the random port you choose is uncommon, you can check using nmap. nmap isn't installed by default so you'll have to install it with your package manager:

```
sudo apt-get install nmap
```

Once 'nmap' is installed use the following command:

```
nmap --top-ports 1000 localhost -v -oG -
```

This will return a list of the 1000 most popular ports which you can reference to see if your port matches.

Open Firewall

Before changing the port, it's important to make sure you don't have a firewall or some other configuration that would block incoming traffic. To check if you have a firewall enabled, run

```
sudo ufw status
```

If ufw is running, you may need to configure it to accept traffic from your desired port. If it's not running, you still may need to deal with your cloud provider security settings. For example, Amazon AWS security instances have security rules which are set up outside the server itself, within their security group rules. Many other cloud providers follow the same model, leaving only port 22 open (possibly also port 80 and 443) to make servers secure by default. Check with your server provider to see if additional steps are required to allow port access.

If ufw is running, you can tell it to allow your port by running

```
sudo ufw allow <port-number>
```

Modify sshd_config

The settings for an SSH server can be modified by editing the file /etc/ssh/sshd_config. Before changing the port on a live server make sure you are certain the port is accessible. If you change the port to one which is blocking incoming requests it's possible that can lock yourself out of the server. To change the default port, simply find the commented line that looks like

```
#Port 22
```

Uncomment the line and switch 22 with your chosen port:

```
Port 7929
```

Note   The default port for an SSH server can also be specified in your client-side SSH config file, so that you don't need to specify it with the -p flag when you connect to the server.

After updating the file, you need to restart the SSH service:

```
sudo service ssh restart
```

Summary

In this chapter, we looked at how to remotely connect to a server or device using SSH and some common configurations. These configurations include turning off password login to use keypair instead, switching default port, and stopping hanging by modifying keep alive settings. We looked at SSH tunnelings and common uses like creating SOCKS proxy.

While the list is hardly comprehensive of all the places and ways SSH is used, it is a good foundation for being able to connect to remote servers with some commonly used settings.

CHAPTER 6

File Transfer

In this chapter, we're going to look at various programs for transferring files between machines.

FTP

One of the most common protocols to transfer files is FTP (*File Transfer Protocol*). To get started using FTP, you should install lftp, a sophisticated file transfer program. This program is primarily used for FTP but can also be used for other protocols:

```
sudo apt-get install lftp
```

With lftp installed, you can enter interactive mode using

```
lftp
```

This will open up an interactive shell where you can run lftp-specific commands. It should look similar to Figure 6-1.

Figure 6-1. *lftp interactive mode*

The lftp shell acts much like the normal bash shell giving you access to several commands like ls and cd. You also gain additional commands. To view the commands available to you, simply enter ? and press enter.

The most important command to know is connect, which is simply used as

```
connect -u <username> <server-address>
```

© Philip Kirkbride 2020
P. Kirkbride, *Basic Linux Terminal Tips and Tricks*, https://doi.org/10.1007/978-1-4842-6035-7_6

After this, you'll be prompted for a password. Once connected, you can download files using

```
get <file-name>
```

Or upload using

```
put <file-name>
```

Note   If you're looking for FTP servers to practice with and don't want to set up your own FTP server, using a Google dork for finding unsecured FTP servers can be useful. A Google dork is a search term used to find a specific application or unsecured website using a search term. A good one for finding FTP servers is `intitle:"index of" inurl:ftp`.

SFTP

Note   When it comes to both SFTP and SCP (next section), you can actually test these commands on your localhost, instead of specifying a remote server. Just use localhost with your username. Of course going from localhost to localhost doesn't provide any additional benefits over a command like `mv`, but it does allow you to test these commands without having a remote server setup.

You're likely familiar with FTP, short for File Transfer Protocol. It's often used with GUI programs like FileZilla for uploading and downloading files to a server. At the height of PHP's popularity, updating the www directory of your server using FileZilla was standard practice.

While programs like FileZilla are still widely used, those programs now make use of a new secure version of FTP called FTPS. FTP has a major weakness which allows an attacker to sniff traffic to the FTP server and obtain user credentials, when those users connect to the server.

Another popular and easy-to-use alternative to FTP is SFTP. SFTP enables file transfer that looks and feels like FTP but over port 22, the same port used for SSH sessions. If you're already using SSH with your server, you should have no problems using SFTP to connect to it. It doesn't require any additional software installation on the server or connecting client. Most installations of SSH should include SFTP, except in rare instances of lightweight builds.

To get started, simply take the command you're already using to connect to your server via ssh and use sftp instead, for example:

```
sftp ubuntu@myserver.com
```

Or if you're using a PEM file for authentication as is common with AWS servers, use

```
sftp -i ~/.ssh/key.pem ubuntu@myserver.com
```

One thing to note before connecting is that the directory where you connect from will be the directory which you intend to download or upload from.

Once logged in to the server, you'll be able to use some of the commands normally available in an ssh session, but not all of them. Most importantly, you'll be able to navigate through your filesystem using ls and cd (*just like with FTP*).

In the case that you want to download a file, navigate to the folder in question and use the get command:

```
get readme.txt
```

If everything is working as expected, you should see some output confirming the download like shown in Figure 6-2.

```
-116-189.compute-1.amazonaws.com
Connected to ec2-35-174-116-189.compute-1.amazonaws.com.
sftp> cd Downloads/
sftp> ls
electrum-3.3.4                      electrum-ltc-3.3.4.1
en1                                 google-free-philip-private.ppk
mbrola-SuSElinux-ultra1.dat         mbrola-linux-alpha
mbrola-linux-i386                   mbrola206a-linux-ppc
mbrola302b-linux-ppc                mbrola_linux_libc5
nordvpn-release_1.0.0_all.deb       readme.txt
sftp> get readme.txt
Fetching /home/ubuntu/Downloads/readme.txt to readme.txt
/home/ubuntu/Downloads/readme.txt            100%   31KB 125.4KB/s   00:00
sftp>
```

Figure 6-2. *Using lftp to get a file from a remote server*

From that point, break the sftp connection by pressing ctrl+c. Once back on your local machine, run ls and you should see the downloaded file.

The other function you'll likely want to make use of for uploading files is put. Again as with get, navigate to the folder containing the file you want to upload before connecting over sftp. Then connect with sftp; once on the server, navigate to where you want to upload the file. Type in put , be sure to include the space after put, then press tab. Pressing tab after put should show you a list of files in the directory. In Figure 6-3, you can see image files for bird, cat, and dog.

```
philip@philip-ThinkPad-T420:/tmp/uploads$ !?sftp
sftp -i ~/.ssh/coinwatch.pem ubuntu@ec2-35-174-116-189.compute-1.amazonaws.com
Connected to ec2-35-174-116-189.compute-1.amazonaws.com.
sftp> cd /tmp
sftp> put
bird.jpg  cat.jpg   dog.jpg
sftp> put █
```

Figure 6-3. *Using autocomplete to see what files can be put*

From this point, I can simply finish typing one of the three options, or if you realize you're in the wrong folder, you can start typing in an alternative path, for example, ../ or /, and then press tab again to assist in finding the file you want to upload.

Note   In the Chapter 5, we looked at creating an ~/.ssh/config file to create shortcuts that include the server, username, and other options. This same config file will also work with both SFTP and SCP.

SCP

SCP, short for secure copy protocol, is another file protocol that usually ships with SSH. The functionality is similar to SFTP, but it does not have the interactive aspects. An upload or download with SCP has to be declared all in a single command, rather than first connecting to a machine and then being able to navigate directories.

Overall it would seem SCP is worse than SFTP given it offers no extra features and is less interactive. However, SCP offers the advantage of being faster than SFTP for file transfer. For small to medium files, this may go unnoticed, but if you're moving a large file, you may decide to go with SCP instead of SFTP. You might also consider using SCP if you're transferring files as part of a script, and interactive mode would actually be a hindrance rather than a benefit.

To download a file from a server, simply run `scp` followed by the `username@ serverName`, then `:/file/location` (*without spaces*), and then as the second argument the path of where you want to save the file on your local machine, for example:

```
scp ubuntu@myserver.com:/tmp/myFile.txt ./
```

Many of the flags which work on `ssh` and `sftp` will also work with `scp` – for example, if you need to use a PEM file to log in to your server:

```
scp -i ~/.ssh/mykey.pem ubuntu@myserver.com:/tmp/myFile.txt ./
```

If you instead need to upload a file to a server, just switch the order of the paths:

```
scp ./ ubuntu@myserver.com:/tmp/myFile.txt
```

Rsync

Note   If you're using a password to log in to your server, you'll need to set up public key authentication, as described in Chapter 5, section "Keypairs with ssh-keygen." Aside from having SSH setup, the only thing your remote server will need installed is `rsync`.

Rsync is another tool for uploading and downloading files on Linux systems, but it functions more like an automatic backup system similar to the service offered by Dropbox. After setup, it will monitor a target folder on one system, and if any files are added or changed, they'll be synced to a remote server. This is handy because unlike some custom backup scripts, it will only save files which are new or changed, as opposed to an `scp` command that runs on a regular interval backing up a folder.

To get started, install `rsync`:

```
sudo apt-get install rsync
```

To use the program, you'll need to run the following command:

```
rsync -r --progress \
  ~/backup ubuntu@<myserver.com>:/home/ubuntu/backup
```

In the preceding command, we are first specifying our local folder ~/backup which is the folder we want to be backed up. After the folder, we specify the username and server ubuntu@<myserver.com> which you'll replace with the information of your server. Then without a space, we have :/home/ubuntu/back which is the folder location where we'll be backing files up to.

While we're specifying our local folder first, that isn't a requirement. If we instead wanted to back up the remote server to a local folder, we would just swap the order of the arguments and instead run the following command:

```
rsync -r --progress \
  ubuntu@<myserver.com>:/home/ubuntu/backup ~/backup
```

The optional flags we're using are -r which causes folders to be backed up recursively and --progress which provides some visual feedback about how far through the backup process you are.

If you're using an identity file, you'll need to use the -e flag and specify the specific SSH command used to start the session. We're using the example of adding an identity file, but if you want to modify the SSH in any way, you can make use of the -e flag. However, in some cases, such as changing the port used for SSH by the remote server, rsync provides its own flag --port (as always you can check the man page for a complete list of options).

```
rsync -r --progress \
  -e "ssh -i /home/philip/.ssh/key.pem" \
  ~/backup ubuntu@myserver.com:/home/ubuntu/backup
```

As mentioned we're making use of the -r flag. Without the -r option, files inside folders will not be backed up. There are several options to be used with rsync; some of the most common ones are listed in Table 6-1.

Table 6-1. *Common rsync options*

Short Flag	Full Flag	Description
-v	--verbose	More detailed output
-q	--quiet	No text output
-a	--archive	Archive files while syncing
-r	--recursive	Sync directories recursively
-b	--backup	Make backup
-u	--update	Don't copy files if destination is newer
-l	--links	Copy symlinks
-n	--dry-run	Trial run
-e	-rsh="command"	Specify remote shell command
-z	--compress	Compress data during sync
-h	--human-readable	Sizes in human-readable format
	--progress	Show progress during sync

Set Up Cron Job for Rsync

We've seen how easy it is to back up a whole folder or group of folders using rsync, but it's not quite automatic yet. To make life a bit easier, we can create a cron job to automate the process of calling the command at a regular interval.

To do this, we'll create a cron job, but first let's move our backup command in a script file. You can create the file in any location you like; one common location for custom scripts is /usr/local/bin/. Open up your script file, in our case we'll use /usr/local/bin/backup.sh, add a shebang, and paste in the rsync command specific to your server and backup folder location:

```
#!/usr/bin/env bash

rsync -r --progress \
  ~/backup ubuntu@myserver.com:/home/ubuntu/backup
```

Make sure to substitute the user, server, and folders to your specific setup. If you want to back up multiple folders, you can add additional rsync commands below the first one. After saving, be sure to add the execution permission to your new file:

```
chmod +x /usr/local/bin/backup.sh
```

Finally, we'll create our cron job by running crontab -e and at the bottom of the file adding

```
0 0 * * * /usr/local/bin/backup.sh
```

With this set, your system should back itself up at midnight everyday.

Two-Way Sync with Unison

We've seen how rsync can make backing up from one machine to another easy, but this isn't quite the same as popular services like Dropbox, which provide two-way synchronization. If you need to synchronize files in two ways, the program to check out is unison which is built on top of rsync but provides two-way synchronization.

Make sure to install unison on both machines you want to synchronize:

```
sudo apt-get install unison
```

As there is no option to specify a .pem key with unison, you'll have to just add it to ssh and let ssh provide it when needed. You can do this by running (*you'll have to run this step every time your system restarts*)

```
ssh-add <path/to/file.pem>
```

With this done, you're ready to run unison:

```
unison -auto -batch \
  ~/backup  \
  ssh://ubuntu@server.com//home/ubuntu/backup/
```

The -auto and -batch flags are recommended to make the process automated; without them you'll be manually asked to verify each file which is synchronized.

Automatically Sync When File Changed with Unison

Unfortunately, the version of unison which is available on some package managers including Ubuntu's does not include the companion binary unison-fsmonitor which monitors the filesystem. This leaves you with two options:

1. Use a cron job to check at a regular interval as we did with rsync.

2. Manually compile unison from source code.

If you want to go with the simple method of using cron, simply refer to the last section about rsync and replace the rsync command in backup.sh with a unison command; you might also want to increase the frequency of the cron job. If you want to compile from source to get the ability to automatically sync instantly when a file is changed, keep reading and we'll walk through the steps needed to compile from source. To avoid any errors make sure to have the same version of rsync on both machines synced.

First off, we'll need to uninstall the package manager version of unison and install ocaml which is the language that unison is written in:

```
sudo apt-get remove unison
sudo apt-get install ocaml
```

Next go to https://github.com/bcpierce00/unison/releases and take note of the latest available version. At the time of writing, it's 2.51.2. Take whatever the version number is and set an environment variable, as we'll use it multiple times:

```
UNISON_VERSION=2.51.2
```

With the version number set, run the following series of commands; notice we make use of the environment variable we set for version number:

```
wget \
  github.com/bcpierce00/unison/archive/v$UNISON_VERSION.tar.gz
tar -xzvf v$UNISON_VERSION.tar.gz
rm v$UNISON_VERSION.tar.gz
pushd unison-$UNISON_VERSION
make
sudo cp -t /usr/local/bin ./src/unison ./src/unison-fsmonitor
popd
rm -rf unison-$UNISON_VERSION
```

You'll need to run the preceding steps on uninstalling, building, and installing unison on both servers you want to sync. Once you've done that, you can run the following command on one of the two servers:

```
unison -batch -auto ~/backup \
  ssh://ubuntu@server.com//home/ubuntu/backup/ \
  -repeat watch
```

With this running, you can try creating a file in the backup directory on either server and see the file get synced.

Note   When setting up unison, be careful not to back up two home directories to each other. During testing, we found that after each backup using home folders, a log file would be updated, itself triggering another backup, causing an infinite loop.

Unison Settings File

As mentioned in our note, we ran into a bug trying to create backup between two home directories due to log files. However, if desired it is possible to modify the location of unison log files and many other aspects of how the program operates. The settings for unison are specified in the file .unison/default.prf. If we wanted to change the location of our logs, we could add the following line.

```
logfile = /tmp/unison.log
```

Other options that can be set include things like ignoring certain file types; see an example of ignoring mp4 files here:

```
ignore = Name *.mp4
```

For additional information on what can be configured on unison, see the official documentation at www.cis.upenn.edu/~bcpierce/unison/docs.html.

Create a Service to Keep Unison Running

While we've got the two-way sync automatically working on both servers, there are still a few problems. Firstly, you're forced to keep a terminal window running with unison, and secondly it will turn off if you restart your computer.

As a solution to these two problems, we're going to create a systemd service which will turn unison on at startup and ensure it keeps running, so that your folders are always synced without you having to run commands or think about it.

The first thing we're going to do is move all our command-line arguments used when calling unison and convert them into a unison configuration file located at ~/.unison/bidirsync.prf. Create ~/.unison/bidirsync.prf and add the following:

```
# Unison preferences
label = bi-directonal sync with server
root = /home/<user>/backup
root = ssh://<user>@<server-name>//home/<user>/backup
batch = true
auto = true
repeat = watch
logfile = /home/<user>/.unison/unison.log
#debug=all
```

If your server requires an identity file like a PEM, you'll also need to add a line specifying the file in the format shown as follows:

```
sshargs = -oIdentityFile=/home/<user>/.ssh/<privkey-name>
```

Test the configuration by running unison bidirsync. Notice that bidirsync is both the name of the file we created and the label in our config file. You can use the ~/.unison/ folder to create as many unison configurations as you want and quickly run them this way.

Now that we have a working configuration, we're going to create a systemd service (see Chapter 11 for more information). First create a new folder ~/.config/systemd/user:

```
mkdir -p ~/.config/systemd/user
```

Then in that folder, create a file called unison.service. It should contain the following (*make sure to update User and Group to your own values*):

```
[Unit]
Description=Unison

[Service]
Environment="PATH=/usr/local/bin:/usr/bin"
```

```
ExecStart=/usr/local/bin/unison bidirsync
User=<yourUser>
Group=<yourUser>
Restart=always
RestartSec=10

[Install]
WantedBy=multi-user.target
```

Once you've created the service file, you can run the following to start it:

```
sudo systemctl start unison
```

You can check that everything is working and see the logs by running

```
systemctl status unison
```

Summary

In this chapter, we looked at several services which can be used for downloading, uploading, and synchronizing files across machines. We started with the classic `ftp` and more secure alternatives like `sftp` and `scp`. Then we looked at `rsync` for synchronizing folders easily and even `unison` which is capable of automatically keeping folders on separate machines synchronized immediately after a change is made on either.

CHAPTER 7

Network Scanning

Often you'll want to see what devices are on your local network, including the device IP addresses. This comes in handy in several situations including but not limited to

- You want to get the IP address of your router.

- You've arrived at a hotel and want to check the network for bugs or hidden devices, like a rogue Raspberry Pi which could have been left behind.

- You want to see the IP addresses of other computers on the network to see if they have any insecurities.

- General curiosity about what devices are on the network.

In this chapter, we'll go over how you can detect what devices are on the network and what ports they have open. In some cases, it's even possible to determine things like the OS a device is running, the version of an application running on a certain port, or the physical location of a server.

Check Connection with Ping

Before we get into scanning networks, it's worth mentioning one of the simplest yet useful commands. `ping` allows you to check that you're connected to the Internet and that your target website is up. To check your connection to the Internet is good, many people will send a `ping` to `8.8.8.8`; this is Google's primary DNS server and is known to be very reliable. You can ping it with

```
ping 8.8.8.8
```

© Philip Kirkbride 2020

P. Kirkbride, *Basic Linux Terminal Tips and Tricks*, https://doi.org/10.1007/978-1-4842-6035-7_7

Note   8.8.8.8 is often used as a dummy server to send pings to, due to its longevity and high uptime. However, since this is a live server used by a business (Google), you may wish to be considerate and not add additional traffic to their load. The website example.com is specifically reserved as an example site, by the Internet Assigned Numbers Authority, to be used for such purposes. For this reason, we'll use example.com going forward instead of 8.8.8.8. However, it is good to be aware that 8.8.8.8 is often used for this purpose so you can identify what is happening if you see it in a script.

You'll get a response back every second or so which tells you the connection is good. You can exit the program with ctrl+c; if you just want to ping once or a set number of times, you can use the -c flag followed by a number. This can be useful if you want to do something only if connected to the Internet or only if a target website is up, for example:

```
ping -c 1 example.com && echo connected
```

If we change the example.com with an IP or website that isn't live, the echo connected will never run.

arp-scan Method

The easiest method is to install a program called arp-scan. arp-scan is a program which sends arp packets to all devices on the network and displays responses which are received.

On Ubuntu/Debian-based systems, you should be able to install it with

```
sudo apt-get install arp-scan
```

Once installed, use the --localnet option to view all devices on your local network; the command requires root permission:

```
sudo arp-scan --localnet
```

The program will return a list of devices including the IP address, unique MAC address, and if possible the manufacturer of the device.

As I write this from my hotel room, I can see the local Cisco router, which not surprisingly can be logged in to using the default username and password of the device.

In addition, I can sometimes see my Android phone which is also connected to the network. For the android device, seeing it depends on whether a response was received upon sending an arp packet, which often doesn't happen when in sleep mode.

It can be useful to note the unique MAC address of a device, for example, if you want to later see if a person is at another location. Say I'm at a friend's house; I might record the MAC address of his laptop and phone. Then later when at a large building on a single network, for example, a library, I could scan the network to see if his device is connected, thus knowing if he is at said location.

nmap Method

While I find arp-scan gives the most complete information for found devices, as it returns IP, MAC address, and manufacturer, there are situations where devices will not be included in the scan – if, for example, a device is present on the network but hasn't been assigned an IP address.

For a more complete list, use this second method. It will require installing nmap, short for "network-mapper". Again on Ubuntu/Debian, you should be able to install it with

```
sudo apt-get install nmap
```

Once installed, you'll want to use option -sn, which stands for no port scan. In older versions of nmap, the option -sP may be used instead of -sn. This option is often known as a "ping sweep".

The full command is as follows, making sure to use root permissions with sudo (otherwise results will differ):

```
sudo nmap -sn 192.168.1.0/24
```

The preceding command assumes your network is using the IP range 192.168.1.*; in some cases, the third number may differ. If you didn't get back any result from the nmap ping sweep, you should manually check the IP range being used by your network. In that case, you can find out by running (the "a" is short for address)

```
ip a
```

In the results, look for the section with your wireless or Ethernet interface (depending on which you're using) and look for your own IP on the local network. In my case, my wireless interface is called wlp3s0, and my local IP address range is 192.168.30.* as shown in Figure 7-1.

```
philip@philip-ThinkPad-T420:~$ ip a
1: lo: <LOOPBACK,UP,LOWER_UP> mtu 65536 qdisc noqueue state UNKNOWN group default qlen 1000
    link/loopback 00:00:00:00:00:00 brd 00:00:00:00:00:00
    inet 127.0.0.1/8 scope host lo
       valid_lft forever preferred_lft forever
    inet6 ::1/128 scope host
       valid_lft forever preferred_lft forever
2: enp0s25: <BROADCAST,MULTICAST> mtu 1500 qdisc noop state DOWN group default qlen 1000
    link/ether 00:21:cc:ba:c8:0d brd ff:ff:ff:ff:ff:ff
3: wlp3s0: <BROADCAST,MULTICAST,UP,LOWER_UP> mtu 1500 qdisc mq state UP group default qlen 1000
    link/ether 10:0b:a9:96:87:74 brd ff:ff:ff:ff:ff:ff
    inet 192.168.30.161/24 brd 192.168.30.255 scope global dynamic noprefixroute wlp3s0
       valid_lft 80778sec preferred_lft 80778sec
    inet6 fe80::5a7e:221e:3122:8e4c/64 scope link noprefixroute
       valid_lft forever preferred_lft forever
4: docker0: <NO-CARRIER,BROADCAST,MULTICAST,UP> mtu 1500 qdisc noqueue state DOWN group default
    link/ether 02:42:db:4b:6e:66 brd ff:ff:ff:ff:ff:ff
    inet 172.17.0.1/16 brd 172.17.255.255 scope global docker0
       valid_lft forever preferred_lft forever
philip@philip-ThinkPad-T420:~$ ■
```

Figure 7-1. *Finding IP address being used locally with* `ip a`

So in my case, I actually need to run

```
sudo nmap -sn 192.168.30.0/24
```

The 0/24 in this command specifies a range in CIDR notation. There are three options for specifying ranges with nmap:

- CIDR notation (*0/24*)

- Range (*1-5*)

- Wildcard (***)

Thus, the same command can be expressed as

```
nmap 192.168.1.0/24
nmap 192.168.1.0-255
nmap 192.168.1.*
```

Note   Want to watch what is happening on the network live? Before running nmap, open up a second terminal and run `ip monitor`. This will allow you to watch everything happening on the network live. Alternatively, if you just want to see activity form nmap, you can add the `-d` flag to your command.

View Open Ports

Once you have the IP address of a device, you often want to see what ports are open. This goes for servers as well, which after all are simply devices located at an IP address somewhere else on the Internet no different than a local computer, smartphone, or IoT device. Situations where this might come in handy include

- Figuring out what type of device is on the network based on open ports

- Finding open ports which may be exploitable by hacks

- Finding an open port which can be visited in your browser or by other means for device interaction

Since we installed nmap previously, I'll assume you have it installed.

The most common way to scan for open ports of a device is to simply use nmap followed by the IP address of the device you want to scan. For example, using the previous tip, I was able to find that my hotel's router has an IP address of 192.168.1.1; I would then use the following command to find open ports:

```
nmap 192.168.1.1
```

This in my case outputs the following:

```
Host is up (0.82s latency).
Not shown: 999 closed ports
PORT    STATE SERVICE
80/tcp open  http
```

> **Note**   Getting this kind of output from nmap is dependent on a device actually being located at the IP you input. It may be that 192.168.1.1 isn't any device on your network.

It shows port 80 is open; this is the basic http port where the web-based interface serves the settings panel for the router.

You might want to check what ports are open on your own machine; you might be surprised what you find:

```
nmap localhost
```

It's important to point out that by default nmap only scans the 1000 most popular ports on the specified device. When a server or device wants to be discreet, less popular ports may be used. If you really want to scan all possible ports, you should use the -p- flag, for example:

```
nmap -p- localhost
```

This will scan all 65535 ports, that is, over 65 times as many ports as the default, so it takes a significantly longer time to complete.

The same method can be used on a web address, for example:

```
nmap -p- example.com
```

This will return open ports on the server for example.com. At the time of writing, only ports 80 and 443 are open – port 80 for http traffic and port 443 for https. Later I'll list some of the most common ports and their most likely use. Keep in mind the phrase "most likely"; there is nothing stopping a server from using a port commonly used for one thing for another thing. Some of the most commonly used ports are shown in Table 7-1.

Sometimes someone might run a service on an unexpected port, for example, running ssh on port 80 instead of port 22, to subvert restrictive network policies that don't allow SSH. The firewall blocks port 22 in an attempt to stop the use of ssh on the network, but if the server is listening on port 80 (normally used for web traffic), the method of blocking becomes ineffective.

Table 7-1. *Commonly vulnerable ports*

Port Number	Common Use
80	http
443	https
21	FTP
22	SSH
25	SMTP
135	Windows RCP
137	NetBIOS
3306	MySQL
3389	RDP

Another common use for running a service on a nondefault port is to avoid exploit bots who might use scanning techniques like those used here. For example, say someone is mass scanning IP addresses to find MySQL instances running on the default port 3306; a server which instead had service running on port 7777 would go undetected. Though with something like MySQL the best policy is to close the port off to the public completely, making it only available to the internal applications which need it. With something like SSH you might not have the option to turn off the port completely. It's for this reason that SSH key authentication is recommended over password authentication, as it makes a brute force attack nearly impossible.

If you want to see a more complete list, you can parse the /usr/share/nmap/ file which lists all services known to nmap. The list is too long to be useful so you may find removing all entries marked as unknown to be useful:

```
cat /usr/share/nmap/nmap-services | grep -v unknown
```

Even after removing all unknown entries we still get over 12,000 results. I recommend reversing the lines so you start with lower-numbered ports. You can do this you can do this by piping the previous command into tac (cat command with lines reversed):

```
cat /usr/share/nmap/nmap-services \
  | grep -v unknown \
```

```
| tac
```

This way you can scroll upward starting at port 1. Alternatively you could pipe the results into 'less', the utlity explored in Chapter 1, to view the results with easy scrolling.

Devices and Ports at Once

If you want to scan all devices on your local network and also scan for open ports on those devices, you can combine the two previous tips into a single command.

This can either be done the easy but slow way or the fast way.

Easy but Slow

The easy but slow way is to simply use nmap for the whole process in a single step, by running nmap on an IP range instead of IP. This means nmap will be attempted for all IPs in the specified range; simply add -p- if you want to scan all ports instead of the 1000 most popular:

```
sudo nmap 192.168.1.0/24
```

Note   Depending on your network, this method can be very slow.

Faster Method

The faster way uses arp-scan to get the IPs, grep to extract them, and finally xargs with nmap to perform the scan on each one. It looks like this:

```
sudo arp-scan --localnet \
  | grep -o \
    '[0-9]\{1,3\}\.[0-9]\{1,3\}\.[0-9]\{1,3\}\.[0-9]\{1,3\}' \
  | xargs nmap
```

OS Detection

If from your results you find some machine IP addresses that look interesting, you can ask nmap to attempt to guess the OS running on the machine:

```
sudo nmap -O <ip-address>
```

If you want to detect the OS of every device scanned using the script from the previous section, you may instead want to use `--osscan-limit` which will limit OS detection scan to promising targets. Or if you want `nmap` to be more aggressive with guessing OS and show closest match, use `--osscan-guess`.

Scanning the Internet with masscan

Masscan is an Internet-scale port scanner, useful for large scale surveys of the Internet, or of internal networks. While the default transmit rate is only 100 packets/second, it can optional go as fast as 25 million packets/second, a rate sufficient to scan the Internet in 3 minutes for one port.

—masscan man page

Note   As with `nmap`, you'll want to build `masscan` from source if you want to get the most up-to-date features (e.g., *--top-ports flag*), though an older version is available in most package managers. You can find the source at `www.github.com/robertdavidgraham/masscan`.

Masscan is a tool very similar to `nmap` but which was released later and has the ability to scan ports at a much faster rate. It's easy to switch between the two as `masscan` uses nmap-compatible syntax. You can even get a list of similar features between `masscan` and `nmap` by running

```
masscan --nmap
```

While `masscan` is much faster than `nmap`, it has less features and is less accurate. Often `masscan` will be used for initial reconnaissance to find targets, and once targets are selected, `nmap` will be used for greater accuracy and detail.

When using `masscan`, you'll likely notice that it runs much slower than the maximum possible speed described in the man pages. This is because there are several other limiting factors to the speed at which `masscan` will run, including things like the rate at which your router can upload and download traffic.

That said, we can run a script equivalent to an `nmap` one to compare:

```
time sudo masscan --top-ports 192.168.1.0/24
```

Once complete, try the same thing in nmap:

```
time sudo nmap 192.168.1.0/24
```

You'll find that masscan runs significantly faster as it doesn't wait for a response before sending the next request, though it will still have to scan each port once devices are found to find which are open.

As mentioned in the description, the default speed is 100 packets per second, though it is possible to increase this all the way to 25 million per second. That rate will be limited by what your network and device can handle. If you want to change the rate, use the --rate flag, for example:

```
sudo masscan -p 22 --rate 1000 192.168.1.0/24
```

When scanning public ranges, be careful as sending massive amounts of unrestricted to a very large range of IPs may trigger red flags for your Internet service provider. It may be better to SSH into a cheap server and test large scans at high speeds from there.

Run Scripts with nmap

Beyond scanning ports and detecting OS, nmap provides advanced capability through script modules. A large variety of these scripts are shipped with the program by default, and additional ones can be installed or written from scratch. To get a complete list of the scripts that come with nmap, check the usr/share/nmap/scripts folder:

```
ls /usr/share/nmap/scripts
```

At the time of writing, there are over 600 prewritten scripts shipped with nmap by default.

Note   The version that is available from apt-get or other package management systems likely isn't the most up to date, as nmap is still a very active project. You can find the most up-to-date version at www.github.com/nmap/nmap.

To use a script, simply pass it in with the --script flag like the following:

```
nmap --script http-headers example.com
```

In this example, we've used a script to get the http-headers of example.com; your results should include headers for both ports 80 and 443, as shown in Figure 7-2.

```
80/tcp    open    http
| http-headers:
|    Accept-Ranges: bytes
|    Age: 444835
|    Cache-Control: max-age=604800
|    Content-Type: text/html; charset=UTF-8
|    Date: Wed, 01 Apr 2020 20:49:01 GMT
|    Etag: "3147526947"
|    Expires: Wed, 08 Apr 2020 20:49:01 GMT
|    Last-Modified: Thu, 17 Oct 2019 07:18:26 GMT
|    Server: ECS (gdl/650D)
|    X-Cache: HIT
|    Content-Length: 1256
|    Connection: close
|
|_   (Request type: HEAD)
```

Figure 7-2. *Header information from http-headers nmap script*

traceroute Script

Some scripts like the ones mentioned earlier can simply be run as is. Others may require being used in conjunction with other options. For example, the `traceroute-geolocation` works with data that comes from the `--traceroute` flag. So using this script requires both:

```
sudo nmap --traceroute \
  --script traceroute-geolocation example.com
```

The `--traceroute` flag is used to trace all hops or intermediating routers; in combination with the `traceroute-geolocation`, we can get the geolocation of each router along the way. An example of results using the '`--traceroute`' flag are shown in Figure 7-3.

```
Host script results:
| traceroute-geolocation:
|   HOP  RTT     ADDRESS                                                      GEOLOCATION
|   1    176.07  _gateway (192.168.1.254)                                     - ,-
|   2    38.11   ipdsl-mex-roma-79-l0.uninet.net.mx (201.154.119.39)         19.437,-99.011 Mexico ()
|   3    179.99  reg-qro-triara-27-hge0-5-0-2.uninet.net.mx (201.125.120.45) 19.437,-99.011 Mexico ()
|   4    186.56  74.125.50.242                                                37.751,-97.822 United States ()
|   5    186.58  209.85.245.223                                               37.751,-97.822 United States ()
|   6    186.60  108.170.236.181                                              37.751,-97.822 United States ()
|_  7    186.57  den03s09-in-f14.1e100.net (216.58.217.14)                    37.406,-122.078 United States (California)
```

Figure 7-3. *Using nmap --traceroute to see the location of the server*

http-enum Script

The `http-enum` script is written to test several paths of a website to detect information that may give hints as to what applications or content management system is running on the server.

```
sudo nmap --script http-enum example.com
```

http-enum is also an example of a script which can be passed an argument. If you want the script to run with a base path, for example, example.com/blog instead of website.com, you can do

```
sudo nmap --script http-enum --script-args \
  http-enum.basepath='blog/' example.com
```

Write Your Own Script for nmap

nmap comes with many useful scripts that are relatively unknown to the majority of people who use it for the port scanning functionality. What is even less known is that you can actually create your own scripts by writing NSE files and placing them in the scripts folder.

NSE stands for Nmap Scripting Engine and is a domain-specific language which is built on top of the Lua programming language. As seen in the previous section, scripts can be used for all kinds of things including

- Network discovery

- Version/OS detection

- Vulnerability detection

- Backdoor detection

- Vulnerability exploitation

Every NSE consists of three sections, in a single file:

- Header

- Rule

- Action

The header section normally contains a description and imports any needed libraries. A very simple example is

```
-- Header --
local shortport = require "shortport"
```

The preceding script imports the shortport library which can be used to determine if a port is of a service type. After the header comes the rule section. Our example app will use the shortport library to check if the port is one commonly used for http:

```
-- Rule --
portrule = shortport.http
```

Next comes the action section of the script. We'll tell our script what to do in the case that the port is one commonly used for http:

```
-- Action --
action = function(host, port)
     return "Hello World!"
end
```

With these three sections written, save your script and save it as /usr/share/nmap/ scripts/testing.nse. Then run the following on a website:

```
sudo nmap --script testing <website.com>
```

If you've copied and run the script correctly, you should see a subsection under any found http ports as shown in Figure 7-4.

```
Not shown: 986 closed ports
PORT        STATE      SERVICE
21/tcp      open       ftp
22/tcp      open       ssh
25/tcp      filtered   smtp
26/tcp      open       rsftp
53/tcp      open       domain
80/tcp      open       http
|_testing: Hello World!
110/tcp     open       pop3
143/tcp     open       imap
443/tcp     open       https
```

Figure 7-4. *Output from the example script*

Our "hello world" NSE script isn't particularly useful but it gives you the outline of the three main parts of an NSE script (header, rule, action). If you want to experiment with making an advanced NSE script, look through the other prebuilt scripts in /usr/ share/nmap/scripts; these provide great examples or starting points for building your own scripts.

Wireshark/tshark

Another tool worth knowing about that we won't go in depth on here is Wireshark. It's a full-featured GUI application for packet analysis. It allows you to capture and analyze traffic on your network. There is a terminal-oriented version of Wireshark called `tshark`. Both versions are available on most package managers. If you want the Wireshark experience but don't have access to GUI on a machine, you can also check out the community project `termshark`, which simulates the UI of Wireshark in the terminal.

Wireshark is commonly used for information security, network quality testing, and quality assurance of software for network use.

While `arp-scan` and `nmap` are the easiest tools for finding devices on the network, Wireshark is actually more powerful in being able to find devices which may be hidden. If, for example, a device does not respond to any requests, `nmap`, `masscan`, `arp-scan`, and `ping` will never be able to find it even with the IP. However, if those devices at some point want to make use of the network and Wireshark is recording, they will be spotted and their existence becomes known.

To see all traffic with `tshark`, simply run it without any options (*root permissions required*):

```
sudo tshark
```

Depending on your network, this will return a fast scrolling screen showing traffic on the network, similiar to that shown in Figure 7-5.

```
File Edit View Search Terminal Help
   134 8.499327614 Ubiquiti_58:64:16 → Broadcast    ARP 60 Who has 192.168.1.151? Tell 192.168.1.
91
   135 8.601716327 HuaweiTe_b3:b8:a3 → Broadcast    ARP 60 Who has 192.168.1.94? Tell 192.168.1.2
54
   136 8.663641534 172.217.5.162 → 192.168.1.112 TLSv1.2 122 Application Data
   137 8.664446164 172.217.5.162 → 192.168.1.112 TCP 66 443 → 56656 [FIN, ACK] Seq=57 Ack=1 Win=2
99 Len=0 TSval=1313636887 TSecr=2041651258
   138 8.664682711 192.168.1.112 → 172.217.5.162 TCP 66 56656 → 443 [FIN, ACK] Seq=1 Ack=58 Win=1
726 Len=0 TSval=2041891262 TSecr=1313636887
   139 8.683288117 172.217.5.162 → 192.168.1.112 TCP 66 443 → 56656 [ACK] Seq=58 Ack=2 Win=299 Le
n=0 TSval=1313636905 TSecr=2041891262
   140 8.707053698        fe80::1 → ff02::1:ff2d:5e20 ICMPv6 86 Neighbor Solicitation for 2806:107e
:c:c654:60e1:ab0:6a2d:5e20 from 00:f8:1c:b3:b8:a3
   141 8.759968315 216.58.193.2 → 192.168.1.112 TLSv1.2 122 Application Data
   142 8.760316239 192.168.1.112 → 216.58.193.2 TCP 66 48590 → 443 [FIN, ACK] Seq=1 Ack=57 Win=50
1 Len=0 TSval=621818446 TSecr=2680395118
   143 8.760899031 216.58.193.2 → 192.168.1.112 TCP 66 443 → 48590 [FIN, ACK] Seq=57 Ack=1 Win=25
3 Len=0 TSval=2680395118 TSecr=621578444
   144 8.760947064 192.168.1.112 → 216.58.193.2 TCP 66 48590 → 443 [ACK] Seq=2 Ack=58 Win=501 Len
=0 TSval=621818447 TSecr=2680395118
   145 8.777831117 216.58.193.2 → 192.168.1.112 TCP 66 443 → 48590 [ACK] Seq=58 Ack=2 Win=253 Len
=0 TSval=2680395136 TSecr=621818446
   146 8.806570877 HuaweiTe_b3:b8:a3 → Broadcast    ARP 60 Who has 192.168.1.65? Tell 192.168.1.2
54
   147 8.858286150 149.154.175.50 → 192.168.1.112 SSL 379 Continuation Data
```

Figure 7-5. Example output when running tshark

As traffic moves quickly, it's often more useful to save the output into a file:

```
sudo tshark > /tmp/output.txt
```

The command will keep running until you cancel by pressing "ctrl+c". The longer you run it, the bigger your sample size will be. This file can later be parsed to extract more specific details and analyzed at your own pace.

If you want to be more specific with the packets which are recorded, tshark has all kinds of filters – for example, if we want to look at a specific device:

```
sudo tshark host <ip-address>
```

If you're going to be parsing through the results looking for a single device, this will save you a lot of time and effort. You can also filter by traffic type, for example, to only show http traffic:

```
sudo tshark -Y http
```

You can show the full path of the http request with

```
sudo tshark -Y http.request.full_uri
```

There are all kinds of filters for tshark and the GUI equivalent Wireshark. We won't go into all of them, but it's a powerful tool worth looking into if you want to analyze local network traffic. Also keep in the GUI version Wireshark is the main version. It's an extremely useful tool and there are full books on making use of it.

More Network Tools

The tools outlined so far can come in handy often, but they're only a small subsection of networking tools available on Linux. Table 7-2 is a longer list of networking tools for Linux that you can research more in depth.

Note   We've included several deprecated utilities in the list. While they're no longer maintained, they're still widely used on older systems or by system admins who continue using them. For this reason, they're worth being aware of, though we'll make sure to list the up-to-date alternatives.

Table 7-2. *Networking utilities*

Port Number	Common Use
dig	Get domain information
netstat	Network statistics (deprecated)
ifconfig	List systems network interfaces (deprecated)
arp	Work with ARP cache (deprecated)
route	Show/manipulate the IP routing table (deprecated)
ip	Show/manipulate routing, network devices, interfaces, and tunnels
ss	Socket statistics
ngrep	Like grep but for network traffic
traceroute	Find route packet takes to get to server
mtr	Network diagnostic tool
nc	Short for "ncat," like cat but for network data. Can also be used as a networking interface module for other programs
nft	Networking tool for packet filtering and classification
iptables	Manage firewall settings (deprecated)

(continued)

Table 7-2. (*continued*)

Port Number	Common Use
sysctl	Configure kernel parameters at runtime (*some related to networking like socket buffer size*)
ethtool	Analyze Ethernet connections
whois	Get whois information on a domain
lsof	Find what programs are using which ports
hping	Like ping but with additional methods and options
socat	Short for "socket cat," like nc (*net cat*) but with more features

Dig

Dig is a DNS lookup utility. If it's not installed on your system, you can find it as part of dnsutils on Debian-based package managers and bind-utils on Fedora, CentOS, and Arch.

Dig is used by passing it a web domain as an argument and will return DNS information on the website. Without options, the information from dig is somewhat cluttered and lacks entries. We recommend using the options +noall and +answer:

```
dig +noall +answer
```

Dig should return all the DNS entries for the domain. Our example in Figure 7-6 includes a query to example.com and another query to yahoo.com. We included a second query to show an example of output when a domain has multiple A records.

```
philip@philip-ThinkPad-T420:~$ dig +noall +answer example.com
example.com.            5734    IN      A       93.184.216.34
philip@philip-ThinkPad-T420:~$ dig +noall +answer yahoo.com
yahoo.com.              363     IN      A       72.30.35.9
yahoo.com.              363     IN      A       72.30.35.10
yahoo.com.              363     IN      A       98.138.219.231
yahoo.com.              363     IN      A       98.138.219.232
yahoo.com.              363     IN      A       98.137.246.7
yahoo.com.              363     IN      A       98.137.246.8
philip@philip-ThinkPad-T420:~$ 
```

Figure 7-6. *Dig queries on example.com and yahoo.com*

Netstat (Deprecated)

Netstat is a multipurpose utility for checking network connections, routing tables, network interface statistics, and other network diagnostics. While you may still see references to netstat and it does work, it has been deprecated.

As netstat is deprecated, it is recommended you use the utilities which have replaced it including dig, ip, and ss.

ifconfig (Deprecated)

Like netstat the utility ifconfig has been deprecated. Despite this, you may find it present on many machines and potentially used within scripts. It's a utility for working with network interfaces. It is recommended you use the ip command which comes with the iproute2 package instead.

If you remember earlier in this chapter, we used the command ip a to find out network IP range. Before ip became the go-to utility for this, running ifconfig was used to do the same thing. ifconfig also has the ability to interact with interfaces, for example, enabling or disabling them (assuming your Ethernet interface is named eth0):

```
ifconfig eth0 up
```

Now that same thing can be done using ip with

```
ip link set eth0 up
```

arp (Deprecated)

arp stands for Address Resolution Protocol, and it is used to map the MAC addresses of devices (globally unique identifying number) to IPs. Computers contain an ARP table which maps MAP and IP addresses. To view all entries in the table, run the following command:

```
arp -a
```

Since arp has now been deprecated, it is recommended you use ip for the same functionality. The equivalent of the preceding function with ip would be

```
ip n
```

where n is short for neighbor. See the man page on arp or ip for more advanced capabilities.

route (Deprecated)

The route command is used to show/manipulate the IP routing table. The simplest command with 'route' is to run it without any options or arguments which will return the IP routing table. The equivalent command with ip is as follows:

ip r

where r stands for route.

ip

As mentioned in the previous section, the ip utility is a replacement for several utilities including ifconfig and 'route', it is included in the iproute2 package. Routes can be seen by running ip route or ip r for short. There are additional route commands for adding or deleting such as ip route del unreachable 10.1.0.0/24, where "unreachable" is the route name and "10.1.0.0/24" is the route.

ss

ss is a utility for monitoring socket use. The initials in the name stand for socket statistics. If ss is not installed, you can find it in most package managers included with iproute2. When running ss stand-alone, you'll get back a long list of all connected sockets as shown in Figure 7-7. To make reading the output more manageable, you can pipe the results into less by running ss | less.

```
philip@philip-ThinkPad-T420:~$ ss
NetidState      Recv-Q  Send-Q                      Local Address:Port       Peer Address:
Port
u_seqESTAB      0       0                            @00012 45538                        *
45539
u_strESTAB      0       0                                 * 48395                        *
48396
u_strESTAB      0       0                                 * 47749                        *
47750
u_strESTAB      0       0                 @/tmp/dbus-YLPpboub 45290                       *
45289
u_strESTAB      0       0                                 * 43531                        *
39901
u_strESTAB      0       0                                 * 40819                        *
42945
u_strESTAB      0       0                                 * 40147                        *
40148
u_strESTAB      0       0         /var/run/dbus/system_bus_socket 28943                  *
26258
u_strESTAB      0       0                                 * 51942                        *
51045
u_strESTAB      0       0                                 * 31248                        *
32231
u_strESTAB      0       0         /var/run/dbus/system_bus_socket 26943                  *
28327
u_strESTAB      0       0                      /run/user/1000/bus 69563                  *
```

Figure 7-7. *Example socket statistics returned from running* ss

It's somewhat difficult to understand what all these sockets are by default. To make things easier, you can add the flag -p which will tell you the process name and ID of each socket connection. This allows you to associate a socket connection with a process running on a machine.

ngrep

ngrep is a network utility which provides grep-like abilities for parsing network data. Given some specific text to listen for, ngrep will monitor network traffic and report any connection data which matches. As an example, we'll view traffic generated by visiting example.com; first we'll tell ngrep to listen for the string "example" as shown in the following:

```
sudo ngrep example
```

ngrep is now actively parsing network traffic for the string "example". If you view example.com in your web browser, you should see a match occur. To demonstrate the importance of https, let's send some unencrypted data to example using curl. Open up a second terminal with ngrep still running and run the following command:

```
curl --data "user=name&password=secret" example.com
```

You should see the request in your window running ngrep. If you look through the text carefully, you should be able to see the user and password fields, as shown in Figure 7-8.

```
T 192.168.30.161:54418 -> 93.184.216.34:80 [AP] #180
  POST / HTTP/1.1..Host: example.com..User-Agent: curl/7.58.0..Accept: */*..C
  ontent-Length: 25..Content-Type: application/x-www-form-urlencoded....user=
  name&password=secret
##
T 93.184.216.34:80 -> 192.168.30.161:54418 [A] #182
  HTTP/1.1 200 OK..Accept-Ranges: bytes..Cache-Control: max-age=604800..Conte
  nt-Type: text/html; charset=UTF-8..Date: Thu, 02 Apr 2020 19:28:28 GMT..Eta
  g: "3147526947"..Expires: Thu, 09 Apr 2020 19:28:28 GMT..Last-Modified: Thu
  , 17 Oct 2019 07:18:26 GMT..Server: EOS (vny/0454)..Content-Length: 1256...
  .<!doctype html>.<html>.<head>.    <title>Example Domain</title>..    <meta
  charset="utf-8" />.    <meta http-equiv="Content-type" content="text/html;
  charset=utf-8" />.    <meta name="viewport" content="width=device-width, i
  nitial-scale=1" />.    <style type="text/css">.    body {.         backgroun
  d-color: #f0f0f2;.         margin: 0;.         padding: 0;.         font-famil
  y: -apple-system, system-ui, BlinkMacSystemFont, "Segoe UI", "Open Sans", "
  Helvetica Neue", Helvetica, Arial, sans-serif;.         .    }.    div {.
      width: 600px;.         margin: 5em auto;.         padding: 2em;.
  background-color: #fdfdff;.         border-radius: 0.5em;.         box-shadow
  : 2px 3px 7px 2px rgba(0,0,0,0.02);.    }.    a:link, a:visited {.         c
  olor: #38488f;.         text-decoration: none;.    }.    @media (max-width:
  700px) {.         div {.         margin: 0 auto;.         width: auto;
```

Figure 7-8. *Unencrypted data recorded using ngrep*

If you run the same command but instead specify https, like shown here

```
curl --data "user=name&password=secret" https://example.com
```

you should still see the request but will not be able to see the data which was sent or even the specific website that was visited.

traceroute

The traceroute utility allows you to send packets to a host and get detailed information on the route taken to get to the host. This might sound familiar as in Chapter 7 we used a 'traceroute' NES script to view the hops made by traffic going from our local machine to a website. The 'traceroute' utility provides this functionality as a stand-alone utility, if we run

```
traceroute example.com
```

we will see the IP addresses of all the machines our packets traveled to before reaching our final destination. This starts with the local router and ends at the IP of the actual website as shown in Figure 7-9.

```
philip@philip-ThinkPad-T420:~/tmp/presidio-research/data$ traceroute example.com
traceroute to example.com (93.184.216.34), 30 hops max, 60 byte packets
 1  _gateway (192.168.30.1)  10.645 ms  15.118 ms  15.708 ms
 2  192.168.100.1 (192.168.100.1)  16.391 ms  16.370 ms  20.346 ms
 3  10.99.128.3 (10.99.128.3)  21.195 ms  21.693 ms  22.087 ms
 4  * * *
 5  10.180.59.75 (10.180.59.75)  28.628 ms  30.877 ms  31.408 ms
 6  10.180.200.172 (10.180.200.172)  36.723 ms  31.901 ms  13.046 ms
 7  fixed-187-190-234-77.totalplay.net (187.190.234.77)  22.643 ms  24.100 ms  1
8.999 ms
 8  93.184.216.34 (93.184.216.34)  15.777 ms  17.218 ms  18.396 ms
 9  93.184.216.34 (93.184.216.34)  16.487 ms  20.883 ms  17.562 ms
philip@philip-ThinkPad-T420:~/tmp/presidio-research/data$ 
```

Figure 7-9. Route taken to example.com shown with traceroute

mtr

The mtr utility is a network diagnostic tool which combines aspects of ping and traceroute. The name mtr is actually short for "my traceroute." Instead of sending a single set of packets like traceroute, mtr continuously sends additional packets after the previous is received (similar to ping). An updating display shows detailed information on the timing as shown in Figure 7-10. If you're having issues with a connection, mtr can help you get an idea of where things go wrong along the way.

```
                          My traceroute  [v0.92]
philip-ThinkPad-T420 (192.168.30.161)                   2020-04-02T15:18:08-0400
Keys:  Help   Display mode   Restart statistics   Order of fields   quit
                                  Packets               Pings
 Host                            Loss%   Snt   Last   Avg  Best  Wrst StDev
 1. _gateway                      0.0%    14    7.8   8.5   1.6  41.8  10.5
 2. 192.168.100.1                 0.0%    14   31.4  18.9   1.9 172.6  44.9
 3. 10.99.128.3                   0.0%    14   87.9  77.8   5.9 122.5  48.0
 4. ???
 5. 10.180.59.75                  0.0%    14    5.9   9.2   4.9  38.1   8.6
 6. 10.180.200.172                0.0%    14   19.8  18.3  12.2  40.5   7.8
 7. fixed-187-190-234-77.totalplay.n 0.0%  14   36.2  33.9  13.1 200.1  49.0
 8. 93.184.216.34                 0.0%    14   14.9  24.6  11.9 139.2  33.3
```

Figure 7-10. Continuously updating route data to example.com shown by mtr

nc

nc is short for network cat, name inspired from the cat utility. nc is a robust utility which provides the ability to connect and listen for connections via TCP or UDP. This means it can even be used for things like opening up a channel between two machines for chat or file transfer (though other tools like SSH are preferred).

nc is often referred to as the "Swiss Army Knife of networking" and can be used for several networking tasks including port scanning, serving a website, or spoofing headers. While many use cases have better options like nmap for port scanning, it can still be useful for some simple things like grabbing headers or spoofing your own headers.

To spoof your own headers, run

```
nc example.com 80
```

You'll then be able to add additional text. You can base your spoof header on the following sample:

```
GET / HTTP/1.1
Host: example
Referrer: duckduckgo.com
User-Agent: fake-browser
```

With the header entered, press enter twice and you'll fetch the website using the spoofed header. You'll get back a response including the header information for the site.

nft – nftables

nftables is an administration tool for nftables framework for packet filtering and classification. While you can find nftables under that name on package managers, the command for running it is actually nft. The "nf" in nftables stands for "net filter," and they're used to filter network traffic. That can be either outgoing or incoming. For example, you might not allow outgoing traffic to a particular IP or not allow incoming traffic to a certain port. nftables works by keeping track of a series of system-wide rules which can be added or dropped and are used during the traffic filtering process.

iptables (Deprecated)

The iptables utility has been deprecated in favor of nftables, its successor. iptables is rule based but lacks features included with nftables like having a single rule to target both ipv4 and ipv6 packets.

sysctl

The sysctl is used to configure kernel parameters at runtime. This is not necessarily only for network issues though some are such as socket size. This might be done for servers which regularly send and receive large files, as tuning socket buffer size can improve network performance for the specific use case.

ethtool

The ethtool utility, short for Ethernet tool, can be used to get in-depth information about your Ethernet connection. This includes things about the data transfer itself and the physical hardware. To view information on your Ethernet interface, you first need to get its name. This can be done with by running

```
ip a
```

Record the name of your Ethernet interface (likely includes an "e") and pass it as an argument to ethtool:

```
ethtool enp0s25
```

In my case, the Ethernet interface name is "enp0s25" but yours will likely be different. One of the most common names for the Ethernet interface is "eth0". When you use the interface as the argument for ethtool, you should get back information about the hardware (even if you're not actively using Ethernet), like shown in Figure 7-11.

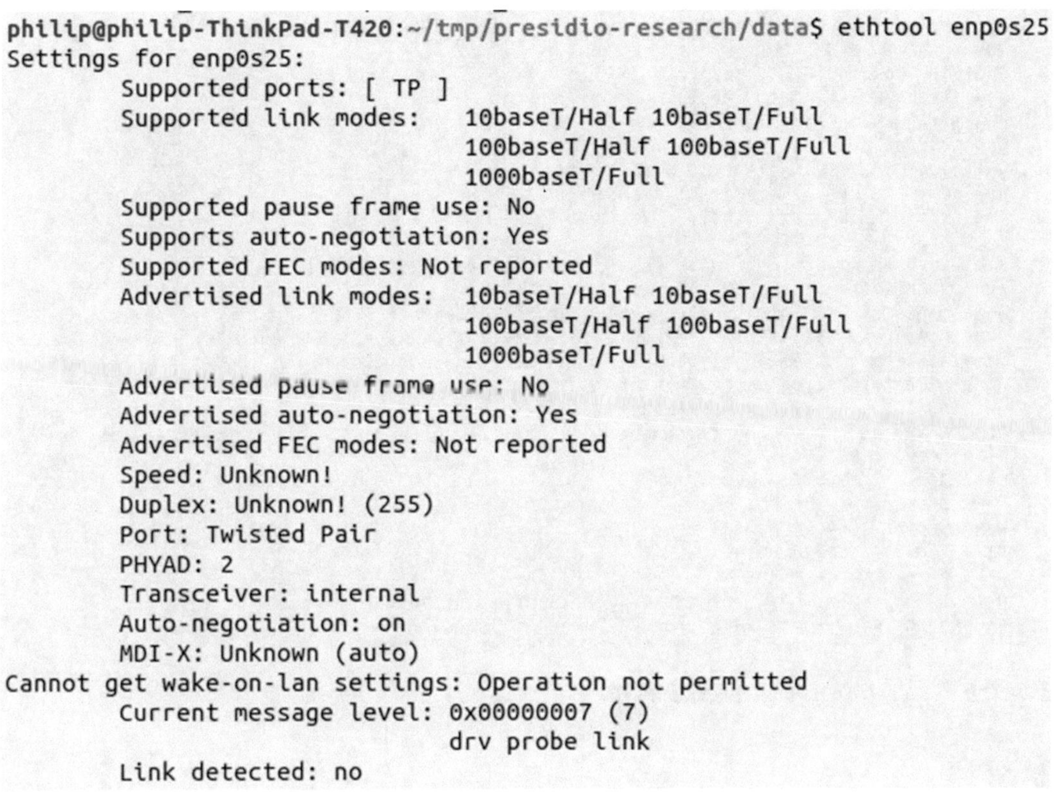

```
philip@philip-ThinkPad-T420:~/tmp/presidio-research/data$ ethtool enp0s25
Settings for enp0s25:
        Supported ports: [ TP ]
        Supported link modes:   10baseT/Half 10baseT/Full
                                100baseT/Half 100baseT/Full
                                1000baseT/Full
        Supported pause frame use: No
        Supports auto-negotiation: Yes
        Supported FEC modes: Not reported
        Advertised link modes:  10baseT/Half 10baseT/Full
                                100baseT/Half 100baseT/Full
                                1000baseT/Full
        Advertised pause frame use: No
        Advertised auto-negotiation: Yes
        Advertised FEC modes: Not reported
        Speed: Unknown!
        Duplex: Unknown! (255)
        Port: Twisted Pair
        PHYAD: 2
        Transceiver: internal
        Auto-negotiation: on
        MDI-X: Unknown (auto)
Cannot get wake-on-lan settings: Operation not permitted
        Current message level: 0x00000007 (7)
                               drv probe link
        Link detected: no
```

Figure 7-11. *Ethernet interface information output from* `ethtool`

whois

`whois` is a utility for retrieving website ownership information provided by registrars. It can be used by simply providing a domain as the argument. For example, running the following command should return ownership and contact information like that shown in Figure 7-12:

```
whois yahoo.com
```

```
philip@philip-ThinkPad-T420:~/tmp/presidio-research/data$ whois yahoo.com
   Domain Name: YAHOO.COM
   Registry Domain ID: 3643624_DOMAIN_COM-VRSN
   Registrar WHOIS Server: whois.markmonitor.com
   Registrar URL: http://www.markmonitor.com
   Updated Date: 2019-12-18T13:37:09Z
   Creation Date: 1995-01-18T05:00:00Z
   Registry Expiry Date: 2023-01-19T05:00:00Z
   Registrar: MarkMonitor Inc.
   Registrar IANA ID: 292
   Registrar Abuse Contact Email: abusecomplaints@markmonitor.com
   Registrar Abuse Contact Phone: +1.2083895740
   Domain Status: clientDeleteProhibited https://icann.org/epp#clientDeleteProhibited
   Domain Status: clientTransferProhibited https://icann.org/epp#clientTransferProhibited
   Domain Status: clientUpdateProhibited https://icann.org/epp#clientUpdateProhibited
   Domain Status: serverDeleteProhibited https://icann.org/epp#serverDeleteProhibited
   Domain Status: serverTransferProhibited https://icann.org/epp#serverTransferProhibited
   Domain Status: serverUpdateProhibited https://icann.org/epp#serverUpdateProhibited
   Name Server: NS1.YAHOO.COM
   Name Server: NS2.YAHOO.COM
   Name Server: NS3.YAHOO.COM
   Name Server: NS4.YAHOO.COM
   Name Server: NS5.YAHOO.COM
   DNSSEC: unsigned
   URL of the ICANN Whois Inaccuracy Complaint Form: https://www.icann.org/wicf/
>>> Last update of whois database: 2020-04-02T23:19:52Z <<<
```

Figure 7-12. *whois information for yahoo.com*

lsof

The lsof stands for "list of open files"; by default it will return a long list which includes all the open files on your system. In terms of networking, the main option you'll want to know for lsof is the -i flag. The -i flag tells lsof to look for IP sockets. It can also be useful to add -P to get the port being connected to. To demonstrate, try running

```
lsof -i -P
```

This should return a list of local ports which are connecting to ports on remote servers and the program associated with said connection. An example of expected output is shown in Figure 7-13.

```
philip@philip-ThinkPad-T420:~/tmp/presidio-research/data$ lsof -i -P
COMMAND    PID    USER   FD   TYPE DEVICE SIZE/OFF NODE NAME
kdeconnec  3040  philip  21u  IPv6  44474      0t0  UDP *:1716
kdeconnec  3040  philip  22u  IPv6  44475      0t0  TCP *:1716 (LISTEN)
brave      3280  philip  40u  IPv4 326252      0t0  TCP philip-ThinkPad-T420:46242->dfw25s34-in-f10.1e100.net:443 (ESTABLISHED)
brave      3280  philip  41u  IPv4 337746      0t0  TCP philip-ThinkPad-T420:39910->104.16.80.80:443 (ESTABLISHED)
brave      3280  philip  42u  IPv4 334924      0t0  TCP philip-ThinkPad-T420:35060->den03s09-in-f3.1e100.net:443 (ESTABLISHED)
brave      3280  philip  43u  IPv4 335528      0t0  TCP philip-ThinkPad-T420:42824->oo-in-f189.1e100.net:443 (ESTABLISHED)
brave      3280  philip  44u  IPv4 239061      0t0  UDP 224.0.0.251:5353
brave      3280  philip  46u  IPv4 392336      0t0  TCP philip-ThinkPad-T420:39870->qro01s14-in-f14.1e100.net:443 (ESTABLISHED)
brave      3280  philip  51u  IPv4 338216      0t0  TCP philip-ThinkPad-T420:39030->qro01s13-in-f14.1e100.net:443 (ESTABLISHED)
brave      3280  philip  52u  IPv4 337669      0t0  TCP philip-ThinkPad-T420:39054->qro01s13-in-f14.1e100.net:443 (ESTABLISHED)
brave      3280  philip  53u  IPv4 238342      0t0  TCP philip-ThinkPad-T420:48006->151.101.50.49:443 (ESTABLISHED)
brave      3280  philip  54u  IPv4 335535      0t0  TCP philip-ThinkPad-T420:37364->den03s09-in-f14.1e100.net:443 (ESTABLISHED)
brave      3280  philip  56u  IPv4 401817      0t0  TCP philip-ThinkPad-T420:41970->ec2-3-228-157-109.compute-1.amazonaws.com:443 (CLOSE_WAIT)
brave      3280  philip  57u  IPv4 338217      0t0  TCP philip-ThinkPad-T420:34434->qro01s18-in-f14.1e100.net:443 (ESTABLISHED)
brave      3280  philip  58u  IPv4 397327      0t0  TCP philip-ThinkPad-T420:39984->qro01s14-in-f14.1e100.net:443 (ESTABLISHED)
brave      3280  philip  59u  IPv4 399070      0t0  TCP philip-ThinkPad-T420:47272->qro02s12-in-f1.1e100.net:443 (ESTABLISHED)
brave      3280  philip  62u  IPv4 400882      0t0  TCP philip-ThinkPad-T420:33620->qro02s15-in-f2.1e100.net:443 (ESTABLISHED)
brave      3280  philip  63u  IPv4 338648      0t0  TCP philip-ThinkPad-T420:32782->151.101.50.217:443 (ESTABLISHED)
brave      3280  philip  64u  IPv4 396241      0t0  TCP philip-ThinkPad-T420:45910->qro01s14-in-f22.1e100.net:443 (ESTABLISHED)
brave      3280  philip  67u  IPv4 393531      0t0  TCP philip-ThinkPad-T420:51406->qro02s11-in-f4.1e100.net:443 (ESTABLISHED)
brave      3280  philip  70u  IPv4 397513      0t0  TCP philip-ThinkPad-T420:40560->104.26.1.240:443 (ESTABLISHED)
brave      3280  philip  71u  IPv4 400890      0t0  TCP philip-ThinkPad-T420:50484->104.28.5.9:443 (ESTABLISHED)
brave      3280  philip  72u  IPv4 401123      0t0  TCP philip-ThinkPad-T420:41340->40.115.22.134:443 (ESTABLISHED)
brave      3280  philip  73u  IPv4 395253      0t0  TCP philip-ThinkPad-T420:56072->qro01s13-in-f5.1e100.net:443 (ESTABLISHED)
brave      3280  philip  75u  IPv4 338733      0t0  TCP philip-ThinkPad-T420:44990->104.26.2.23:443 (ESTABLISHED)
brave      3280  philip  81u  IPv4 396753      0t0  TCP philip-ThinkPad-T420:55702->151.101.1.69:443 (ESTABLISHED)
brave      3280  philip  83u  IPv4 398093      0t0  TCP philip-ThinkPad-T420:56752->dfw06s48-in-f106.1e100.net:443 (ESTABLISHED)
brave      3280  philip  85u  IPv4 396375      0t0  TCP philip-ThinkPad-T420:60280->104.26.3.165:443 (ESTABLISHED)
brave      3280  philip  86u  IPv4 395111      0t0  TCP philip-ThinkPad-T420:57312->qro01s13-in-f1.1e100.net:443 (ESTABLISHED)
brave      3280  philip  89u  IPv4 399913      0t0  TCP philip-ThinkPad-T420:41112->dfw25s12-in-f42.1e100.net:443 (ESTABLISHED)
brave      3280  philip  90u  IPv4 394941      0t0  TCP philip-ThinkPad-T420:45700->104.16.86.20:443 (ESTABLISHED)
brave      3280  philip  91u  IPv4 395871      0t0  TCP philip-ThinkPad-T420:33252->151.101.48.134:443 (ESTABLISHED)
brave      3280  philip  93u  IPv4 394794      0t0  TCP philip-ThinkPad-T420:60708->104.16.29.34:443 (ESTABLISHED)
brave      3280  philip  96u  IPv4 394598      0t0  TCP philip-ThinkPad-T420:35204->den03s09-in-f3.1e100.net:443 (ESTABLISHED)
brave      3280  philip  98u  IPv4 395877      0t0  TCP philip-ThinkPad-T420:40580->104.26.1.240:443 (ESTABLISHED)
brave      3280  philip  99u  IPv4 398078      0t0  TCP philip-ThinkPad-T420:53482->qro02s11-in-f14.1e100.net:443 (ESTABLISHED)
brave      3280  philip 101u  IPv4 399416      0t0  TCP philip-ThinkPad-T420:51420->172.217.195.189:443 (ESTABLISHED)
brave      3280  philip 102u  IPv4 397250      0t0  TCP philip-ThinkPad-T420:56756->dfw06s48-in-f106.1e100.net:443 (ESTABLISHED)
```

Figure 7-13. *Example output from* `lsof -i -P`

hping

`hping` is an offensive security networking tool which takes its name from `ping`. Like `ping` it sends packets over the network to a destination, but it has advanced options allowing for the crafting of custom packets, specifying things like destination port and spoofed source IP for both TCP and UDP. In addition, it has some built-in methods like the `--flood` option which can be used for DDOS-like attacks, like SYN flood attack.

The current version is 3 and is integrated into both the command and name on most package managers:

```
sudo apt-get install hping3
```

On offensive security operating systems like Kali Linux, you'll actually find `hping` installed by default. An example of SYN flood attack is shown later. A SYN flood attack involves opening several connections without finishing the handshake. It can be used to test if your network is safe from these attacks; the following is an example of performing a SYN flood attack, to test switch the IP used with the target device on your network:

```
hping3 --rand-source -S -d 500 -p 21 --flood 127.168.1.110
```

The preceding command combines a few options. The first `--rand-source` tells hping to spoof a random IP address as its source. Then `-S` flag specifies the SYN packet network, `-d  500` is the size of the packets, `-p  21` is the destination port, and finally `--flood` turns on flooding mode which sends many requests.

socat

socat is similar to nc (netcat) but has more advanced features. Also like netcat, it takes its name from cat, standing for "socket cat." It can be found on most package managers as socat. Anything that can be done with netcat is possible with socat, but it also has some additional features like multiple clients on a single port and options for working with UDP.

Summary

In this chapter, we looked at some networking techniques, particularly related to port scanning. We also briefly looked at some popular networking tools that can be used for working with networks through analysis, configuration, and opening communication channels.

CHAPTER 8

System Monitoring

Another common task you'll find yourself wanting to do while maintaining a Linux system is monitoring things like system processes, memory, and network use. This helps you to gauge how much of your capacity you're making use of. Knowing what resources might be running low gives you insights into how the system load might be reduced or where resources should be increased. In this chapter, we'll look at tools for doing different types of monitoring.

Top

Whenever a system or device is experiencing performance issues, one of the first things you'll want to do is check what programs are running and how much system resources they're using. The simple go-to for this is top which comes installed on most Linux systems. Running it will list all currently running processes. You can quickly kill a process without leaving top by pressing z and entering the process ID (PID) of your target process.

If you find yourself using top often, you might consider installing htop. htop is an enhanced version of top with an improved visual interface and shows the full path of the process.

If you prefer using built-in tools like top, or you're on a machine where you can't install htop, you can actually use a combination of keyboard commands to get something that looks almost identical to htop and in some ways better.

With top open, press zxcVm1t0 (as a sequence, not at the same time) and you'll end up with something that looks like in Figure 8-1.

© Philip Kirkbride 2020
P. Kirkbride, *Basic Linux Terminal Tips and Tricks*, https://doi.org/10.1007/978-1-4842-6035-7_8

```
top - 01:50:39 up 1 day, 11:54,  2 users,  load average: 1.21, 1.13, 1.03
Tasks: 320 total,   1 running, 261 sleeping,   0 stopped,   0 zombie
%Node0  :    7.4/2.7    10[||||||                                               ]
%Cpu0   :    8.6/3.3    12[|||||||||                                            ]
%Cpu1   :    7.0/2.0     9[|||||                                                ]
%Cpu2   :    8.4/3.2    12[|||||||                                              ]
%Cpu3   :    5.6/2.3     8[||||                                                 ]
KiB Mem :   29.5/16305400 [|||||||||||||||||||                                  ]
KiB Swap:    0.0/2097148  [                                                     ]

  PID USER       PR  NI    VIRT    RES    SHR S  %CPU %MEM     TIME+ COMMAND
    1 root       20        225676   9252   6536 S   0.1  1:43.64 /sbin/init+
  268 root       19  -1    232964  99136  97716 S   0.6  0:04.18   - /lib/s+
  291 root       20         47396   5580   3140 S   0.0  0:03.79   - /lib/s+
  819 systemd+   20        146108   3324   2764 S   0.0  0:00.30   - /lib/s+
  824 systemd+   20         72336   7568   5428 S   0.0  0:03.43   - /lib/s+
 1000 root       20          4684   2004   1756 S   0.0  0:13.52   - /usr/s+
 1001 root       20        434400   9736   8184 S   0.1  0:00.14   - /usr/s+
 1002 root       20        177624  17352   9400 S   0.1  0:00.10   - /usr/b+
 1003 root       20        294752   7016   6012 S   0.0  0:02.55   - /usr/l+
 1004 avahi      20         50540   7008   3152 S   0.0  2:32.61   - avahi-+
 1020 avahi      20         47076    340        S   0.0             - av+
 1006 root       20         38428   3236   2944 S   0.0  0:00.27   - /usr/s+
 1013 root       20        503804  12116   8636 S   0.1  0:10.70   - /usr/l+
```

Figure 8-1. *top after running* zxcVm1tO

We can take it a level further by entering alternate display mode by pressing A; this splits the screen into four separate field groups. Once in alternate display mode, you can switch between field groups by pressing g which will promote you to enter the field number. If you switch between each field group and enter zxcVm1tO, you'll end up with a neat-looking multifield display as shown in Figure 8-2.

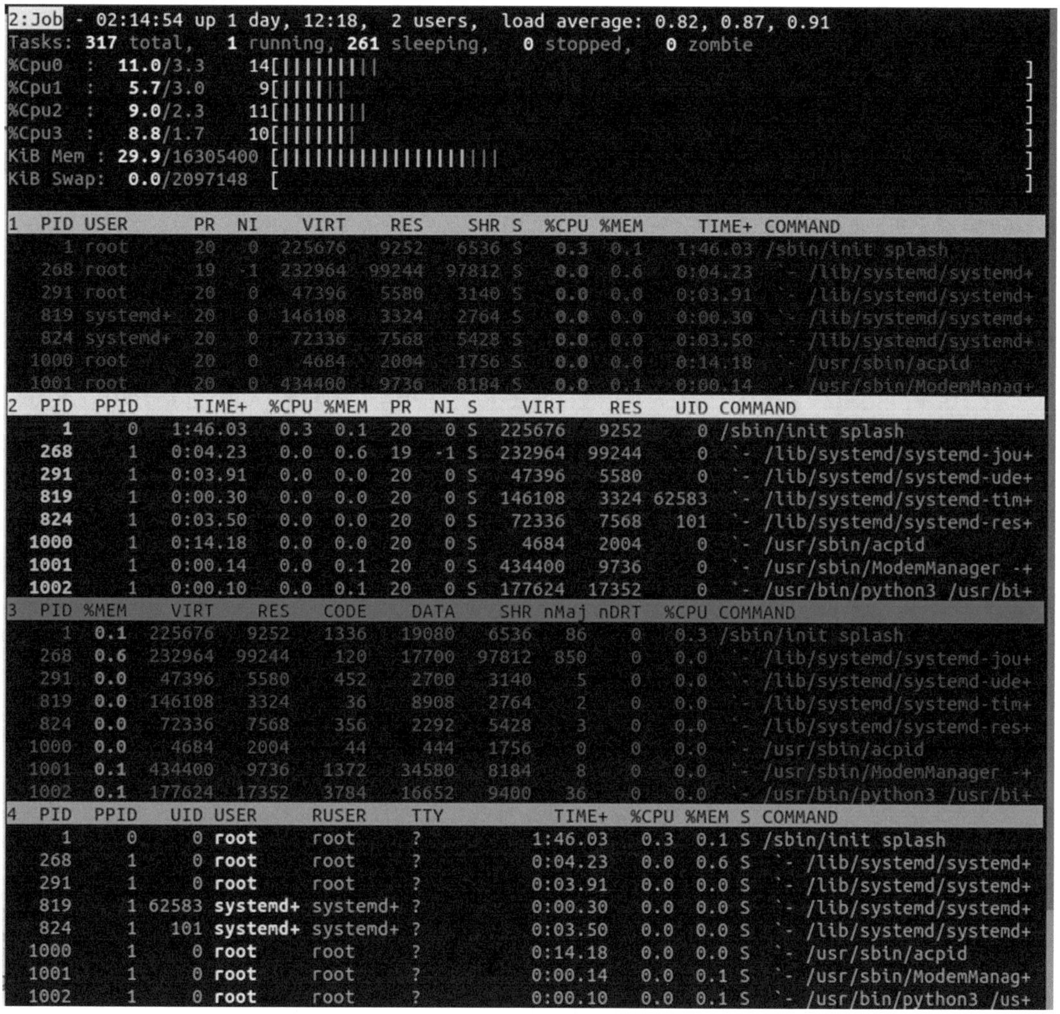

Figure 8-2. *Styled multi-tab top*

Of course you're probably thinking that looks great but that's a lot of steps to run every time you open top. To save these settings, all you have to do is press W. This will save whatever your current configuration in top, and it will look the same when you reopen it.

If you want to go back to the defaults, simply delete the configuration file that was created; by default it should be ~/.toprc.

Top-Like Programs

There are several programs which are inspired by top and either monitor some specific aspect of the system not available in top or provide the same information in a different layout. In this section, we'll go over some of the popular programs which take both their name and format from top.

htop

This is a program very similar to top which provides an improved graphic interface by default in comparison to top as shown in Figure 8-3. It is not installed by default on most distros but is available via many package management systems such as apt on Debian/Ubuntu.

```
File  Edit  View  Search  Terminal  Help

  1  [|||||||||||||||         40.5%]   Tasks: 189, 668 thr; 2 running
  2  [|||||||||||||||         42.7%]   Load average: 1.89 2.05 1.53
  3  [|||||||||||||||         41.9%]   Uptime: 1 day, 00:45:37
  4  [|||||||||||||||         43.5%]
Mem[|||||||||||||||||||||  4.24G/15.5G]
Swp[                          0K/2.00G]

  PID USER      PRI  NI  VIRT   RES   SHR S CPU% MEM%   TIME+  Command
31590 philip     20   0 1108M  389M  110M R 86.7  2.5  0:59.98 /opt/brave.com/br
 2850 philip     20   0 3587M  269M  125M S 36.7  1.7 12:36.39 /usr/bin/gnome-sh
31715 philip     20   0 1108M  389M  110M S 25.3  2.5  0:01.20 /opt/brave.com/br
31595 philip     20   0 1108M  389M  110M S 25.3  2.5  0:04.48 /opt/brave.com/br
31592 philip     20   0 1108M  389M  110M S 24.7  2.5  0:03.93 /opt/brave.com/br
31719 philip     20   0 1997M  309M 90176 S 19.3  1.9  0:09.15 /home/philip/bin/
 2693 philip     20   0  721M  118M 91108 S 16.7  0.7 21:46.57 /usr/lib/xorg/Xor
30857 philip     20   0 1669M  236M  115M S  6.7  1.5  1:22.87 /snap/spotify/41/
30626 philip     20   0 3255M  373M  111M S  3.3  2.4  0:51.64 /snap/spotify/41/
 2860 philip      9 -11 1906M 14264 10584 S  2.7  0.1  0:43.71 /usr/bin/pulseaud
31721 philip     20   0 1997M  309M 90176 S  2.0  1.9  0:00.27 /home/philip/bin/
30837 philip     20   0  877M  107M 95592 S  2.0  0.7  0:15.10 /snap/spotify/41/
31705 philip     20   0 33812  5044  3880 R  1.3  0.0  0:01.31 htop
30878 philip     20   0 1669M  236M  115M S  1.3  1.5  0:18.94 /snap/spotify/41/
F1Help  F2Setup F3SearchF4FilterF5Tree  F6SortByF7Nice -F8Nice +F9Kill   F10Quit
```

Figure 8-3. *htop running with default settings*

atop

This is an advanced system & process monitor which is similar to top but is suited for long-running analysis. It provides the ability to output the results of system monitoring as a log file for analysis. As shown in Figure 8-4, it has a simple loop but provides the feature of exporting as logs not available in top or htop.

It is not preinstalled on most distros by default, but it is widely available in package management systems including Debian and RHEL.

```
 File  Edit  View  Search  Terminal  Help
ATOP  -  philip-ThinkPad-T420    2020/03/31   13:18:20   -------------       10s elapsed
PRC │  sys      1.98s │  user    10.70s │  #proc      320 │  #zombie      1 │  #exit       2 │
CPU │  sys      18% │  user    105% │  irq        0% │  idle      275% │  wait       1% │
cpu │  sys       5% │  user     26% │  irq        0% │  idle       68% │  cpu000 w  0% │
cpu │  sys       4% │  user     28% │  irq        0% │  idle       68% │  cpu001 w  0% │
cpu │  sys       5% │  user     26% │  irq        0% │  idle       69% │  cpu002 w  0% │
cpu │  sys       4% │  user     26% │  irq        0% │  idle       70% │  cpu003 w  0% │
CPL │  avg1    2.36 │  avg5    2.21 │  avg15    1.72 │  csw      71637 │  intr    28075 │
MEM │  tot    15.5G │  free    7.0G │  cache    3.5G │  buff    883.7M │  slab   647.0M │
SWP │  tot     2.0G │  free    2.0G │          │  vmcom   12.9G │  vmlim    9.8G │
DSK │          sda │  busy      2% │  read       0 │  write      168 │  avio 1.29 ms │
NET │  transport  │  tcpi     103 │  tcpo     107 │  udpi       6 │  udpo       6 │
NET │  network    │  ipi      109 │  ipo       74 │  ipfrw      0 │  deliv    109 │
NET │  wlp3s0    0% │  pcki     105 │  pcko     110 │  si   14 Kbps │  so   66 Kbps │
NET │  lo      ---- │  pcki       3 │  pcko       3 │  si    0 Kbps │  so    0 Kbps │

  PID  SYSCPU   USRCPU    VGROW    RGROW   ST EXC    THR  S  CPUNR    CPU  CMD         1/13
 2850   0.16s    2.91s    4576K    4140K   -- -      15  S      0    31%  gnome-shell
30458   0.09s    2.43s  23764K   -3988K   -- -      17  S      2    26%  brave
31719   0.24s    0.95s      0K     196K   -- -      13  S      0    12%  Telegram
31980   0.11s    1.00s  -3292K   -24.4M   -- -      13  S      3    11%  brave
 2693   0.40s    0.70s   -720K   -1128K   -- -       5  S      3    11%  Xorg
12647   0.22s    0.49s   -0.3G   -4520K   -- -      34  S      3     7%  brave
30857   0.03s    0.67s      0K      52K   -- -      11  S      1     7%  spotify
```

Figure 8-4.   atop running with default settings

By default the log files from atop will be saved to the folder /var/log/atop/. These log files can be read by passing them to atop with the -r flag as shown in the following, except substitute the atop_20200310 with the file name of the log you want to open:

```
atop -r /var/log/atop/atop_20200310
```

iftop

This is inspired by top but specializes in monitoring network usage rather than CPU or memory use. When given a network interface, it will listen to all incoming and outgoing traffic and provide information such as origin port and which external servers are using the network most. Due to accessing network interfaces, using iftop requires sudo permissions.

It is not installed by default on most distros but widely available. We'll look at this program further later in the chapter as part of a section on monitoring networking traffic.

ntop

A more advanced alternative to iftop is ntop which also monitors network traffic. However, unlike the other programs here, it is a GUI-based system which is accessed via the browser. While this makes it less lightweight, it does provide some more advanced visualizations like that shown in Figure 8-5.

Unlike the other programs mentioned so far, you won't find ntop with its standard name on package managers. Instead you'll find it under the name ntopng:

```
sudo apt-get install ntopng
```

Figure 8-5. *Applications page in ntop*

Once installed and started, it will run on port 3000 and provide several admin pages with statistics and visualizations based on network use.

iotop

This is another program inspired by top which focuses on filesystem read and write usage. Threads are listed in order of disk read and disk write usage. The package is widely available on both Debian- and RHEL-based systems. Like iftop using iotop will require sudo permissions to run. iotop contains the basic information of each process like user and command, as well as disk write and IO> (which is the measure of the % of time a process has spent on IO). See Figure 8-6 for an example of iotop in action.

```
File  Edit  View  Search  Terminal  Help
Total DISK READ :      0.00 B/s | Total DISK WRITE :    1222.20 K/s
Actual DISK READ:      0.00 B/s | Actual DISK WRITE:    1577.89 K/s
  TID  PRIO  USER     DISK READ   DISK WRITE   SWAPIN     IO>    COMMAND
32535 be/4 root       0.00 B/s    0.00 B/s    0.00 %   0.37 % [kworker/~3-iwlwifi]
32444 be/4 philip     0.00 B/s  821.11 K/s    0.00 %   0.16 % brave [Th~PoolForeg]
  300 be/3 root       0.00 B/s   52.97 K/s    0.00 %   0.13 % [jbd2/sda4-8]
  399 be/4 philip     0.00 B/s  348.12 K/s    0.00 %   0.00 % brave --t~PoolForeg]
    1 be/4 root       0.00 B/s    0.00 B/s    0.00 %   0.00 % init splash
    2 be/4 root       0.00 B/s    0.00 B/s    0.00 %   0.00 % [kthreadd]
    3 be/0 root       0.00 B/s    0.00 B/s    0.00 %   0.00 % [rcu_gp]
    4 be/0 root       0.00 B/s    0.00 B/s    0.00 %   0.00 % [rcu_par_gp]
    6 be/0 root       0.00 B/s    0.00 B/s    0.00 %   0.00 % [kworker/~H-kblockd]
    8 be/0 root       0.00 B/s    0.00 B/s    0.00 %   0.00 % [mm_percpu_wq]
    9 be/4 root       0.00 B/s    0.00 B/s    0.00 %   0.00 % [ksoftirqd/0]
   10 be/4 root       0.00 B/s    0.00 B/s    0.00 %   0.00 % [rcu_sched]
   11 rt/4 root       0.00 B/s    0.00 B/s    0.00 %   0.00 % [migration/0]
   12 rt/4 root       0.00 B/s    0.00 B/s    0.00 %   0.00 % [idle_inject/0]
   14 be/4 root       0.00 B/s    0.00 B/s    0.00 %   0.00 % [cpuhp/0]
   15 be/4 root       0.00 B/s    0.00 B/s    0.00 %   0.00 % [cpuhp/1]
   16 rt/4 root       0.00 B/s    0.00 B/s    0.00 %   0.00 % [idle_inject/1]
   17 rt/4 root       0.00 B/s    0.00 B/s    0.00 %   0.00 % [migration/1]
   18 be/4 root       0.00 B/s    0.00 B/s    0.00 %   0.00 % [ksoftirqd/1]
   20 be/0 root       0.00 B/s    0.00 B/s    0.00 %   0.00 % [kworker/~H-kblockd]
   21 be/4 root       0.00 B/s    0.00 B/s    0.00 %   0.00 % [cpuhp/2]
```

Figure 8-6. *io running with default settings*

slabtop

This is a top-style program for monitoring kernel slab cache information, shown in Figure 8-7. It's mainly good for those who need to worry about kernel-level issues.

Like iftop and iotop, using slabtop will require sudo permissions.

```
File  Edit  View  Search  Terminal  Help
Active / Total Objects (% used)      : 2183230 / 2275893 (95.9%)
Active / Total Slabs (% used)        : 68434 / 68434 (100.0%)
Active / Total Caches (% used)       : 113 / 155 (72.9%)
Active / Total Size (% used)         : 640422.24K / 674066.56K (95.0%)
Minimum / Average / Maximum Object : 0.01K / 0.30K / 16.81K

  OBJS ACTIVE  USE OBJ SIZE  SLABS OBJ/SLAB CACHE SIZE NAME
658164 653079   0%   0.10K  16876      39      67504K buffer_head
409290 401842   0%   0.19K  19490      21      77960K dentry
280050 276303   0%   1.05K   9335      30     298720K ext4_inode_cache
122196 122105   0%   0.04K   1198     102       4792K ext4_extent_status
111180 108797   0%   0.13K   3706      30      14824K kernfs_node_cache
 87087  80862   0%   0.20K   2233      39      17864K vm_area_struct
 66688  59482   0%   0.06K   1042      64       4168K anon_vma_chain
 52640  48079   0%   0.57K   1880      28      30080K radix_tree_node
 45312  41363   0%   0.03K    354     128       1416K kmalloc-32
 40384  32679   0%   0.25K   1262      32      10096K filp
 39882  35399   0%   0.09K    867      46       3468K anon_vma
 35532  33067   0%   0.58K   1316      27      21056K inode_cache
 30705  30587   0%   0.69K   1335      23      21360K squashfs_inode_cache
 30272  27581   0%   0.06K    473      64       1892K kmalloc-64
 20064  17668   0%   0.65K    836      24      13376K proc_inode_cache
 17850  17189   0%   0.02K    105     170        420K lsm_file_cache
```

Figure 8-7. slabtop running with default settings

More on Viewing Processes

The programs listed like top and atop can be great for viewing processes. It's also possible to manually query all running tasks using ps and then pipe them through to other programs. When running ps alone, you'll get a list of processes running in your current terminal session. The list will likely be small only including bash and the ps process itself, like in Figure 8-8.

```
philip@philip-ThinkPad-T420:/etc/systemd/system$ ps
   PID TTY              TIME CMD
  4477 pts/0       00:00:00 bash
 14183 pts/0       00:00:00 ps
philip@philip-ThinkPad-T420:/etc/systemd/system$ ▮
```

Figure 8-8. *Running ps in a fresh terminal*

However, if your terminal has been open for a while and you've backgrounded some processes, you may see more. We can create a background process manually to demonstrate with the following steps:

1. Run sleep for 500 seconds and background the process sleep 500 &.

2. Run ps and observe the new process.

3. Take the PID from the sleep command and end the process with kill kill 123.

4. Run ps again and observe the difference.

These steps should result in an additional process for sleep being returned by ps like shown in Figure 8-9.

```
philip@philip-ThinkPad-T420:~$ sleep 500 &
[1] 14823
philip@philip-ThinkPad-T420:~$ ps
   PID TTY              TIME CMD
 14634 pts/1      00:00:00 bash
 14823 pts/1      00:00:00 sleep
 14826 pts/1      00:00:00 ps
philip@philip-ThinkPad-T420:~$ kill 14823
philip@philip-ThinkPad-T420:~$ ps
   PID TTY              TIME CMD
 14634 pts/1      00:00:00 bash
 14832 pts/1      00:00:00 ps
[1]+  Terminated              sleep 500
philip@philip-ThinkPad-T420:~$ ▮
```

Figure 8-9. *ps with a background process*

Of course, most of the time, you're going to want to see all the processes running on your machine, not just the ones in your current terminal session. To get all running processes, you can run ps -e or ps -ef, the difference being the adding f shows more details. The detailed ps view is shown in Figure 8-10.

```
philip@philip-ThinkPad-T420:/etc/systemd/system$ ps -ef
UID          PID  PPID  C STIME TTY          TIME CMD
root           1     0  0 11:03 ?        00:00:16 /sbin/init splash
root           2     0  0 11:03 ?        00:00:00 [kthreadd]
root           3     2  0 11:03 ?        00:00:00 [rcu_gp]
root           4     2  0 11:03 ?        00:00:00 [rcu_par_gp]
root           6     2  0 11:03 ?        00:00:00 [kworker/0:0H-kb]
root           8     2  0 11:03 ?        00:00:00 [mm_percpu_wq]
root           9     2  0 11:03 ?        00:00:00 [ksoftirqd/0]
root          10     2  0 11:03 ?        00:00:24 [rcu_sched]
root          11     2  0 11:03 ?        00:00:00 [migration/0]
root          12     2  0 11:03 ?        00:00:00 [idle_inject/0]
root          14     2  0 11:03 ?        00:00:00 [cpuhp/0]
root          15     2  0 11:03 ?        00:00:00 [cpuhp/1]
root          16     2  0 11:03 ?        00:00:00 [idle_inject/1]
root          17     2  0 11:03 ?        00:00:00 [migration/1]
root          18     2  0 11:03 ?        00:00:00 [ksoftirqd/1]
root          20     2  0 11:03 ?        00:00:00 [kworker/1:0H-kb]
```

Figure 8-10. *Running ps -ef to see system-wide processes*

While we could use grep to parse processes by user, ps provides some built-in flags that make this easy, for example, ps -u philip or by specific PID with ps --pid 123. Either of these can be used with -e to get more details.

Kill a Process

Commands often used in conjunction with ps are kill and killall. When running ps, we saw that there is a column that displays PID, short for process ID. If a process isn't running right, hanging, or we just want to end it, one way is using the kill command. Simply pass it the PID, for example, given a PID of 123:

kill 123

If you want to match the process by name instead of PID, you can use killall, for example, if Firefox was frozen and we wanted to force quit:

killall firefox

Another option very similar to killall is pkill. pkill can also match a service by name but will include more matches, as unlike killall it does not require an exact match if you make use of the -i for pattern matching. For example, if we instead just pass in "Firef", we will still kill the process:

```
pkill -i Firef
```

The same style of command can be used with pgrep to find processes without killing them. For example, if we run the following command with Firefox open, we'll get a list of PIDs associated with the program:

```
pgrep -i Firef
```

To make the preceding command a little bit more useful, add the -l flag to get the exact program name for each process or -a even more information.

Visualize Process Tree with pstree

Another concept to keep in mind is the fact that processes exist in a hierarchy, with some processes having parent and child processes; this is visualized in Figure 8-11. When you run ps in your terminal, for example, it is a child process of the terminal process. If we run sleep 500 and then close the terminal, the child process sleep 500 will automatically terminate with the termination of the parent process. However, this isn't always the case; in some cases, a child will continue running after the parent closes and inherit the parent's parents.

Our terminal process itself is the child of another process, likely systemd depending on your Linux distribution. Thus, if a process continued running after closing the terminal, in our case, the new parent would be systemd.

A great tool for visualizing this relationship is pstree which can be used to show all processes running on our system, like ps but in a visualization showing the parent/child relationships between processes. Try running it with the -p flag which will make sure process ID is also returned. It should return a very long list of processes all stemming from a single process with PID of 1 on the left.

```
philip@philip-ThinkPad-T420:~$ pstree -p
systend(1)─┬─ModemManager(1166)─┬─{ModemManager}(1263)
           │                    └─{ModemManager}(1267)
           ├─NetworkManager(1151)─┬─dhclient(10638)
           │                      ├─{NetworkManager}(1290)
           │                      └─{NetworkManager}(1294)
           ├─accounts-daemon(1165)─┬─{accounts-daemon}(1178)
           │                       └─{accounts-daemon}(1186)
           ├─acpid(1138)
           ├─apache2(1359)─┬─apache2(4123)
           │               ├─apache2(4124)
           │               ├─apache2(4125)
           │               ├─apache2(4126)
           │               └─apache2(4127)
           ├─atop(10547)
           ├─atopacctd(1181)
           ├─avahi-daemon(1157)───avahi-daemon(1183)
           ├─bluetoothd(1170)
           ├─boltd(1709)─┬─{boltd}(1721)
           │             └─{boltd}(1723)
           ├─brave-browser-d(3005)───brave(3013)───brave(3017)───brave(3021)─┬─brave(3117)─┬─{brave}(3122)
           │                                                                 │             ├─{brave}(3123)
           │                                                                 │             └─{brave}(3124)
           │                                                                 └─brave(3129)─┬─{brave}(3131)
           │                                                                               ├─{brave}(3133)
           │                                                                               ├─{brave}(3134)
           │                                                                               ├─{brave}(3135)
           │                                                                               ├─{brave}(3143)
```

Figure 8-11. *Running pstree with -p flag to show process IDs*

As mentioned when we run a command in our terminal, it is actually a child process of the terminal process. To demonstrate this, run the following commands:

```
sleep 500 &
pstree -p | grep -A 5 -B 5 pstree
```

This creates a sleep process in the background, gets pstree, and then greps for the pstree process so we can find our current terminal process. The -A flag stands for get five lines above the match and -B is get five lines below. The result should be similar to that shown in Figure 8-12.

```
philip@philip-ThinkPad-T420:~$ pstree -p | grep -A 5 -B 5 pstree
grep: warning: GREP_OPTIONS is deprecated; please use an alias or script
    |               |                        |-{gnome-shell-cal}(2679)
    |               |                        |-{gnome-shell-cal}(2685)
    |               |                        |-{gnome-shell-cal}(2686)
    |               |                        `-{gnome-shell-cal}(2868)
    |               |-gnome-terminal-(14625)-+-bash(14634)-+-grep(15911)
    |               |                        |             |-pstree(15910)
    |               |                        |             `-sleep(15909)
    |               |                        |-{gnome-terminal-}(14626)
    |               |                        |-{gnome-terminal-}(14627)
    |               |                        `-{gnome-terminal-}(14628)
    |               |-goa-daemon(2676)-+-{goa-daemon}(2687)
philip@philip-ThinkPad-T420:~$ █
```

Figure 8-12. *Grepping pstree to see a specific process*

Notice the pstree process highlighted in green and the sleep process below it. They both stem from the bash process, which itself is stemming from gnome-terminal.

Process Nice Value

When using top, you may have noticed the column marked "NI." This refers to the "nice" values which is a key concept in Linux. Every process has a nice value of -20 to 19. The lower the number, the more priority the process gets in scheduling. One way to think about it is that nice processes (e.g., *10 nice value*) wait in queue, while not nice processes butt ahead (*-20 nice value*), and really nice processes (*19 nice value*) let others butt ahead in line. Of course this is a simplification as the nice value is relative to that of others in queue.

As mentioned you can view the nice value for processes in top under the column NI. Another method is by using ps with the -o flag followed by the columns you want to see (*include ni*), for example:

```
ps ax -o pid,ni,cmd
```

This will return the process ID, nice value, and command for all running processes as shown in Figure 8-13.

```
philip@philip-ThinkPad-T420:~$ ps ax -o pid,ni,cmd
 PID  NI CMD
   1   0 /sbin/init splash
   2   0 [kthreadd]
   3 -20 [rcu_gp]
   4 -20 [rcu_par_gp]
   6 -20 [kworker/0:0H-kb]
   8 -20 [mm_percpu_wq]
   9   0 [ksoftirqd/0]
  10   0 [rcu_sched]
  11   - [migration/0]
  12   - [idle_inject/0]
```

Figure 8-13. *Getting command, PID, and nice value with ps*

Notice that several of the commands started during the startup process (*we can tell because PID is close to 1*) have a nice value of -20 as they're considered to be vital for running the OS.

You also might notice some processes marked with - (depending on your OS); these are system-level processes which are governed by a different set of priorities (they always run first). For the most part, you won't need to worry about these lower-level processes.

Other Priority Systems

As mentioned earlier, some processes are governed by different sets of priorities. The normal processes that we're mainly concerned with in user space are governed by SCHED_OTHER.

The other main schedulers SCHED_FIFO and SCHED_RR are for real-time processes which need to run before all normal processes. These two schedulers have the same priority but different in how they schedule. FIFO stands for first in first out (e.g., *first come first serve*), while RR stands for round robin (*taking turns, until process completed*).

You likely won't need to deal with these schedulers if you're not working at the kernel level. If you're curious to see the real-time and absolute priority values for processes, you can run

```
ps -e -o class,rtprio,pri,nice,cmd
```

From the output, you'll find several processes that have a higher absolute priority than those listed as -20 nice value; these are real-time processes.

Change Nice Value

Now that you know about nice, how do you use it? You can change the nice value of any running process with the renice command. Generally, changing nice values isn't a common task. However, there are few reasons you might want to do it. Say, for example, you've created a custom script that cleans up old log files by compressing them and sending them to a long-term storage service. You may want to give this process a high nice value so that users making use of the server are always given a higher priority than the backup process, which has no deadline or urgency.

Let's create a process to work with:

```
sleep 500&
```

Take the process ID that is returned (*1234 in our example*) and use it with renice:

```
renice -n 19 1234
```

Now if we check the nice value using ps, we should see the value has updated.

```
ps -o ni 1234
```

Zombie Process

In the following section, we'll be compiling a C program to explore the idea of zombie processes. It's somewhat technical and knowledge of zombie processes is not critical. If you find this section too technical, feel free to skip ahead.

This section will require you to have a C compiler installed and the libraries used here. They're all available in the build-essential package on Debian-based systems.

```
sudo apt-get install build-essential
```

Another concept worth understanding when looking at processes is zombies. A zombie process is a child process which has exited, but has not been cleared by its parent process. Most programs will remove their child processes quickly after they exit, so zombie processes are rather rare. Despite the nefarious name, zombie processes are fairly harmless and won't have a negative impact on your machine's performance.

To demonstrate, we'll create a C program to make our own zombie process.

```c
#include <stdlib.h>
#include <sys/types.h>
#include <unistd.h>

int main () {

  // Create variable with type of process identification
  pid_t child_pid;

  // Fork main process creating a child
  child_pid = fork ();

  // Both main script and forked child run the code below the fork point

  // Child process will have a PID of 0 within script
  if (child_pid > 0) {
    // Only parent process runs this section
    sleep (500);
  }
  else {
    // Only forked child runs this section, exiting immediately
    exit (0);
  }
}
```

```
  return 0;
}
```

After writing the preceding C program, save it as `zombie.c`. Next you'll need to compile it by running

```
cc zombie.c -o zombie
```

Once you successfully compile `zombie`, we can demonstrate what a zombie process looks at. Run the executable and background it:

```
./zombie &
```

Next we'll use some of the previous commands to view the process. First run `ps` with no options. You should see an entry for both the parent process `zombie` and the child which will be followed by `<defunct>`, as shown in Figure 8-14; this indicates the process is in a zombie state.

```
philip@philip-ThinkPad-T420:/tmp$ ./zombie &
[1] 7449
philip@philip-ThinkPad-T420:/tmp$ ps
  PID TTY          TIME CMD
 7259 pts/0     00:00:00 bash
 7449 pts/0     00:00:00 zombie
 7450 pts/0     00:00:00 zombie <defunct>
 7451 pts/0     00:00:00 ps
philip@philip-ThinkPad-T420:/tmp$ █
```

Figure 8-14. *Creating a zombie process*

If you were to run `top`, you'd also see an indication that a zombie process is running in the top right, shown in Figure 8-15.

```
2:Job - 17:34:13 up  3:24,  1 user,  load average: 1.08, 1.06, 1.00
Tasks: 313 total,   2 running, 251 sleeping,   0 stopped,   1 zombie
%Cpu0  :  10.3/3.1    13[|||||||||||||||
%Cpu1  :  12.2/3.0    15[|||||||||||||||||
%Cpu2  :  12.7/3.0    16[||||||||||||||||||
%Cpu3  :  15.4/1.7    17[||||||||||||||||||||
KiB Mem : 25.8/16302604 [|||||||||||||||||||||||||||||||||
KiB Swap:  0.0/2097148  [
```

Figure 8-15. *View zombie count in top*

As mentioned, zombie processes are fairly harmless and are already technically not running. Thus, running kill 7450 (based on the process ID in Figure 8-14) will be ineffective. The only way a zombie process can be killed is by killing its parent.

```
kill 7449
```

Of course this is a problem if you want the program in question to keep running. Our recommendation is to let the zombie processes deal with themselves as they generally don't cause problems.

Check Available Disk Space

Another common issue with servers or embedded devices is running out of disk space. I've encountered a few situations where a device that stopped working had simply run out of space to write to, as a result of a program which failed to compress or delete old log files over a period of many months.

The easiest way to check available disk space is with the utility df, short for "free space." To find your available disk space, run the command

```
df -h
```

The preceding command will return a list of partitions with information about each. One of these partitions will be the main one used by your system. You can find it by looking at the "Mounted on" column and finding the one with a value of "/".

The next thing you'll want to look at for that partition is the "Size" and "Use%". This will tell you how much disk space you have in total and what percentage is currently used.

For a complete list of the columns returned by df, see Table 8-1. This table also includes the inodes used column which can be enabled with the -i flag and the type column enabled with -T flag.

Notice we used the -h flag in the preceding example; this stands for "human readable." Without the -h flag, df will still work but shows the space available in KB rather than converting large amounts to MB or GB. Making use of -h is recommended unless you have a specific reason for wanting all values in KB.

Table 8-1. *Information returned by the df command*

Column	Description
Filesystem	The name of the filesystem
Size	Size of the partition (hidden by default, show with -h)
1K-blocks	Size of the system in 1K-blocks (replaced by size when using -h)
Used	Amount of space used
Available	Amount of space available
Use%	Amount of space used shown as a percentage
Mounted On	The directory location of the partition
IUsed	inodes used on partition (hidden by default, show with -i)
Type	Partition filesystem type (hidden by default, show with -T)

Find Largest Files on System

If you find that you are low on system space, you might want to search for large files on your system. Here is an example for getting anything over 100M:

```
sudo find / -xdev -type f -size +100M -exec ls -la {} \; \
  | sort -nk 5 \
  | tac
```

The preceding command is assuming you want to look at every file on the system. If you instead want to only include files within a specific folder, you can modify the find command's first argument, for example, say I wanted to only search for files in the folder for user philip, I would then use

```
sudo find /home/username -xdev -type f \
  -size +100M -exec ls -la {} \; \
    | sort -nk 5 \
    | tac
```

If you only want to find files and directories with contents totaling over a GB, you can instead do

```
sudo du -ahx / | grep -E '\d*\.?\d*+G\s+'
```

Note   It's also possible to get and print size with `find` by combining the `-size` and `-printf` flags; however, find only displays sizes in KB, which is hard to read compared to GB. See `man find` for more details.

Monitor Device Network Use

Another statistic you might want to check is the network usage of a system as a whole as well as a breakdown by process or networking interface. This can be useful on a device with limited Internet access or expensive bandwidth, for example, an IoT device or even laptop connected via a GSM SIM card. In such a situation, programs which use excessive data can be very expensive.

Even if you're not on a system with limited data, it can be useful to see what programs are using your Internet connection. If you see something that surprises you, you may want to investigate further. There are a few good programs I use for network monitoring, each slightly different.

bmon – Monitor Each Network Interface

With bmon, you can monitor each interface (e.g., Wi-Fi, Ethernet). This is great in the GSM SIM card situation described earlier. Imagine you have a device which has both Wi-Fi and 5G. You likely don't mind high network usage over the Wi-Fi interface but will want to ensure 5G use stays below a certain level.

Given this situation, you might write your software to detect what Internet interface is being used and reduce or increase data use based on the connection type. bmon gives you a way to ensure that such measures are actually working by breaking down how much data was transmitted over each interface.

bmon won't be installed by default, but it is available on most package managers. When opening it by running bmon in the terminal, you'll see an interface like that shown in Figure 8-16. If your terminal window isn't maximized, the bottom section with green/red graphs may be hidden.

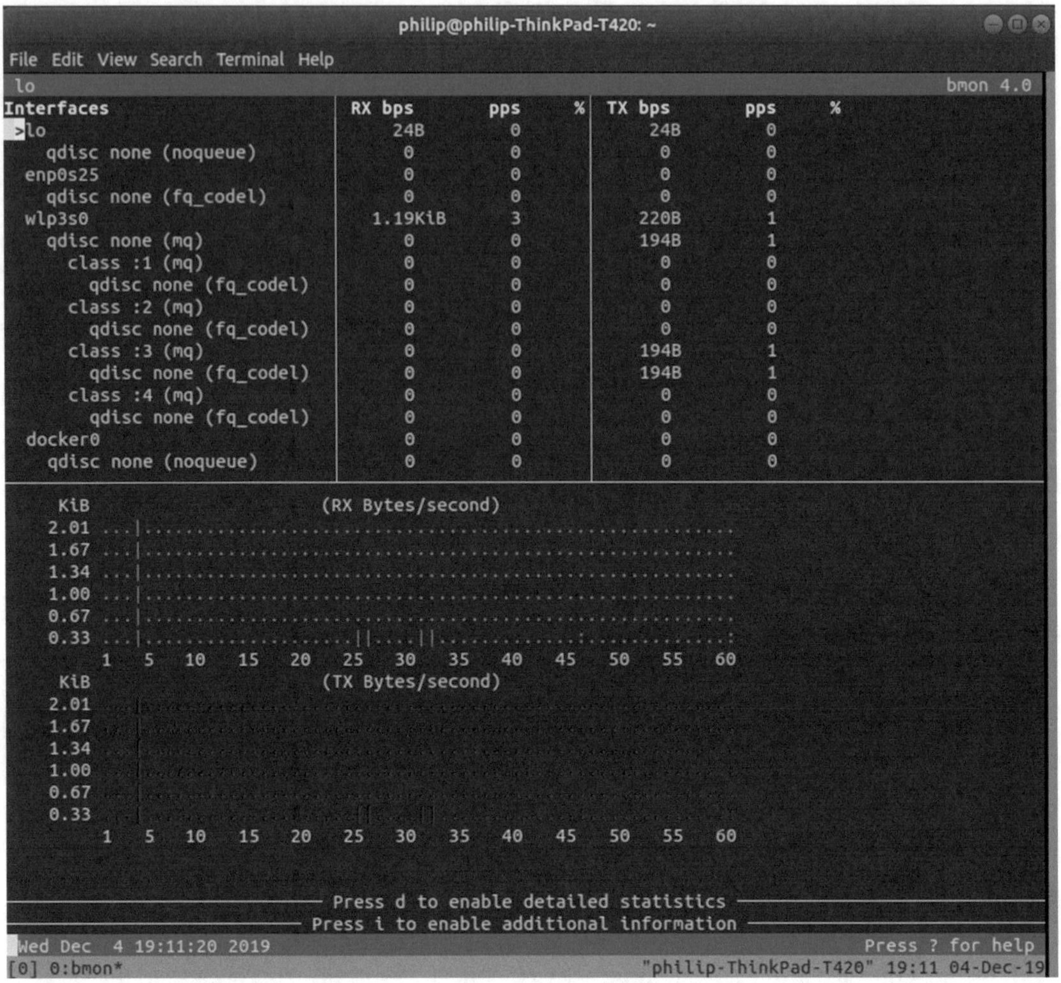

Figure 8-16. Running bmon

nethogs – List Programs by Bandwidth Use

Most of the time, you won't be interested in what interfaces are being used, but instead will want to know what programs are using the most bandwidth. For this install and run nethogs; you'll see an interface like shown in Figure 8-17. Keep in mind if you close the program, it'll start from scratch again when you open it later. To get a clear picture of use over time, you'll want to open nethogs and let it run over time. After coming back a few hours or even days later, you'll have a better idea of which programs use the most bandwidth.

```
NetHogs version 0.8.5-2

     PID USER        PROGRAM                    DEV      SENT       RECEIVED
    3077 philip      ..ome/philip/Documents/Telegr  wlp3s0   0.134     0.326 KB/sec
    2879 philip      ..pt/brave.com/brave-dev/brav   wlp3s0   0.026     0.026 KB/sec
    7750 philip      nmap                       wlp3s0   0.000     0.000 KB/sec
       ? root        unknown TCP                         0.000     0.000 KB/sec

  TOTAL                                                  0.160     0.351 KB/sec
```

Figure 8-17. *Running nethogs*

iftop

Another option is iftop, yet another program in the top family. Instead of monitoring by interface or application, iftop lets us monitor which external IP addresses are being communicated with the most based on traffic size.

When starting iftop, you need to specify the network interface. If you don't know your network interfaces, you can get it by running

ip a

You'll get back a list of interfaces with lots of details; the interface is the key value on the left. In my case, the Wi-Fi interface is called wlp3s0, as shown in Figure 8-18. You can normally tell which interface is Wi-Fi because it will include a "w".

```
3: wlp3s0: <BROADCAST,MULTICAST,UP,LOWER_UP> mtu 1500 qdisc mq state UP group default qlen 1000
    link/ether 10:0b:a9:96:87:74 brd ff:ff:ff:ff:ff:ff
    inet 10.177.13.190/8 brd 10.255.255.255 scope global dynamic noprefixroute wlp3s0
       valid_lft 85994sec preferred_lft 85994sec
    inet6 fe80::1f80:ad8f:8d2d:7577/64 scope link noprefixroute
       valid_lft forever preferred_lft forever
```

Figure 8-18. *Wi-Fi interface returned from* ip a

Once you have the interface you want to monitor, pass it to iftop with the -i flag:

sudo iftop -i wlp3s0

This will result in a list of external IP addresses and amount of data which is being uploaded and downloaded, as shown in Figure 8-19.

```
            195Kb              391Kb            586Kb             781Kb           977Kb
L_____I_____I_____I_____I_____I
philip-ThinkPad-T420          => 149.154.175.53                  5.88Kb  1.66Kb   991b
■                             <=                                 51.9Kb  12.0Kb  4.74Kb
philip-ThinkPad-T420          => 149.154.175.50                  3.33Kb   765b    451b
                              <=                                 1.41Kb   330b   1.66Kb
philip-ThinkPad-T420          => _gateway                         604b    367b    217b
                              <=                                 1.05Kb   462b    376b
224.0.0.251                   => 172.20.5.152                      0b      0b      0b
                              <=                                   560b    317b    262b
224.0.0.251                   => 172.20.6.47                       0b      0b      0b
                              <=                                   952b    190b     48b
224.0.0.251                   => 172.20.12.174                     0b      0b      0b
                              <=                                   0b      84b     42b
philip-ThinkPad-T420          => 151.101.1.69                     0b      42b     10b
                              <=                                   0b      42b     10b
philip-ThinkPad-T420          => gru06s26-in-f4.1e100.net         0b      42b     10b
                              <=                                   0b      42b     10b
philip-ThinkPad-T420          => yul02s04-in-f14.1e100.net       208b     42b     10b
                              <=                                 208b     42b     10b
────────────────────────────────────────────────────────────────────────────────────
TX:          cum:   72.7KB  peak:    14.2Kb          rates:   10.0Kb  2.95Kb  3.15Kb
RX:                 52.6KB           56.3Kb                   56.3Kb  13.7Kb  8.44Kb
TOTAL:              125KB            66.3Kb                   66.3Kb  16.6Kb  11.6Kb■
```

Figure 8-19. *Monitoring Wi-Fi with iftop*

To make things a bit cleaner, you can press s to hide the source on the left-hand side (*given they will mostly be local sources*). Then press p to show the origin port. Port is much more useful than source as it gives us a better idea of the origin program and a way to dig deeper if we want to investigate a connection further. The iftop interface with source replaced with port is shown in Figure 8-20.

```
            195Kb              391Kb            586Kb             781Kb           977Kb
L_____I_____I_____I_____I_____I
* :52582                      => gru06s28-in-f14.1e100.net:https  34.4Kb  6.89Kb  13.5Kb
                              <=                                 4.23Kb   867b   12.4Kb
* :56214                      => 40.115.22.134:https              0b     1.24Kb   317b
                              <=                                   0b     5.44Kb  1.36Kb
* :47412                      => gru10s10-in-f14.1e100.net:https  27.0Kb  5.40Kb  2.67Kb
                              <=                                 5.72Kb  1.14Kb   571b
* :34976                      => 149.154.175.53:https            1.02Kb   543b    670b
                              <=                                 2.55Kb  1.56Kb  7.16Kb
* :37138                      => _gateway:domain                   0b      66b     16b
                              <=                                   0b      388b     97b
* :51014                      => 151.101.200.133:https             0b     106b     26b
                              <=                                   0b     108b     27b
* :51016                      => 151.101.200.133:https             0b     106b     26b
                              <=                                   0b     108b     27b
* :51018                      => 151.101.200.133:https             0b     106b     26b
                              <=                                   0b     108b     27b
* :51020                      => 151.101.200.133:https             0b     106b     26b
                              <=                                   0b     108b     27b
────────────────────────────────────────────────────────────────────────────────────
TX:          cum:   1.30MB  peak:    90.7Kb          rates:   62.7Kb  14.7Kb  18.4Kb
RX:                 2.23MB           268Kb                    12.7Kb  10.3Kb  38.1Kb
TOTAL:              3.53MB           289Kb                    75.4Kb  25.0Kb  56.4Kb■
```

Figure 8-20. *Viewing traffic by outgoing port in iftop*

Other Programs for Monitoring

sysstat

Another program that can be used to monitor system use over a long period of time, similar to atop but more comprehensive, is sysstat. Rather than checking the current status of the system, sysstat is best used by letting it run in the background and then reading the daily reports. It works by running a cron job every 10 minutes and recording system data.

It's likely available by default, but if not, you can install with

```
sudo apt-get install sysstat
```

First open up /etc/default/sysstat and ensure the following line is set to true; by default on Ubuntu, it will be set to false:

```
ENABLED="true"
```

Then enable it with systemctl:

```
sudo systemctl enable --now sysstat
```

After these simple steps, your system will start to save system data in the /var/log/sysstat folder. A new file will be created for each day of the month, for example, if you start on the 26th, the file would be /var/log/sysstat/sa26. You can view the data for the current day by running

```
sar
```

Once it's been running for a while, sar will return something like shown in Figure 8-21.

```
philip@philip-ThinkPad-T420:~$ sar
Linux 5.0.0-37-generic (philip-ThinkPad-T420)    12/28/2019      _x86_64_        (4 CPU)

01:03:58 AM       CPU     %user     %nice   %system   %iowait    %steal     %idle
01:04:58 AM       all     11.94      0.00      3.75      0.08      0.00     84.22
01:05:01 AM       all     11.95      0.00      3.03      0.08      0.00     84.93
01:15:01 AM       all      8.88      0.00      2.50      0.23      0.00     88.39
01:25:01 AM       all      4.07      0.00      1.01      0.03      0.00     94.89
Average:          all      6.74      0.00      1.85      0.13      0.00     91.28

01:28:50 AM   LINUX RESTART      (4 CPU)

01:35:01 AM       CPU     %user     %nice   %system   %iowait    %steal     %idle
01:45:01 AM       all      2.36      0.10      0.62      0.08      0.00     96.84
01:55:01 AM       all      0.25      0.00      0.19      0.01      0.00     99.55
Average:          all      1.31      0.05      0.40      0.05      0.00     98.19
```

Figure 8-21. *Running sar*

As mentioned, these stats are saved in the /var/log/sysstat folder. If you want to view a previously monitored day, specify the file to open with sar:

```
sar -f /var/log/sysstat/sa27
```

Note that once you've been using sysstat for over a month, the files will start to be overwritten. If you want to keep the logs for longer, you'll have to back them up manually.

Load Average

Load average refers to the average number of threads running or waiting to run. There are a number of ways you can get this information, the easiest being to run

```
uptime
```

This should return the amount of time the system has been running, users logged in, and three different values for load average. The three different values are the average over 1 minute, 5 minutes, and 15 minutes. Using these three values, you can get an idea of whether load is increasing or decreasing.

If you're already using top regularly now, you can find the same three load average values on the top line.

It's important to keep in mind that load average is measured by threads in the queue regardless of how many CPUs a computer has. A load average of two on a single CPU machine is a higher rate of saturation than a load average of three on a machine with two CPUs. Imagine each thread is a person at a grocery store waiting to pay for their goods and each CPU is a cashier. Knowing how many people are waiting in line is not necessarily useful without knowing the number of cashiers in the store.

A more useful statistic to consider is load average divided by CPUs. If the load average divided by the number of CPUs is greater than 1, this could indicate that your system is overloaded. Consider the concept of niceness explored earlier. If a process with a nice value of 19 is running but the load average is always higher than the available CPUs, it may never end up executing, as it keeps allowing the new processes which enter the line to run first.

According to one rumor when the IBM 7094 at MIT was shut down in 1973, they found a low-priority process that had been submitted in 1967 and had not yet been run. This was exactly the situation described where a queue had always existed, and because the process had low priority, it kept waiting in line, always allowing newer high-priority tasks to run first. This problem is often referred to as resource starvation.

Note   If you forget how many CPUs are on a machine, you can always use `lscpu` and look for the row titled "CPU(s)."

Users

In the last section, we saw that the third value returned by uptime is actually users logged in. If you end up seeing a number you didn't expect, you can get more information on the users currently logged in using either who or w. If your system has it, w is preferred as it is a rewrite of who which includes more user details. Simply run

w

You'll get back a list of users and the TTY they're using. If a user is using multiple TTYs, they'll be listed multiple times. An example of a user using a single TTY is shown in Figure 8-22.

```
philip@philip-ThinkPad-T420:~$ w
 14:55:23 up 26 min,  1 user,  load average: 0.79, 0.81, 0.74
USER     TTY      FROM             LOGIN@   IDLE   JCPU   PCPU WHAT
philip   :0       :0               14:28    ?xdm?  1:32   0.00s /usr/lib/gdm3/g
philip@philip-ThinkPad-T420:~$ ▌
```

Figure 8-22.   *Viewing logged in users with w*

An example of a user using a multiple TTY (*via tmux, a program for keeping terminal sessions open but backgrounded*) is shown in Figure 8-23.

```
ubuntu@ip-172-31-58-133:~$ w
 19:56:16 up 141 days, 18:35, 11 users,  load average: 3.92, 4.27, 4.30
USER     TTY      FROM             LOGIN@   IDLE   JCPU   PCPU WHAT
ubuntu   pts/0    200.57.229.98    19:41    0.00s  0.41s  0.03s w
ubuntu   pts/1    tmux(6894).%16   25Oct19 22:15m  3:06   3:06 python3 -m merc
ubuntu   pts/2    tmux(6894).%23   27Oct19 16days  5:23   5:20 node bot.js
ubuntu   pts/4    tmux(6894).%13   28Sep19 40days  9.81s  7.75s node ./bin/www
ubuntu   pts/5    tmux(6894).%47   27Nov19 28days  2:11   2:09 node index.js
ubuntu   pts/6    tmux(6894).%27   03Nov19 12days  3:53   3:51 node bot.js
ubuntu   pts/7    tmux(6894).%28   04Nov19 16days  5:39   5:36 node bot.js
ubuntu   pts/8    tmux(6894).%32   07Nov19 23days  7:42   7:41 node bot.js
ubuntu   pts/9    tmux(6894).%34   11Nov19 29days  1:42   1:40 node /home/ubun
ubuntu   pts/10   tmux(6894).%53   01Dec19 16days  5:15   5:13 node bot.js
ubuntu   pts/12   tmux(6894).%52   27Nov19 16days  8:04   0.00s sh -c node bot.
ubuntu@ip-172-31-58-133:~$
```

Figure 8-23. *Running w with several tmux sessions open*

Log Folder

When monitoring or debugging a system, you'll want to be aware of system log folders. One of the best places to look is /var/log, the system folder for miscellaneous logs. Navigate into the folder and view the files:

```
cd /var/log
ls
```

You should see several different files and folders here depending on what services are running and how long your system has been up. The contents of my log folder are shown in Figure 8-24.

```
philip@philip-ThinkPad-T420:/var/log$ ls
alternatives.log         atop              dpkg.log.8.gz     nordvpn
alternatives.log.1       auth.log          dpkg.log.9.gz     openvpn
alternatives.log.10.gz   auth.log.1        faillog           postgresql
alternatives.log.2.gz    auth.log.2.gz     fontconfig.log    speech-dispatcher
alternatives.log.3.gz    auth.log.3.gz     gdm3              syslog
alternatives.log.4.gz    auth.log.4.gz     gpu-manager.log   syslog.1
alternatives.log.5.gz    boot.log          hp                syslog.2.gz
alternatives.log.6.gz    bootstrap.log     installer         syslog.3.gz
alternatives.log.7.gz    btmp              journal           syslog.4.gz
alternatives.log.8.gz    btmp.1            kern.log          syslog.5.gz
alternatives.log.9.gz    .cups             kern.log.1        syslog.6.gz
apache2                  dist-upgrade      kern.log.2.gz     syslog.7.gz
apport.log               dpkg.log          kern.log.3.gz     sysstat
apport.log.1             dpkg.log.1        kern.log.4.gz     tallylog
apport.log.2.gz          dpkg.log.10.gz    lastlog           tor
apport.log.3.gz          dpkg.log.2.gz     mail.err          unattended-upgrades
apport.log.4.gz          dpkg.log.3.gz     mail.err.1        wtmp
apport.log.5.gz          dpkg.log.4.gz     mail.log          wtmp.1
apport.log.6.gz          dpkg.log.5.gz     mail.log.1
apport.log.7.gz          dpkg.log.6.gz     mongodb
apt                      dpkg.log.7.gz     mysql
philip@philip-ThinkPad-T420:/var/log$ █
```

Figure 8-24. *Example of contents in /var/log*

If you're on a Debian system like Ubuntu, the main log file will be /var/log/syslog. If you're on a non-Debian system like CentOS, you should instead look for /var/log/messages. We'll open it up with

```
less /var/log/syslog
```

You'll see all kinds of messages from different programs.

The program responsible for writing these logs on most systems is rsyslogd. It can be customized by editing the /etc/rsyslog.conf file.

Note   Aside from syslog, another good method for checking logs is systemd's journalctl; see the Journalctl section in Chapter 11.

Other sysstat Utilities

When you install and enable sysstat, you actually get a whole box of utilities and binaries which process and display system data in various ways. These utilities are listed in Table 8-2.

Table 8-2. *sysstat utilities list*

Command	Description
sar	Collects data and displays all system activities
sadc	"System activity data collector" runs in the background
sa1	Runs from cron and processes data collected
sa2	Creates daily summary, runs from cron
sadf	Exports sar reports to CSV, JSON, XML, etc.
iostat	For viewing I/O use
mpstat	For viewing process-related stats
pidstat	Views data by process ID
cifsiostat	Views CIFS (*Common Internet File System*) stats; this is a Microsoft filesystem which can be enabled in Linux by Samba

vmstat

vmstat is an older system monitoring tool which returns system information related to system memory, processes, interrupts, paging, and block I/O. It isn't installed on most systems but can be found as vmstat on most package managers.

It takes two input values; the first is the sampling period in seconds, and the second is how many samples to take. So if we run with inputs of 1 and 10 like the following:

```
vmstat 1 10
```

we get back ten rows. The first line is always the summary since boot. Then we get nine rows each printed 1 second after the   last, showing the average of a 1-second sample. An example of running vmstat for ten periods of 1 second is shown in Figure 8-25.

```
philip@philip-ThinkPad-T420:~$ vmstat 1 10
procs -----------memory---------- ---swap-- -----io---- -system-- ------cpu-----
 r  b   swpd   free    buff   cache   si   so    bi    bo   in   cs us sy id wa st
 0  0      0 11270964 160072 2132964    0    0  1406   228  645 1675 26  6 67  1  0
 0  0      0 11270384 160072 2133788    0    0     0     0  726 1298  2  1 98  0  0
 0  0      0 11265344 160072 2139180    0    0     0     0  741 1345  4  2 94  0  0
 2  0      0 11270888 160080 2133108    0    0     0   884  863 1459  5  2 92  0  0
 0  0      0 11284412 160080 2129292    0    0     0     0  804 1529  5  2 92  0  0
 0  0      0 11278428 160080 2128300    0    0     0     0 1141 2023  8  2 90  0  0
 0  0      0 11277952 160080 2128512    0    0     0   512  787 1341  4  2 93  0  0
 0  0      0 11271400 160080 2134668    0    0     0     0  701 1298  3  2 94  0  0
 0  0      0 11269888 160088 2136452    0    0     0   100  833 1477  2  1 97  0  0
 1  0      0 11283244 160088 2128768    0    0     0     0  727 1268  1  1 99  0  0
philip@philip-ThinkPad-T420:~$ ▮
```

Figure 8-25. *Getting 9-second long samples with vmstat*

Due to the compressed space used to show the table, it can be difficult to interpret the column values. Table 8-3 lists the short forms and what they mean.

Table 8-3. *List of vmstat columns*

Sequence	Description
r	Threads waiting in queue for CPU
b	Threads blocked on I/O
swpd	Total swap used in KB
free	Total free memory
buff	Memory used as buffers
cache	Memory used as cache
si	Memory swapped in from disk
so	Memory swapped to disk
bi	Blocks received from block device
bo	Blocks sent to block device
in	Interrupts per second
cs	Context switches per second
us	Time spent running non-kernel code

(continued)

Table 8-3. (*continued*)

Sequence	Description
sy	Time spent running kernel code
id	Time spent idle
wa	Time spent waiting for I/O
st	Time stolen from virtual machine

r – Threads Waiting for Runtime

As we mentioned when talking about load average, threads in a queue are processes waiting to be run on a CPU. Thus, this column is essentially the same as load average. However, the first line returned will be the average since starting your machine (if vmstat was already installed). This gives you an average for the full runtime which isn't available with top or uptime.

For the values below the top line, you'll be getting the value for the instant when the sample is taken rather than an average.

b – Threads Blocked by I/O

Threads blocked by I/O are threads which have been put into a waiting state by the kernel while it waits for a process reading or writing to storage. If you have a high number of threads blocked by I/O, it may indicate that there are issues related to your storage device or simply that a process which makes heavy use of I/O is running.

swpd – Total Swap Used

Swap refers to disk space that has been allocated to act as RAM when actual RAM memory is full. Swap memory is significantly slower than normal RAM and can cause programs relying on said memory to run slowly. If you're often using swap memory, your system may be in need of RAM, or alternatively a program may be needlessly using more RAM than is necessary.

free – Total Free Memory

This shows the total amount of unused memory on your system in KB. This is similar to the free column which is shown when running the `free` command. This gives you an idea of how close you are to using all your RAM.

buff – Memory Used in Buffers

This is similar to cache but specific to file metadata; see the following section for more details.

cache – Memory Used as Cache

Sometimes memory will be used to cache data which is being accessed regularly by programs. This speeds up programs but can make it appear that you have less RAM available than is actually the case; this often happens if your system has been running for a long time.

If you have a low value for `free` but a high value for `cache`, you still won't need to worry about swap being used as memory from buffers can be reallocated. If however `cache` + `buff` + `free` added together are close to 0, it's a sign that your machine is strained for resources.

si – Memory Swapped In from Disk

As mentioned previously, data or metadata (*as is the case with buffers*) are often stored in memory to increase the speed at which programs operate. We talked about how if more memory ends up being needed for something else this memory can be freed up. In other cases, the data cached in memory might be swapped out for other data.

With swapping this data actually contains aspects of the executing program itself, for example, data structures produced by a program which only exist while the program is running. This swapping is what the `si` column measures. `si` is the memory swapped from disk per second.

The use of swap indicates that a system doesn't have enough memory available for caching and has resorted to using disk space. If you have consistent or high rates of swap, it means your system doesn't have enough memory.

so – Memory Swapped Out from Disk

As the name hints, this goes hand in hand with memory swapped in. While swapping in is the process of loading data back into memory from disk, swapping out is the process where data is first saved to disk.

bi – Blocks Received from Block Device

This is essentially the amount of data which has been read from disk storage devices. By default, blocks have a size of 512 bytes.

bo – Blocks Sent to Block Device

This is the amount of blocks saved to disk via block device.

in – Interrupts per Second

An interrupt is a signal which requires immediate handling. For example, when a key is pressed on the keyboard, an interrupt is created which requires handling. In the same way, when an incoming signal is produced from a network card connected to the Internet, an interrupt is created. Interrupts can be viewed directly by looking at the file / proc/interrupts.

Interrupts occurring is a normal part of system operation, but if interrupts are higher than normal, there may be a hardware issue. A next step might be looking in /proc/ interrupts and finding what device is responsible for the high count.

cs – Context Switches

A context switch occurs when the CPU switches between one process and another without having finished the first. A context switch requires saving the state of the first process so that it can be finished at a later time. There is a cost associated with context switching, as resources are required for saving the state of the first process and loading the state back up later.

If you're seeing an abnormally high amount of context switching, it is likely related to a specific program which is using multithreading badly.

us – Time Spent Running Non-kernel Code

As the title says, us is time spent running non-kernel code. The kernel as we mentioned previously is the core of Unix-like systems which connects the physical hardware to user-level software. All "time spent" values are measured as a percentage of time, so a value of 2 would indicate 2% of the time during the period measured was spent on non-kernel code.

sy – Time Spent Running Kernel Code

This is the percentage of time spent running kernel code; an easy way to think of this is, time spent on system processes outside the user level. An abnormally high value for time spent on system processes could indicate hardware problems, memory bottlenecks, or kernel-level locking issues.

id – Time Spent Idle

This is the percentage of time spent idle. This is used for comparing with us and sy. Notice that adding us, sy, id, and wa (*which we'll look at next*) should add up to around 100% (can be slightly off due to rounding). If you're not running a lot of programs in the background while testing vmstat, it's likely that the majority of time will be spent idle. A low number for time spent idle indicates your system is doing a lot of processing.

wa – Time Spent Waiting for I/O

The fourth category of "time spent" on vmstat is the percentage of time spent waiting for I/O. In the section on b, we mentioned how threads can be blocked while waiting to write to disk or while reading from disk. wa gives us a measure of how much CPU time was lost while waiting for I/O. Having a high % of time spent waiting for I/O could indicate our disk storage is slow or that we're simply doing a lot of reading and writing to disk. If you're finding that waiting for I/O seems to be taking a lot of your system's time, you can possibly lower this percentage by upgrading the underlying hardware with disk storage that has higher read/write speeds.

If you'd like to simulate a process that causes a high amount of disk reading and writing to observe the effect in vmstat, you can run the following code snippet:

```
(cd /tmp &&
```

```
(sync ; vmstat 1 & PID1=$! ; \
cat </dev/zero >test & PID2=$! ; \
sleep 3 ; kill $PID2 ; sync ; kill $PID1))
```

This snippet moves into the /tmp directory, starts vmstat, and then starts reading zeros from /dev/zero and writing them to /tmp/test. PID1 and PID2 contain the process IDs of both running processes and kill them after sleeping 3 seconds. When running this command, you should see the wa value ramp up to some high values.

st – Time Stolen from Virtual Machine

Just like it sounds, the st value indicates the amount of time a virtual machine running on your system spends waiting to gain access to the resources allocated to it. This is only relevant if your system is running a virtual machine. Consistently having a value above 0 may indicate that you've allocated too much memory to virtual machines, meaning your primary system has to steal time from them, or you simply don't have enough memory to run your hosted virtual machines and primary system.

nmon

The 'nmon' system monitoring tool can display CPU, memory, network, disks (mini graphs or numbers), filesystems, NFS, top processes, resources (Linux version and processors) and power micro-partition information. What makes nmon unique is that it allows you to mix and match between these different statistics to create your own custom display screen. nmon is not installed by default, but it can be found on most package managers as nmon.

When you first open nmon by simply running the command with no options, you'll see a start screen similar to Figure 8-26.

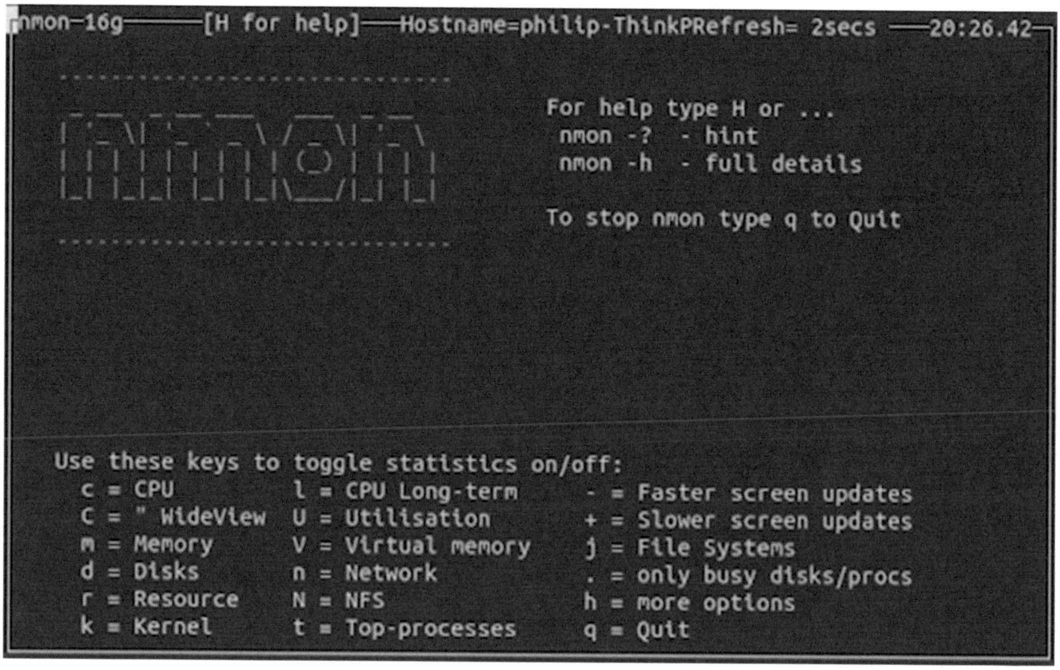

Figure 8-26. *Running nmon*

From here you can press any of the buttons listed at the bottom to toggle on
that particular statistic. If we press n, for example, the screen will display network
information; if we then press c, we'll be viewing both network and CPU information like
shown in Figure 8-27.

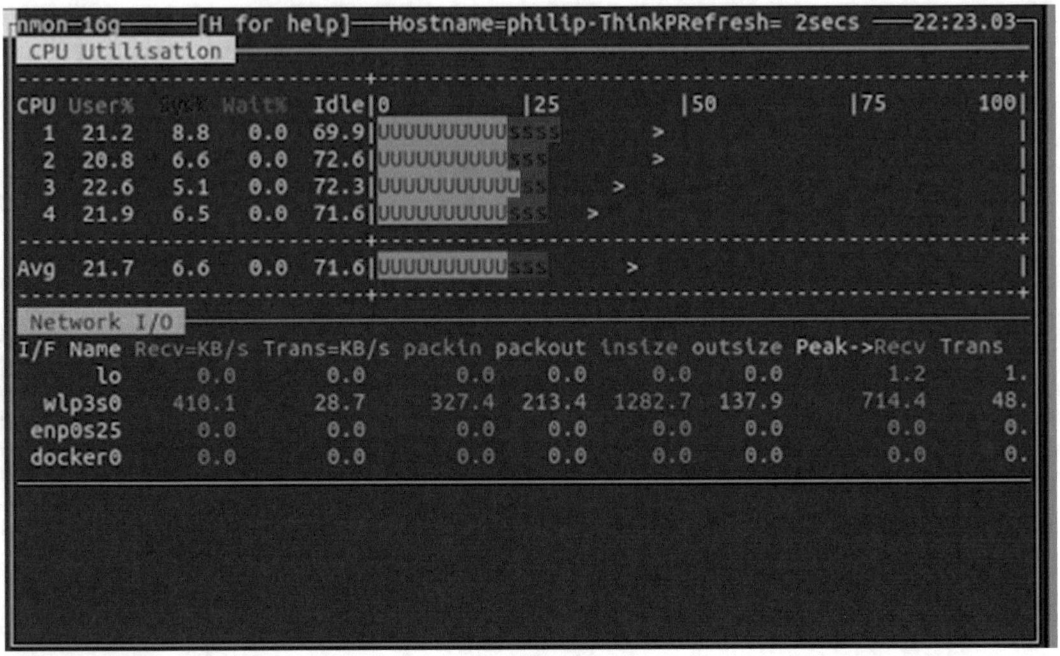

Figure 8-27. Viewing CPU and network info in nmon

The only limit to how many different stats you can view at once is your screen size. At any time, you can remove a section by pressing the same button which was used to activate it.

Advanced Network Monitoring with Snort

Another monitoring system worth mentioning is Snort, an open source network intrusion prevention and detection system. Snort works by analyzing network traffic in real time and checking it against a set of defined rules. Common rule sets include

- Checking IP addresses against blacklists

- Checking for abnormal amount of requests from an IP

- Checking content of requests

- Rules specific to certain services like FTP, SSH, or https

- Any custom rules

Snort also allows the system administrator to connect rules to trigger actions such as sending a notification to the system admin or blocking requests from the offending IP. Snort is completely open source and several community-maintained rule sets exist, there are also premium rule sets which are updated regularly and made available as a paid service.

We won't go into detail about how to install or set up `snort` though it is available from most package managers. The setup process is rather long and outside the scope of this book, but it is worth looking into if the use case is applicable to your setup.

Nagios

Another open source full-suite network monitoring system complete with web-based GUI is Nagios. It can be used to monitor resources across multiple machines and infrastructure, with features including

- Alerts based on potential issues

- Monitor your websites to record any downtime

- Capture port use (*http, SMTP, SNMP, FTP, SSH, POP, etc.*)

- Extensive logs for network requests

As with Snort, the Nagios server is more useful for those running a medium- to large-sized infrastructure for providing web-based services.

Summary

In this chapter, we looked at various programs and commands which can be used to monitor Linux systems, from basic process monitoring with `top` or `atop` to more specific monitoring programs like `nethogs` and `iftop`.

CHAPTER 9

Hardware Details and /dev

In this chapter, we'll look at some useful commands for checking the details of the hardware on the machine you're using or connecting to. When connecting to a machine via SSH, you may not know all the details about what kind of hardware you're dealing with. Even if you're using a machine you're used to or some embedded device, you may not know all the details. Additionally, if you are completely familiar with the hardware of a device, you may be able to find hardware issues by checking the details to see if they match up with what you've expected.

A missing folder within the /dev/ directory or device missing when running lshw may alert you to some hardware which has either failed to mount or is broken.

Commands for Hardware Details

In this section, we'll look at commands and programs which can give you a better idea of what kind of hardware is on the system you're using.

Everyone knows about ls, but there is a whole list of hardware query commands which take their name from the command. Some of them useful for finding out information about the underlying hardware of a machine are listed in Table 9-1.

Table 9-1. *Useful commands for getting hardware details*

Command/Application	Description
lspci	Lists all PCI devices
lsblk	Lists all block devices
sudo fdisk –l	Similar to lsblk but with more detailed information including sectors
lscpu	Lists information about the CPU architecture

(continued)

© Philip Kirkbride 2020
P. Kirkbride, *Basic Linux Terminal Tips and Tricks*, https://doi.org/10.1007/978-1-4842-6035-7_9

Table 9-1. (*continued*)

Command/Application	Description
lshw	In-depth list of hardware details. Can also be run with the -short flag to show a condensed version
ls /dev	The /dev folder on Linux systems
ls -l /sys/block	Lists hard disks attached and bus ID. You will likely also see several virtual devices named loop
lsusb	Displays information about USB buses in the system and the devices connected to them
cat /proc/cpuinfo	Provides data about the processor
free -h	Displays free memory, -h for human readable
df -m	Lists mounted filesystems
ip a	Lists network interfaces
netstat -i	Cleaner alternative to ifconfig for listing interfaces
hdparm	Gets/sets SATA/IDE device parameters
uname -r	Displays kernel version

The /dev/ Folder

Another folder that can be used to gain insights into connected hardware is the /dev folder. The /dev folder contains many files and folders related to mounted devices, as well as some other nonhardware files with special use cases. Table 9-2 shows an extensive list of files which can be found in the /dev folder. Your system likely won't have them all.

Note   All files which end in a number like js0 can have multiple instances; each subsequent instance is named with the number incremented, in this case, js1, js2, and so on.

Table 9-2. *Examples of devices in the /dev/ folder*

Folder/File	Description
/dev/dsp	Digital signal processor
/dev/fd0	Floppy disk reader
/dev/fb0	Framebuffer device
/dev/js0	Analogue joystick
/dev/lp0	Parallel printer
/dev/usb/lp0	USB printer
/dev/cdrom	CD ROM
/dev/dvd	DVD
/dev/rtc	Real-time clock
/dev/sda	Hard drive
/dev/ttyS0	Serial port

This list is by no means complete. Essentially, any I/O device which can be connected to your computer will show up in the /dev folder.

Special Files in the /dev/ Folder

In addition to physical devices, you'll also find some special files within the /dev/ folder. These represent pseudo-devices with some special behavior. Table 9-3 shows a list of the popular ones.

Table 9-3. *Special files in the /dev/ folder*

Folder/File	Description
/dev/null	A special file that discards anything thrown into it
/dev/random	A special file that produces random output
/dev/urandom	Same as random but does not block when system runs out of entropy

(continued)

Table 9-3. (*continued*)

Folder/File	Description
/dev/stdin	Standard input of processes
/dev/stdout	Standard output of processes
/dev/stderr	Standard output of errors from processes
/dev/zero	A special file that returns all zeros
/dev/tty0	Teletypewriter (*see the following note*)
/dev/loop0	Pseudo-device that makes file available as a block device

Next we'll look at some of these special files a little more in depth.

Teletypewriter

TTY (*teletypewriter*) is a device which can be used to both send and receive text over various mediums. The name originates from the historical teleprinters which predate screen-based computers. Teletypewriters were commonly used at Bell since the early 1900s; see Figure 9-1 for an example. Bell would later create Unix in 1971 which includes a virtual teletypewriter as a core concept.

Figure 9-1. *Historical example of a teletypewriter from Bell Telephone Magazine 1921*

When typing in Unix terminal, you're actually inputting text into a virtual or pseudo TTY which takes inputs and can return outputs. Of course in the case of the on-screen terminal, it's simulated hardware. At any one time, your system likely has several TTYs. To see them all, simply run

```
ls /dev/ | grep tty
```

It's likely too many to count manually; if you're curious as to how many, you can pipe the result into `wc -l` and get the amount of lines:

```
ls /dev/ | grep tty | wc -l
```

In my case, I have 98. Why so many? Well some of these TTYs represent normal terminal sessions, while others have special use cases. For example, `tty0` is a special alias TTY which always points to the current terminal. TTYs may also be used to contain processes or applications in the background. Try running

```
ps ax
```

This will return a list of processes; take note of the TTY column which shows the parent TTY for some processes. Some processes may be listed as ?, which means they're unbound to a terminal, running in the background.

It is also possible to attach your screen to some of these TTYs directly by pressing ctrl+alt+F1, replace F1 with the terminal number in question (*F1, F2, F3, etc.*). On many OS, `tty1` will be used for X Server; thus, moving to another terminal will cause your computer to seem to leave the OS completely (*music turns off, can no longer see applications or system menus*).

stdin, stdout, and stderr

The special files `stdin`, `stdout`, and `stderr` are short for "standard in," "standard out," and "standard error." They're more akin to a stream of I/O than a file per se, but because (almost) everything is represented as a file in Linux, these aspects of the operating system have associated files.

If you open them, you'll find they're completely empty though you can direct text into them which is what is done in the background of the operating system, for example:

```
echo hello > /dev/stderr
```

It's worth knowing what stdin, stdout, and stderr are. You'll likely encounter them even if not referred to by their file name directly. The system of converting "standard in" to "standard out" and "standard error" via a process is visualized in Figure 9-2.

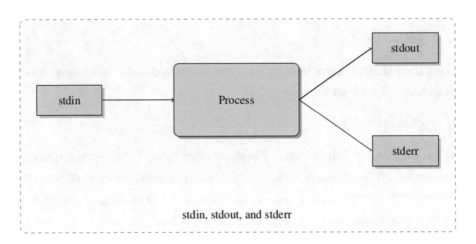

Figure 9-2. *Diagram of a process transforming standard input into standard output and standard error*

/dev/null

A commonly used special device file is /dev/null. This file is like a blackhole you send input in, but nothing ever comes out. This may sound rather useless at first, but it can actually be used to silence a process that otherwise would print output to the terminal or log files.

To show an example, we'll use the ping command and redirect our output to /dev/null. There are two types of output we can redirect, standard output (represented by 1) and standard error (represented by 2).

In order to test redirecting both standard out and standard error to /dev/null, we're going to create a file which simply writes one message to standard out and another to standard error. I'm creating mine at /tmp/out.sh:

```
#!/usr/bin/env bash
echo Working
>&2 echo Error
```

After saving the file, be sure to add the execution permission:

```
chmod +x /tmp/out.sh
```

Next let's try running it:

```
/tmp/out.sh
```

Next try running it with the following redirection:

```
/tmp/out.sh 1>/dev/null
```

You should now only get back the error as standard output is directed to `/dev/null` the blackbox. Let's do the same thing but switch the 1 to a 2:

```
/tmp/out.sh 2>/dev/null
```

As you likely expected, now we only see the output but not the error. It's also possible to redirect both at once. For both the syntax is a little bit different:

```
/tmp/out.sh > /dev/null 2>&1
```

Figure 9-3 shows the expected output for each command.

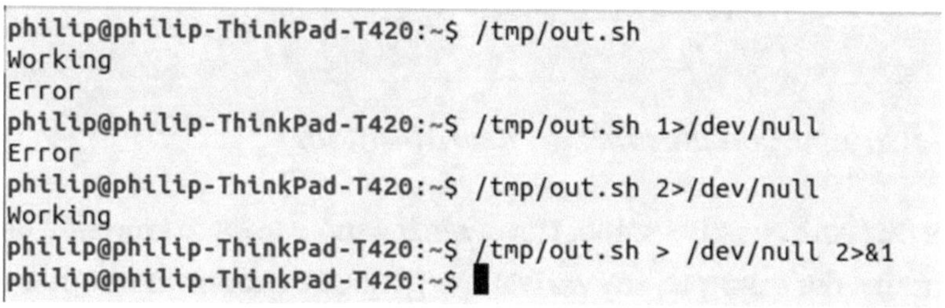

```
philip@philip-ThinkPad-T420:~$ /tmp/out.sh
Working
Error
philip@philip-ThinkPad-T420:~$ /tmp/out.sh 1>/dev/null
Error
philip@philip-ThinkPad-T420:~$ /tmp/out.sh 2>/dev/null
Working
philip@philip-ThinkPad-T420:~$ /tmp/out.sh > /dev/null 2>&1
philip@philip-ThinkPad-T420:~$ █
```

Figure 9-3. *Redirecting to /dev/null*

/dev/random and /dev/urandom

Another useful special device is random and urandom. These are both essentially the same thing in that they both act as a device which inputs completely random data. Thus, it serves as a pseudo-random number generator. Like most pseudo-random number generators, it relies on some inputs to create entropy.

The entropy that is used for input is the result of random aspects of the state of the system such as mouse movements, key presses, and other device inputs (e.g., *speed of a drive*). Using this entropy, random characters are generated in the `/dev/random` and `/dev/urandom`.

The main difference between random and urandom is that if random runs out of entropy, it will block a program relying on it, whereas urandom will not. Generally, urandom should be preferred.

To get an idea of the kind of data in /dev/urandom, let's get the first 500 characters using head:

```
head -c 500 /dev/urandom
```

This should return a long string of unreadable characters like shown in Figure 9-4.

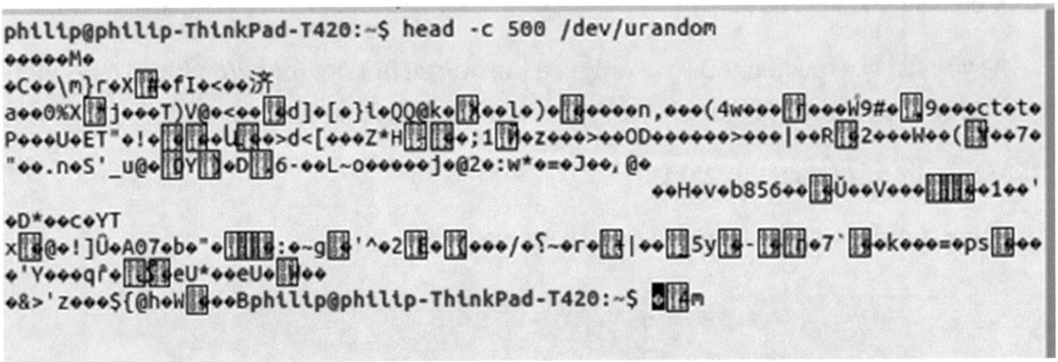

Figure 9-4.   Example contents inside /dev/urandom

Of course this isn't exactly usable. However, it can be used to generate useful random data for programs. For example, say we want to generate a random number to use with a program. We could use od, short for octal dump, to generate a human-readable number:

```
od -vAn -N1 -tu1 < /dev/urandom
```

The preceding example generates an unsigned number of 1 byte size (0–255). If we wanted to instead do 2 bytes, we could run

```
od -vAn -N2 -tu2 < /dev/urandom
```

/dev/zero

Another special file you'll find in the /dev folder is zero. Reading this file will return a stream of null 0s which goes on forever. To demonstrate /dev/zero, let's create a file with 512 bytes of null 0s:

```
dd if=/dev/zero of=/tmp/zero count=1
```

If you open /tmp/zero after this, you should see something like in Figure 9-5 (*depending on how your text editor interprets null character*).

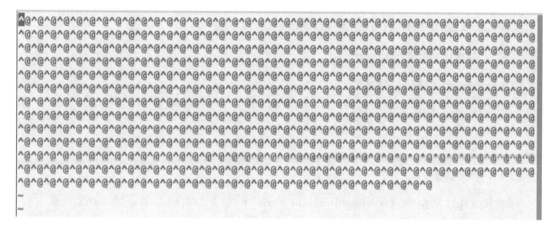

Figure 9-5. *Example output from /dev/zero*

This is mainly used for creating dummy files. It can also be used for zeroing out memory on a computer. When a file is deleted on the computer, the underlying memory still exists, but it has been marked as free space that can be used.

By creating large files that are all zeros, this underlying data can be removed, though this method has been criticized, in favor of using random data instead of zeros, as advanced methods can still recover this data.

A more thorough way of doing this would be to use the shred command, for example:

```
shred /dev/sda
```

It will not only delete the contents of a drive but make them difficult to recover.

What Is the Kernel?

You've likely already heard references to the Linux kernel, but what exactly is it? The Linux kernel is the core component of all Linux operating systems and is the part which everything else is built around. The word kernel originally refers to the very center of a nut or fruit. In the same way, the Linux kernel is at the very center of all Linux systems.

The Linux kernel controls all communications between the physical hardware of a system and the inner software. Many developers and Linux users will never have to interact with the kernel directly, yet it is worth knowing what this refers to.

The Linux kernel is responsible for things including

- Memory management

- Process management

- Device drivers

- System calls

- Security

Much of this happens without the user even being aware of it. The hierarchy of hardware, kernel, and processes is visualized in Figure 9-6.

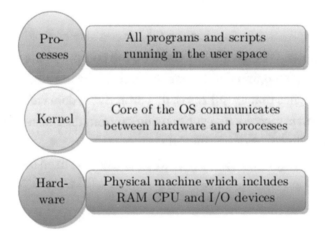

Figure 9-6. *Userspace, kernel, and hardware stack*

Getting Kernel Version

You can find out what version of the Linux kernel you're using by running

```
uname -r
```

For more complete information on the version, you can run

```
cat /proc/version
```

This will return more complete information on your kernel like shown in Figure 9-7. In addition to the version, the identity of who compiled the kernel is listed, compiler used, type of compile, and the date/time of compile.

```
philip@philip-ThinkPad-T420:~$ uname -r
5.0.0-37-generic
philip@philip-ThinkPad-T420:~$ cat /proc/version
Linux version 5.0.0-37-generic (buildd@lcy01-amd64-023) (gcc version 7.4.0 (Ubuntu 7.4.0-1
ubuntu1~18.04.1)) #40~18.04.1-Ubuntu SMP Thu Nov 14 12:06:39 UTC 2019
philip@philip-ThinkPad-T420:~$
```

Figure 9-7. *Displaying kernel version*

Configure and Mount a Drive

Often when setting up a server, either in person or in the cloud, the default storage space won't be enough to store data on. In this section, we'll look at how to attach a drive to the filesystem.

As mentioned in the section on /dev/, all connected drives will show up in the /dev/ folder. However, these will show as a single file not a folder which can be explored. In order to have the drive treated as a filesystem, it needs to be mounted.

The first step in mounting the drive is figuring out which file it is in the /dev folder. You can do this by running mount and grepping instances of "/dev/sd":

```
mount | grep /dev/sd
```

This will list all drives connected followed by their mount point, as shown in Figure 9-8.

```
philip@philip-ThinkPad-T420:~$ mount | grep /dev/sd
/dev/sda4 on / type ext4 (rw,relatime,errors=remount-ro
/dev/sda1 on /boot/efi type vfat (rw,relatime,fmask=007
philip@philip-ThinkPad-T420:~$
```

Figure 9-8. *Displaying mountable drives*

Take note of the highlighted section /dev/sda4 on / type ext4. This tells us a few things about the sda4 drive. Firstly, it is mounted as the root of our system / and secondly the format is ext4.

The `mount` command will not list every device; to get a better view of things, try running `lsblk`, which should return a list like that shown in Figure 9-9.

```
philip@philip-ThinkPad-T420:~$ lsblk | grep sd
sda        8:0      0 223.6G  0 disk
├─sda1     8:1      0    512M  0 part /boot/efi
├─sda2     8:2      0     16M  0 part
├─sda3     8:3      0   92.3G  0 part
└─sda4     8:4      0  130.8G  0 part /
philip@philip-ThinkPad-T420:~$
```

Figure 9-9. *Viewing drives and partitions with lsblk*

Notice that in this case we can see the relationship between `sda` (*the physical drive*) and the partitions on that disk (*sda 1 through 4*).

In my case, `sda3` is a partition previously used for a Windows install. As it's no longer needed, I'll format it and mount it. Whenever formatting double check that the drive doesn't have data you need and is in fact the correct partition name. After formatting the partition, all data will be lost.

The steps we'll be taking:

1. Delete the windows partition

2. Create a new partition

3. Format the partition

4. Mount the partition

5. Ensure partition is always mounted on startup

Delete Partition

To delete the partition, first you'll enter `fdisk` interactive mode for the drive in question:

```
sudo fdisk /dev/sda
```

You'll be asked to enter a command; enter d for delete. Then enter the partition number, in my case, 3. To make the changes final, enter the w command for write. The deletion process will then start as shown in Figure 9-10.

```
philip@philip-ThinkPad-T420:/media$ sudo fdisk /dev/sda

Welcome to fdisk (util-linux 2.31.1).
Changes will remain in memory only, until you decide to write them.
Be careful before using the write command.


Command (m for help): d
Partition number (1-4, default 4): 3

Partition 3 has been deleted.

Command (m for help): w
The partition table has been altered.
Syncing disks.
```

Figure 9-10. *Deleting a partition with fdisk*

Now if you run lsblk | grep sd again, we'll see one less partition.

Create Partition

Next we'll use the freed up space to create a new partition. Again open fdisk:

```
sudo fdisk /dev/sda
```

This time enter the command n for new. First you'll be asked to choose a number; we'll use 3 to replace the deleted one. Next you'll be asked to choose the sector on the hard drive to start the new partition. In most cases, the default will be the lowest available position and is a good choice.

After choosing the starting sector, you'll be asked about the ending sector; you can specify a specific location in memory or specify the size of the partition. We'll simply choose the default option which will use all remaining space to create our partition. In my case, I was also asked if I want to remove the ntfs signature, which is a Windows-specific thing; it is safe to remove. An example of the process is shown in Figure 9-11.

```
philip@philip-ThinkPad-T420:/media$ sudo fdisk /dev/sda

Welcome to fdisk (util-linux 2.31.1).
Changes will remain in memory only, until you decide to write them.
Be careful before using the write command.


Command (m for help): n
Partition number (3,5-128, default 3): 3
First sector (1083392-468862094, default 1083392):
Last sector, +sectors or +size{K,M,G,T,P} (1083392-194664447, default 194664447):

Created a new partition 3 of type 'Linux filesystem' and of size 92.3 GiB.
Partition #3 contains a ntfs signature.

Do you want to remove the signature? [Y]es/[N]o: Y

The signature will be removed by a write command.

Command (m for help): w
The partition table has been altered.
Syncing disks.

philip@philip-ThinkPad-T420:/media$ █
```

Figure 9-11. *Create a partition with fdisk*

After the partition is created, you'll want to run the following command to have the partition table reread:

partprobe

Format Partition

We now have a new /dev/sda3 file, but we still need to format it. We'll do this using the mkfs command, short for "make filesystem."

sudo mkfs.ext4 /dev/sda3

Or:

sudo mkfs -t ext4 /dev/sda3

Mount Partition

With the partition formatted, we can now mount it to our filesystem. First you'll want to create a folder which will be mounted to. The recommended locations for mounting are /mnt and /media though these folders have different recommended uses. The /mnt folder is for manually mounted drives, while /media is where automatically mounted removable drives (e.g., *USB portable drives*) will appear.

However, technically, there is nothing stopping you from mounting a device anywhere you'd like. In my case, I'll create a folder called /mnt/drive1:

```
sudo mkdir /mnt/drive1
```

Once created, let's mount the drive to it:

```
sudo mount /dev/sda3 /mnt/drive1
```

System Link from Partition to ~/

It may seem awkward having your storage outside your home directory as it's out of the way and you won't have permission by default. What you can do to deal with this is to create system links to other folders within your home directory.

For example, say we want more space for a movie collection that will be located at ~/ Movies. First go into /mnt/drive1 and create the folder:

```
sudo mkdir Movies
```

Next make yourself the owner of the directory:

```
sudo chown $USER:$USER /mnt/drive1/Movies
```

Now that we have permission to use ~/Movies, we'll create a symbolic link in our home directory that acts as a shortcut, meaning we never have to go outside the home directory to use it (*be sure to use full path for the first argument*):

```
ln -s /mnt/drive1/Movies/ ~/
```

Now if you go to your home directory, you should see a Movies folder. Anything which is saved into the ~/Movies folder will actually be saved onto our newly mounted drive.

Making Mounted Partition Persistent

We have our partition working perfectly; you might think we're done. Unfortunately, if we now restart our machine, it will start back up without sda3 mounted. In order to make the new partition mount to /mnt/drive1 on every startup, we need to do one more thing.

When starting up, the system looks at the file /etc/fstab to determine what drives need to be mounted. Before we make an entry, let's look at what values are needed:

1. UUID of block device (*find with lsblk -d -fs <file>*)

2. Folder to mount

3. Filesystem type

4. Mount options (*use default or see man*)

5. Should filesystem be dumped (*normally 0*)

6. Fsck order (*use 1 for main partition, 2 for others*)

To get the UUID of the partition, run the following using your own partition location:

```
lsblk -d -fs /dev/sda3
```

Once you have the six values needed, open up /etc/fstab to edit. The values we'll be using are shown in the second uncommented line of Figure 9-12.

```
 /etc/fstab: static file system information.
#
# Use 'blkid' to print the universally unique identifier for a
# device; this may be used with UUID= as a more robust way to name devices
# that works even if disks are added and removed. See fstab(5).
#
# <file system> <mount point>   <type>  <options>       <dump>  <pass>
# / was on /dev/sda4 during installation
UUID=0b794822-d885-4db1-849b-1bc97337d932 /              ext4    errors=remount-ro 0       1
UUID=289826a6-f8dc-4171-b062-ef7fa2bdde0c /mnt/drive1 ext4 defaults 0 2
# /boot/efi was on /dev/sda1 during installation
UUID=65B2-C1AE  /boot/efi       vfat    umask=0077      0       1
/swapfile                       none            swap    sw              0       0
~
~
~
```

Figure 9-12. *Editing /etc/fstab*

Be careful when editing /etc/fstab as an incorrect entry will cause your system to go into emergency mode on restart. If that happens, don't panic, simply use the command line in emergency mode to open /etc/fstab and comment out the line you added.

You can reduce any chance of errors by running

```
sudo findmnt --verify
```

This will pick up on things like mismatch between file type on disk and that declared but is not 100% foolproof at catching errors.

lm-sensor

After installing `lm-sensor`, you first need to let the application detect what sensors are on your system. Do this with

```
sudo sensors-detect
```

It will ask several questions which you can reply "yes" to enable. In most cases, the default responses are fine so you can just press enter. Once done with the setup process, you can run

```
sensors
```

This will return sensor, fan, and other data which are available as shown in Figure 9-13.

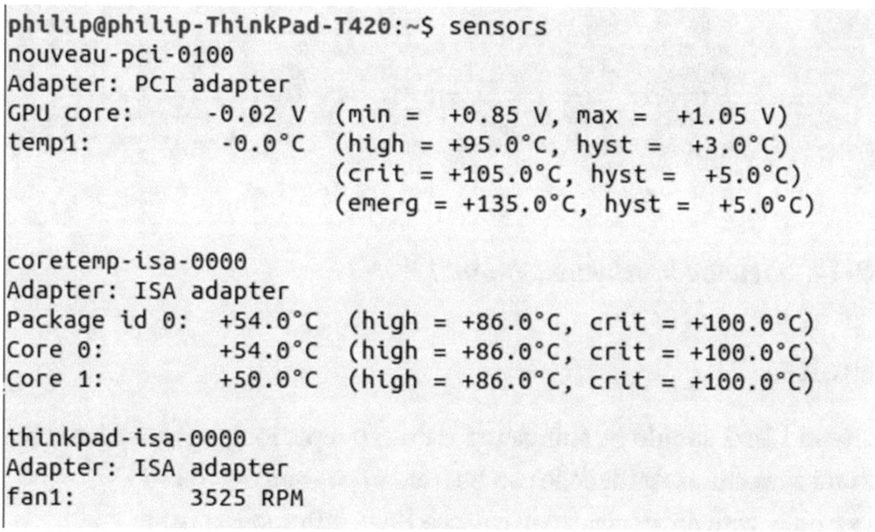

```
philip@philip-ThinkPad-T420:~$ sensors
nouveau-pci-0100
Adapter: PCI adapter
GPU core:      -0.02 V  (min =  +0.85 V, max =  +1.05 V)
temp1:         -0.0°C  (high = +95.0°C, hyst =  +3.0°C)
                       (crit = +105.0°C, hyst =  +5.0°C)
                       (emerg = +135.0°C, hyst =  +5.0°C)

coretemp-isa-0000
Adapter: ISA adapter
Package id 0:  +54.0°C  (high = +86.0°C, crit = +100.0°C)
Core 0:        +54.0°C  (high = +86.0°C, crit = +100.0°C)
Core 1:        +50.0°C  (high = +86.0°C, crit = +100.0°C)

thinkpad-isa-0000
Adapter: ISA adapter
fan1:          3525 RPM
```

Figure 9-13. *Viewing sensors with lm-sensor*

inxi

A program similar to lshw that can be installed for an improved experience when getting hardware information is i-nex. It can be installed with

```
sudo apt-get install inxi
```

By default, it will return very basic data on a single line of output. To get full details, run with the -F flag:

```
inxi -Fxz
```

This should return a detailed list of hardware information as shown in Figure 9-14.

```
philip@philip-ThinkPad-T420:~$ inxi -F
System:    Host: philip-ThinkPad-T420 Kernel: 5.0.0-37-generic x86_64 bits: 64
           Desktop: Gnome 3.28.4 Distro: Ubuntu 18.04.3 LTS
Machine:   Device: laptop System: LENOVO product: 4180F98 v: ThinkPad T420 serial: N/A
           Mobo: LENOVO model: 4180F98 serial: N/A
           UEFI: LENOVO v: 83ET78WW (1.48 ) date: 01/21/2016
Battery    BAT0: charge: 66.5 Wh 79.4% condition: 83.7/94.0 Wh (89%)
CPU:       Dual core Intel Core i5-2540M (-MT-MCP-) cache: 3072 KB
           clock speeds: max: 3300 MHz 1: 926 MHz 2: 1143 MHz 3: 992 MHz 4: 1025 MHz
Graphics:  Card-1: Intel 2nd Generation Core Integrated Graphics Controller
           Card-2: NVIDIA GF119M [Quadro NVS 4200M]
           Display Server: x11 (X.Org 1.20.4 ) drivers: i915,nouveau
           Resolution: 1600x900@60.01hz
           OpenGL: renderer: Mesa DRI Intel Sandybridge Mobile version: 3.3 Mesa 19.0.8
Audio:     Card-1 Intel 6 Series/C200 Series Family High Def. Audio Controller
           driver: snd_hda_intel
           Card-2 NVIDIA GF119 HDMI Audio Controller driver: snd_hda_intel
           Sound: Advanced Linux Sound Architecture v: k5.0.0-37-generic
Network:   Card-1: Intel 82579LM Gigabit Network Connection (Lewisville) driver: e1000e
           IF: enp0s25 state: down mac: 00:21:cc:ba:c8:0d
           Card-2: Intel Centrino Advanced-N 6205 [Taylor Peak] driver: iwlwifi
           IF: wlp3s0 state: up mac: 10:0b:a9:96:87:74
```

Figure 9-14. *Viewing hardware with inxi*

dmidecode

While lshw and inxi should be sufficient for most people looking to see basic hardware details about a machine, dmidecode can be used to go even deeper.

For example, with dmidecode, you can see BIOS information using

```
sudo dmidecode -t bios
```

Running the command stand-alone as `sudo dmidecode` will return all system information in detail including things like serial number and manufacturer which can't be found with less detailed utilities. When using it stand-alone, you may want to pipe to `less` for easy reading:

```
sudo dmidecode | less
```

For motherboard, you can run

```
sudo dmidecode -t baseboard
```

There are all kinds of options that can be specified via `-t` to specify specific hardware info; see the man page for more complete information.

Summary

In this chapter, we looked at several ways you can explore the underlying hardware of a system using tools like `lshw`, `inxi`, and `dmidecode`. We also looked at how connected hardware will appear in the `/dev/` folder which contains hardware devices and a number of special files like `/dev/null` and `/dev/urandom` useful for various tasks. We interacted with a hard drive in the `/dev` folder by using the `mount` command to mount it in the `/mnt` directory.

CHAPTER 10

Parsing Text

No matter what you're doing on Linux, you'll likely find yourself needing to parse text at some point. As Linux is largely file based, there is a huge need for utilities which can parse large amounts of text to find specific values, format, and process it.

There are several utilities that can be used for parsing text. In this chapter, we'll look at several of these utilities and how you can see them to parse text.

grep

grep is one of the most commonly used command-line tools. It allows you to find a specific string in a set of text. For example, given a file with several lines, we can find the line with the text we're looking for. As an example, let's find the root user in the /etc/passwd file.

```
cat /etc/passwd | grep root
```

You should get back a single entry as shown in Figure 10-1.

```
philip@philip-ThinkPad-T420:~$ cat /etc/passwd | grep root
root:x:0:0:root:/root:/bin/bash
philip@philip-ThinkPad-T420:~$ ▮
```

Figure 10-1. *Grepping root from /etc/passwd*

Or even better, we can perform grep directly on a file itself without the need for a pipe:

```
grep root /etc/passwd
```

You can also do the inverse and find lines without, to do that add the -v flag which stands for invert matches:

© Philip Kirkbride 2020

P. Kirkbride, *Basic Linux Terminal Tips and Tricks*, https://doi.org/10.1007/978-1-4842-6035-7_10

```
cat /etc/passwd | grep -v root
```

This should return similar entries for every other user on your system. The -v flag is only one of many options that can be used with grep; see Table 10-1 for more.

Table 10-1. *Options for grep*

Flag	Description
-e	Regex pattern
-i	Ignore uppercase/lowercase
-v	Invert matches
-c	Cont matches
-n	Get X lines before match and show line number (*requires number input*)
-h	Don't show file name before matched line (*default when grepping a single file*)
-x	Exact line match
-f	Load regex from a file
-o	Only output the matched parts of a line
-A	Show N lines after match (*requires number input*)
-B	Show N lines before match (*requires number input*)
-C	Show N lines before and after match (*requires number input*)

cut

While grep can parse files to return the relevant lines in a file, sometimes there is the need to parse the text in a line itself. For parsing a single line, cut works well. cut can be used to split the contents of a line by character, byte, or custom delimiter, for example, with byte:

```
echo hello world | cut -b 1,2
```

The preceding command will return "he" as this is the content of the first and second byte of "hello world". It's also possible to do from byte X to the end of a line, for example:

```
echo hello world | cut -b 7-
```

This should return just "hello". cut doesn't need to receive its input from a pipe; you can also read from a file directly. When reading from a file, the same transformation will be applied to every line. For example, let's get the 1st to the 9th byte from every line in the /etc/passwd file:

```
cut -b 1-9 /etc/passwd
```

You should get back a line for each user as shown in Figure 10-2.

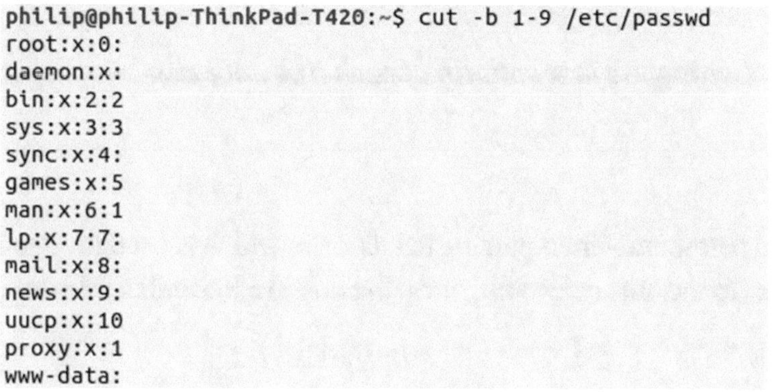

```
philip@philip-ThinkPad-T420:~$ cut -b 1-9 /etc/passwd
root:x:0:
daemon:x:
bin:x:2:2
sys:x:3:3
sync:x:4:
games:x:5
man:x:6:1
lp:x:7:7:
mail:x:8:
news:x:9:
uucp:x:10
proxy:x:1
www-data:
```

Figure 10-2. *Grepping root from /etc/passwd*

Note   With normal text files, the -b and -c flags will act the same since a single character is a byte long.

Of course in the preceding example, the result isn't particularly useful; we've gotten several usernames, but as not all users are the same length, some lines get extra data and others get cut off. The most commonly used mode is -d for delimiter. For example, let's get just the usernames. We provide the character we want to use as a delimiter, in our example each username is preceded by a ":". Then we specify what section of the cut text we want to return with the -f flag:

```
cut -d : -f 1 /etc/passwd
```

This should return a list of all users as shown in Figure 10-3.

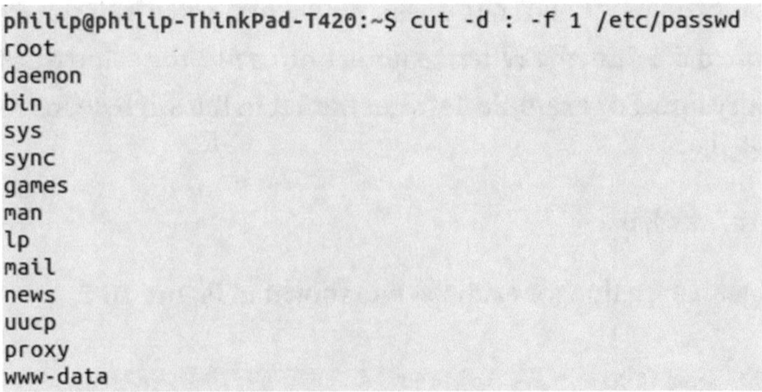

```
philip@philip-ThinkPad-T420:~$ cut -d : -f 1 /etc/passwd
root
daemon
bin
sys
sync
games
man
lp
mail
news
uucp
proxy
www-data
```

Figure 10-3. Getting the first column of each line with cut

uniq

Another useful command when parsing text is uniq, which is used for parsing out duplicate lines. To test this command, let's first create a file with some duplicate lines:

```
printf 'Hello %d\n' 1 1 1 2 2 3 > /tmp/hello.txt
```

The file /tmp/hello.txt should now contain six lines, three of which are unique. To confirm, first cat the contents of the file, and then do a second cat piped into uniq:

```
cat /tmp/hello.txt
uniq /tmp/hello.txt
```

Your contents should be similar to those shown in Figure 10-4.

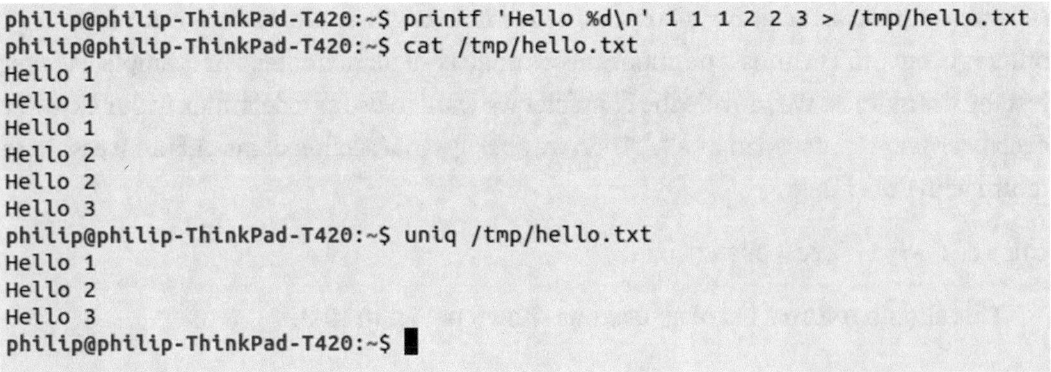

```
philip@philip-ThinkPad-T420:~$ printf 'Hello %d\n' 1 1 1 2 2 3 > /tmp/hello.txt
philip@philip-ThinkPad-T420:~$ cat /tmp/hello.txt
Hello 1
Hello 1
Hello 1
Hello 2
Hello 2
Hello 3
philip@philip-ThinkPad-T420:~$ uniq /tmp/hello.txt
Hello 1
Hello 2
Hello 3
philip@philip-ThinkPad-T420:~$ 
```

Figure 10-4. Using uniq

It's important to note that the unique feature only applies to duplicates which are next to each other. If we add another "Hello 1" to the end of the file, for example, it will still be printed as a unique line. *Be sure to use >> and not > as a single redirect symbol will overwrite the file rather than add to it*:

```
echo Hello 1 >> /tmp/hello.txt
uniq /tmp/hello.txt
```

Notice how the first and last lines are the same like in Figure 10-5.

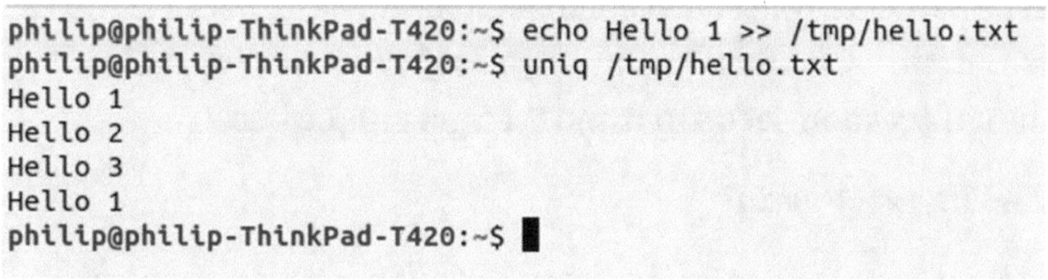

```
philip@philip-ThinkPad-T420:~$ echo Hello 1 >> /tmp/hello.txt
philip@philip-ThinkPad-T420:~$ uniq /tmp/hello.txt
Hello 1
Hello 2
Hello 3
Hello 1
philip@philip-ThinkPad-T420:~$ 
```

Figure 10-5. *Using uniq when duplicate lines aren't next to each other*

If we want to only print completely unique lines, we'll have to first parse the file with sort which we'll look at in the next section.

Some options to be aware of which can be used with sort are shown in Table 10-2.

Table 10-2. *Options for uniq*

Flag	Description
-c	Count occurrences of each line
-d	Only show repeated lines
-i	Case insensitive
-s	Skip first N characters on each line (*requires number input*)
-u	Only show unique lines
-w	Only compare the first N lines (*requires number input*)

sort

The sort utility is used for sorting lines in a file. To demonstrate, let's create a file which has numbers 1–5, followed by those same numbers again:

```
seq 1 5 > /tmp/numbers.txt && seq 1 5 >> /tmp/numbers.txt
```

Next let's view the output and then view the output a second time piping through sort:

```
cat /tmp/numbers.txt
sort /tmp/numbers.txt
```

The output from the first command should be in the order 1, 2, 3, 4, 5, 1, 2, 3, 4, 5, whereas the second command will sort the numbers as 1, 1, 2, 2, ...

This can be particularly useful in combination with uniq, because you can ensure alike lines are next to each other. Assuming you still have the /tmp/hello.txt file created in the uniq section, let's sort it and then get unique lines:

```
sort /tmp/hello.txt | uniq
```

With the combination of sort and uniq, you'll only get back one instance of each line, as shown in Figure 10-6.

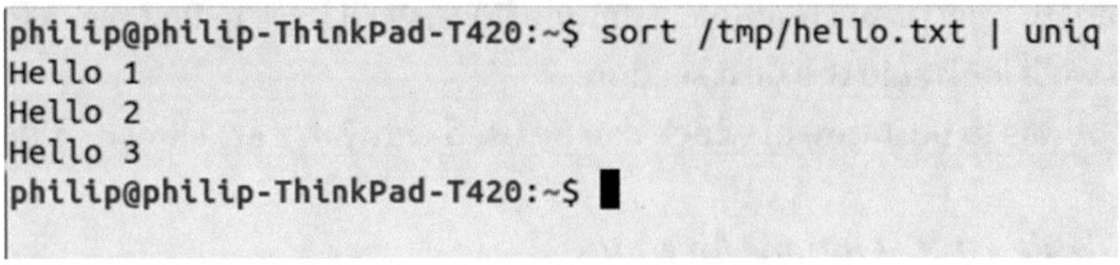

```
philip@philip-ThinkPad-T420:~$ sort /tmp/hello.txt | uniq
Hello 1
Hello 2
Hello 3
philip@philip-ThinkPad-T420:~$ █
```

Figure 10-6. *Using sort with uniq to only show a single instance of each line*

The same effect can be accomplished with sort alone using the -u option:

```
sort -u /tmp/hello.txt
```

As with the other utilities we've covered, sort has some useful options shown in Table 10-3.

Table 10-3. *Options for sort*

Flag	Description
-r	Reverse sort (*can be combined with other options*)
-n	Sort numerically
-d	Dictionary sort, considers only blank and alphanumeric characters
-k	Sort by column (*requires number input*)
-u	Only show unique lines
-M	Sort by month (*assumes month names in lines*)
-V	Version number sort

Regex

Regex isn't a utility itself but a standard form of text parsing which is used by several utilities and programming languages. Regex is short for regular expressions. A regular expression provides a pattern by which a string is tested again. A simple example, say we want to match either "Hello" or "Hi". The regular expression for that would be

```
(Hello|Hi)
```

grep has a special -E option for extended regex. So we can use the expression with grep. Before we do that, let's add a line that says "Hi 1" to the /tmp/hello.txt file we made in the last section:

```
echo "Hi 1" >> /tmp/hello.txt
```

With that done, run the following:

```
grep -E '(Hello|Hi)' /tmp/hello.txt
```

You should get back a match on every line, with the part that matched highlighted, like shown in Figure 10-7.

```
philip@philip-ThinkPad-T420:~$ grep -E '(Hello|Hi)' /tmp/hello.txt
Hello 1
Hello 1
Hello 1
Hello 2
Hello 2
Hello 3
Hello 1
Hi 1
philip@philip-ThinkPad-T420:~$ █
```

Figure 10-7. *Regex with grep*

The same regex format can be used with several utilities and programming languages: Perl, JavaScript, Python, and Ruby, just to name a few. For example, if you have perl installed, you can use the exact same regex:

```
perl -pe '(Hello|Hi)' /tmp/hello.txt
```

Beyond one word or another, we can actually use wildcards or specific classes to match again. Imagine you're writing software to validate serial codes for a product, and they come in the pattern of "number number number letter letter number." This pattern can be expressed as

```
[0-9][0-9][0-9][a-zA-Z][a-zA-Z][0-9]
```

Notice that for letters we're using [a-zA-Z]; this indicates that we'll accept both capital and lowercase. If we instead only wanted capital letters, we could do [A-Z].

Now let's say we wanted to make our serial code a bit harder to guess so we want the first number to be either 3, 5, or 8. We would update the expression using [358] for the first character:

```
[358][0-9][0-9][a-zA-Z][a-zA-Z][0-9]
```

This same pattern can be applied with both letters and numbers, for example, [123ABC] would match any of the characters listed. Another common similar use might be phone numbers:

```
[0-9]{3}[-][0-9]{3}[-][0-9]{4}
```

The preceding example introduces a new element we haven't used yet. Instead of defining each character in the number, we can do the short form [0-9]{3}, meaning three instances of [0-9]. So we have a three-digit number, followed by a dash, a three-digit number followed by a dash, and then a four-digit number.

One downside of the preceding regex is that it explicitly requires the dash. You can make any character optional by following it with ?. So if we want to take our same regex and make the dash optional, we would end up with

[0-9]{3}[-]?[0-9]{3}[-]?[0-9]{4}

Notice the addition of the two ?. So now our regex will match phone numbers with or without the dash. If you're from a country other than the USA/Canada, you may have to further adjust the regex to match the pattern used in your locale. In addition, this regex doesn't take into account things like the possibility of using "()" around numbers. However, using these simple elements, you can modify the regex to handle any type of phone number format.

To test the phone number example, let's open up the numbers.txt file created in the section on sort. Then add a line which contains a phone number in the format "519-555-0100". With that done, run the following command:

```
grep -E '[0-9]{3}[-]?[0-9]{3}[-]?[0-9]{4}' /tmp/numbers.txt
```

This should return only the newline added with the phone number.

Another common regex is for finding emails. This isn't a comprehensive example but one which will work for most phone numbers:

```
\S+@\S+\.\S+
```

In this example, we're making use of \S which is any nonspace character followed by +, meaning one or more of the previous characters. Thus, together \S+ means any amount of nonspace characters. Then we have an "@" symbol followed by another \S+; after that, we have \.; normally . is a wildcard character, but with the backslash, it takes on the literal meaning of ".". Then we finish off with another \S+.

Just like with phone numbers, if we add an email to the /tmp/numbers.txt file we made, we can test the regex as part of a command:

```
grep -E '\S+@\S+\.\S+' /tmp/numbers.txt
```

Table 10-4 contains a list of commonly used symbols in regex.

Table 10-4. *Regex symbols*

Special Charachter	Description
\s	Matches any space or tab
\S	Matches any nonspace character
\d	Matches any digit
\D	Matches any nondigit character
\w	Matches any word character
\W	Matches any nonword character
.	Matches any character
^	Start of line
$	End of line
*	Matches preceding character zero to any amount of times
+	Matches preceding character one or more times
?	Matches preceding character zero or one time
|	Or symbol used for either or expression

awk

awk is a pattern scanning and processing language and command-line utility tool. It excels at working with formatted text data. As an example, create the file /tmp/users.txt with the following text:

```
Jesse 4557389203 jesse@gmail.com xl 1991 1
Matt 8839293940 matt@hotmail.com s 1983 1
Jeff 8493739304 jeff@outlook.com l 1980 3
Sarah 4939304952 sarah@email.com m 1974 2
```

We'll use this file as sample data to process. Given the preceding data, we wanted to look at all the emails. We could run

```
awk '{ print $3 }' /tmp/users.txt
```

This should print out all the information for the third column as specified by $3, as shown in Figure 10-8.

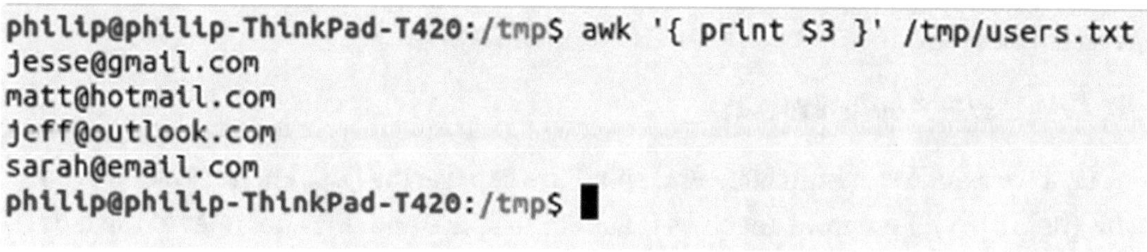

```
philip@philip-ThinkPad-T420:/tmp$ awk '{ print $3 }' /tmp/users.txt
jesse@gmail.com
matt@hotmail.com
jeff@outlook.com
sarah@email.com
philip@philip-ThinkPad-T420:/tmp$ ▮
```

Figure 10-8. *Printing third column in a file with awk*

We can mix and match these values and format them as we like, for example, getting the email and size and separating them by a space:

```
awk '{ print $3" "$4 }' /tmp/users.txt
```

Or say we want to generate a sentence (example output in Figure 10-9) using the information for each row of data:

```
awk '{ print "Hello "$1", thanks for buying a "$4" shirt" }'\
  /tmp/users.txt
```

```
philip@philip-ThinkPad-T420:/tmp$ awk '{ print "Hello "$1", thanks for buying a "$4" shirt" }'\
>   /tmp/users.txt
Hello Jesse, thanks for buying a xl shirt
Hello Matt, thanks for buying a s shirt
Hello Jeff, thanks for buying a l shirt
Hello Sarah, thanks for buying a m shirt
philip@philip-ThinkPad-T420:/tmp$ ▮
```

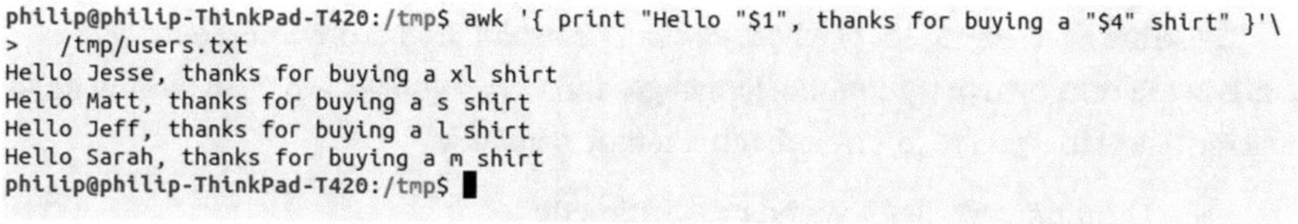

Figure 10-9. *Using columns as variables with awk*

We can also use basic search functionality to find specific rows, for example:

```
awk "/Jeff/" /tmp/users.txt
```

This should return the row with user Jeff, as shown in Figure 10-10.

```
philip@philip-ThinkPad-T420:/tmp$ awk "/Jeff/" /tmp/users.txt
Jeff 8493739304 jeff@outlook.com l 1980 3
philip@philip-ThinkPad-T420:/tmp$ █
```

Figure 10-10. *Searching for a string with awk*

The regex we looked at previously is compatible with awk as well. Say we want to get all users who are size "l" for large. We'll create some regex to find cases of "l" with a space /s on either side:

```
awk "/\sl\s/" /tmp/users.txt
```

Or if we want to get both large and small, we can use the (...|...) pattern like we did with (Hello|Hi). Remember each \s is actually a space and does not refer to the letter itself. So \ss\s actually means " s ":

```
awk "/(\sl\s|\ss\s)/" /tmp/users.txt
```

This should return entries with both small and large, as shown in Figure 10-11.

```
philip@philip-ThinkPad-T420:/tmp$ awk "/(\sl\s|\ss\s)/" /tmp/users.txt
Matt 8839293940 matt@hotmail.com s 1983 1
Jeff 8493739304 jeff@outlook.com l 1980 3
philip@philip-ThinkPad-T420:/tmp$ █
```

Figure 10-11. *Get users with size small or large using awk*

Any regex can be used with awk; simply put it in between the / / as we've seen.

These are a few examples of where awk can be useful. It's hardly comprehensive as awk is actually its own programming language, and whole books have been written about making use of it. If you're interested, other features include

- Creating .awk files invoked by awk directly

- Ability to define and use variables

- Support for writing stand-alone functions inside an awk script

- Built-in functions like a random number generator

- Support for if, else, and loops

sed

sed stands for stream editor, and it will be present on most Linux installations. There is significant overlap between what awk and sed can do. They both can be used to search text for matches or perform operations on data. For example, if we wanted to search for the row in /tmp/users.txt like we did with awk, we could do

```
sed -n "/Jeff/p" /tmp/users.txt
```

The -n flag disables sed automatically printing the file, and instead we'll only print the lines we specify. Then the p at the end of our match pattern stands for print.

Overall, I would recommend learning awk over sed as it's simpler to use and a more complete tool for more situations. However, there are a few things which are simpler with sed than awk. One of those things is finding and replacing text.

Let's take our sample data and replace "Jeff" with "Jeffery":

```
sed -i 's/Jeff/Jeffery/g' /tmp/users.txt
```

The -i here enables edit in place so the file we're reading from is changed. Then the s/ tells sed to use the substitute command. We then match Jeff, and on the other side of the /, we specify the replacement. Finally, the /g at the end specifies that this is a global change, rather than simply replacing the first match.

However, there is a small problem with the preceding command. If ran a second time, it will try to replace "Jeff" in "Jeffery." As with awk, we can specify matching of a space with \s and then use a literal space in our replace section:

```
sed -i 's/Jeff\s/Jeffery /g' /tmp/users.txt
```

You might recognize the \s from the regex table. As with awk, regex syntax is compatible with sed.

Using JQ to Work with JSON

Many of the older programs that are used on Linux were written in a time before JSON became the standard for information sharing between web apps. While programs like sed and grep are powerful for parsing and text manipulation, they are not well suited for dealing with JSON. The most popular command-line program for dealing with JSON is JQ, so much so that it has started to ship standard on many distributions such as Ubuntu.

JQ is a very fast JSON processor written in C. I asked the author if JQ stands for JSON Query, and he said that would make sense but he didn't intend for it to stand for anything. Nonetheless, you can think of it as a way to query and work with JSON.

Note   In this section, we'll be using Open Trivia DB as an example API to fetch JSON from. Feel free to substitute this for any other API. Of course you'll have to modify the commands specifically for the data you're working with. Some interesting APIs that don't require getting an API key include

Open Trivia DB – www.opentb.com

TheSportsDB – www.thesportsdb.com

The simplest thing you can do with JQ is pipe valid JSON into it and receive back a colored result, for example, with Open Trivia DB:

```
curl -s https://opentdb.com/api.php?amount=3 | jq
```

This should return the same JSON but color coded for easy reading as shown in Figure 10-12.

```
philip@philip-ThinkPad-T420:~$ curl -s https://opentdb.com/api.php?amount=3 | jq
{
  "response_code": 0,
  "results": [
    {
      "category": "Science: Computers",
      "type": "multiple",
      "difficulty": "medium",
      "question": "What does AD stand for in relation to Windows Operating Systems? ",
      "correct_answer": "Active Directory",
      "incorrect_answers": [
        "Alternative Drive",
        "Automated Database",
        "Active Department"
      ]
    },
```

Figure 10-12. Curl request being parsed with JQ

Already you'll find working with JQ is easier, especially if the server you're requesting had originally serve the JSON in a compressed format. Also notice that for `curl` we used the `-s` flag; without this, you'll see a little progress bar which needlessly wastes space.

Of course this is just the beginning; JQ is much more than a simple pretty print. Let's take the same data and work with it a little bit. Say, for example, we only want to display the first question from our query (*keep in mind the questions are random each request*).

```
curl -s https://opentdb.com/api.php?amount=3 \
  | jq '[ .results][0][0]'
```

We simply add [0] to get the first element in the array, similar to C-like languages you might be familiar with like JavaScript. In this situation, the results we actually wanted were wrapped in an outer array that contained only our target array, so it ended up being [0][0].

If you're familiar with working with arrays and objects in JavaScript or other languages, doing more complex things will come very easily to you. Say now we want to take the first question and select only the question text.

```
curl -s https://opentdb.com/api.php?amount=3 \
  | jq '[ .results][0][0]'.question
```

If the database format remains the same when you're reading this and you've copied the command correctly, you should see a question text displayed on your screen. Let's think back to our section on pipes and send the result to cowsay (not installed by default) just for fun.

```
curl -s https://opentdb.com/api.php?amount=3 \
  | jq '[ .results][0][0]'.question \
  | cowsay
```

The output should look something like Figure 10-13.

```
philip@philip-ThinkPad-T420:~$ curl -s https://opentdb.com/api.php?amount=3 \
>   | jq '[ .results][0][0]'.question \
>   | cowsay
 _____
/ "What was the unofficial name for \
\ Germany between 1919 and 1933?"   /
 -------------------------------
        \   ^__^
         \  (oo)_____
            (__)\       )\/\
                ||----w |
                ||     ||
```

Figure 10-13. Using JQ to get a question and piping it to cowsay

We can expand on the preceding example to create a full command line–based quiz game, by saving the result of the curl request in a script and fetching the questions and answers to display separately. For a full example of a command-line quiz bot which prints a list of potential answers and checks if the user responds with the correct answer, see the following link:

```
https://github.com/Apress/basic-linux-terminal-tips-and-tricks
```

Summary

In this chapter, we looked at utilities for parsing text from the command line and scripts. For plain text files or piped input, these include grep, cut, uniq, sort, awk, and sed. We saw that regex is extremely useful for matching patterns of text and is supported by several utilities and most popular programming languages. Finally, we saw how we can work with JSON which is often returned from web APIs by using the program JQ.

CHAPTER 11

systemd

We've explored looking at processes directly using tools like ps; another way to look at the processes running on a system is from the daemon perspective. A daemon is a long-running process which operates in the background of a system; often they're automatically started on system start by an init program like systemd. The "d" in systemd comes from the concept of daemon, as it acts as a controller for all daemons running on the system.

systemd is a scheduling system which has become widely used across Linux distributions. It is often the subject of both praise and criticism. Its central role in controlling system functionality in a number of areas including logging, scheduling, service monitoring, and system init has led some to say it is too centralized and goes against the Unix philosophy of each program doing one thing well. Defenders of systemd would point out that it is actually a collection of several binaries like systemctl and journald which each do one thing and work together to create a larger system.

Whatever you think of systemd, it has become so widespread that it's nearly impossible to avoid if you're using any popular Linux distribution. It was originally developed in 2010 at Red Hat as a way to replace older init systems particularly SysV-style init. By 2015 systemd had come to replace SysV init and other init systems on most popular distributions including CentOS, RHEL, Debian, Ubuntu, and SUSE.

systemctl

If your system is running systemd, you should have a command-line program called systemctl, short for system control. systemctl can be used to monitor, query, and modify the services and processes which are controlled by systemd. See Figure 11-1 for a visualization of the subtasks which are monitored and controlled by systemd.

© Philip Kirkbride 2020
P. Kirkbride, *Basic Linux Terminal Tips and Tricks*, https://doi.org/10.1007/978-1-4842-6035-7_11

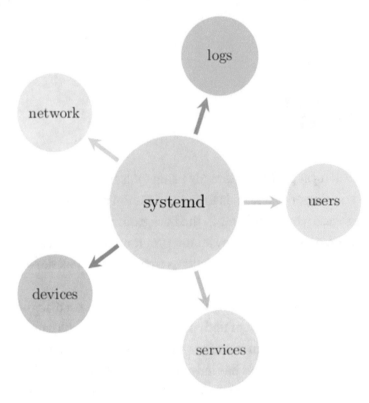

Figure 11-1. *Many uses of systemd*

systemctl is the system control which connects various aspects of the system keeping track of each service status, turning services on/off based on settings, and parsing service output and moving it to log files.

Running systemctl without any flags will return a list of active systemd units, like shown in Figure 11-2.

Figure 11-2. *Example output from running systemctl*

Stop, Start, Disable, and Enable Services

We've already used some of the commands we'll go over here, but it's worth reiterating as they're some of the most common commands you'll want to use for managing services with systemd.

Stop a Service

If a service is running and you want to stop it via systemd, simply run the following with sudo; we'll use the printing service cups as an example (no output shown on success):

```
sudo systemctl stop cups
```

Get Status of a Service

Next to ensure the service is off, we'll use the status command. This can come in useful in many situations when you're unsure of the status of a service.

```
sudo systemctl status cups
```

You'll get back not only the status of the service but the latest logs; see Figure 11-3 for an example. The addition of recent logs is a feature which was not present in the old System V service command.

```
philip@philip-ThinkPad-T420:/var/log$ systemctl status cups
● cups.service - CUPS Scheduler
   Loaded: loaded (/lib/systemd/system/cups.service; enabled; vendor preset: enabled)
   Active: inactive (dead) since Mon 2019-12-23 19:40:27 EST; 46s ago
     Docs: man:cupsd(8)
  Process: 4044 ExecStart=/usr/sbin/cupsd -l (code=exited, status=0/SUCCESS)
 Main PID: 4044 (code=exited, status=0/SUCCESS)

Dec 23 12:09:30 philip-ThinkPad-T420 systemd[1]: Started CUPS Scheduler.
Dec 23 19:40:27 philip-ThinkPad-T420 systemd[1]: Stopping CUPS Scheduler...
Dec 23 19:40:27 philip-ThinkPad-T420 systemd[1]: Stopped CUPS Scheduler.
philip@philip-ThinkPad-T420:/var/log$ █
```

Figure 11-3. *Getting the status of a specific program with systemctl*

Notice the logs at the bottom which display a time and messages for starting and stopping.

Start a Service

Next let's turn the service back on; as you may have guessed, it can be done with the following command:

```
sudo systemctl start cups
```

After running start, rerun the status command and confirm that cups is running again.

Disable a Service

Stop and start deal with the state of a service in the current session. Disable and enable deal with the state of a service during the startup of a new session after a machine is turned on. Simply using stop on a service will result in it restarting every time the computer is stopped. To fully turn off a service for good, the disable command should be used:

```
sudo systemctl disable cups
```

Again, after running, check the status and observe the differences.

Enable a Service

As you probably guessed, the opposite of disable is enable:

```
sudo systemctl enable cups
```

After testing disabling a command, be sure to turn the service back to enabled if you want it to continue starting on boot.

Unit Files

Programs communicate their configurations to systemd via unit files, which are ini files located in the /etc/systemd/system/ folder. The simplest unit file just tells systemd to keep the program running. Let's create an example program and unit file to demonstrate; call it logTime.sh. I've created mine in the /tmp folder since I don't plan to keep it.

```
#!/usr/bin/env bash

while true
  do
    echo time is $(date)
    sleep 5
  done
```

Once you've written the script, give it executable permission with the following command:

```
chmod +x logTime.sh
```

Go into the folder /etc/systemd/system; this is where you can place unit files which configure programs to work with systemd. We'll create the simplest possible unit file for our script which simply logs time; name the file logTime.service. You'll need to have root permissions to edit and create files in /etc/systemd/system.

```
[Service]
ExecStart=/tmp/logTime.sh
```

With the unit file saved, you can now turn on the service.

```
sudo systemctl start logTime
```

Next we'll get the status of the daemon.

```
sudo systemctl status logTime
```

This should return some information telling us the service is active and show the most recent logs, like shown in Figure 11-4.

```
philip@philip-ThinkPad-T420:/etc/systemd/system$ sudo systemctl start logTime
philip@philip-ThinkPad-T420:/etc/systemd/system$ sudo systemctl status logTime
● logTime.service
   Loaded: loaded (/etc/systemd/system/logTime.service; static; vendor preset: enabled)
   Active: active (running) since Sat 2019-12-14 10:06:08 EST; 8s ago
 Main PID: 6832 (bash)
    Tasks: 2 (limit: 4915)
   CGroup: /system.slice/logTime.service
           ├─6832 bash /tmp/logTime.sh
           └─6852 sleep 5

Dec 14 10:06:08 philip-ThinkPad-T420 systemd[1]: Started logTime.service.
Dec 14 10:06:08 philip-ThinkPad-T420 logTime.sh[6832]: time is Sat Dec 14 10:06:08 EST 2019
Dec 14 10:06:13 philip-ThinkPad-T420 logTime.sh[6832]: time is Sat Dec 14 10:06:13 EST 2019
```

Figure 11-4. *Starting custom unit file and checking status*

You can actively watch the logs as they are generated using journalctl.

sudo journalctl -u logTime -f

This can be useful when you want to investigate some specific service that is running on your machine. If it doesn't seem to be acting right or is taking too much resources, looking at the logs may give you hints as to the issue.

There are several other options that can be set in the unit file. The following is a more complete unit file with comments to describe what each line does:

[Unit]
# Description of what the program does
Description=Log time every 5 seconds
# List services needed for this service to work
After=time-sync.target

[Service]
# Path to executable
ExecStart=/tmp/logTime.sh
# Policy for restarting when stops
Restart=always
# Working directory for executable
WorkingDirectory=/tmp
# The user the process will run under
User=philip
# User group for the process
Group=philip

```
# Set environment variables
Environment=MYVAR=var

[Install]
# Which programs require the unit
# multi-user.target is when linux start
# Adding this line makes the program start when system is booting
WantedBy=multi-user.target
```

If you manually modify a service file, you'll need to do a soft reset on systemd with the following command:

```
sudo systemctl daemon-reload
```

Even though the final line tells the program to turn on during boot, it needs to be enabled to actually take the unit file into account.

```
sudo systemctl enable logTime
```

This will activate the service. If you want to disable the service, simply run

```
sudo systemctl disable logTime
```

The disable command is extremely useful. Say, for example, you check running services and see a program that you aren't using and don't need. You kill the process or turn it off, only to find that the next time you restart your computer, it's back again. If you encounter that situation, systemctl disable may be able to solve it.

After you finish this section, make sure to delete the service file we created in /etc/systemd/system. If you created the executable in the /tmp directory like we did here, the service will fail after your first restart if you don't remove it by deleting the service file.

Find Running Services

When you log in to a machine, you'll likely want to figure out what services are already running. The command we previously looked at systemctl, for enabling and disabling our logTime service, can also be used to get a complete list of services running on a machine.

`systemctl` is short for system control and is systemd's command for controlling the services on a system. Given that, nearly all services will be launched through systemd (*at least the ones that automatically start after a restart*).

The simplest command you can do with `systemctl` is run it stand-alone:

```
systemctl
```

This will return a list of processes which are currently active on the system, as shown in Figure 11-5.

```
UNIT                                                                                    LOAD   ACTIVE SUB      DESCRIPTION
proc-sys-fs-binfmt_misc.automount                                                       loaded active running  Arbitrary Executable File
sys-devices-pci0000:00-0000:00:01.0-0000:01:00.0-backlight-acpi_video1.device loaded active plugged   /sys/devices/pci0000:00/00
sys-devices-pci0000:00-0000:00:01.0-0000:01:00.0-drm-card1-card1\x2dLVDS\x2d2-nv_backlight.device loaded active plugged   /sys/d
sys-devices-pci0000:00-0000:00:01.0-0000:01:00.1-sound-card1.device                     loaded active plugged   GF119 HDMI Audio Controlle
sys-devices-pci0000:00-0000:00:02.0-backlight-acpi_video0.device                        loaded active plugged   /sys/devices/pci0000:00/00
sys-devices-pci0000:00-0000:00:02.0-drm-card0-card0\x2dLVDS\x2d1-intel_backlight.device loaded active plugged   /sys/devices/pci
sys-devices-pci0000:00-0000:00:16.3-tty-ttyS4.device                                    loaded active plugged   6 Series/C200 Series Chips
sys-devices-pci0000:00-0000:00:19.0-net-enp0s25.device                                  loaded active plugged   82579LM Gigabit Network Co
sys-devices-pci0000:00-0000:00:1b.0-sound-card0.device                                  loaded active plugged   6 Series/C200 Series Chips
sys-devices-pci0000:00-0000:00:1c.1-0000:03:00.0-net-wlp3s0.device                      loaded active plugged   Centrino Advanced-N 6205 [
sys-devices-pci0000:00-0000:00:1f.2-ata1-host0-target0:0:0-0:0:0:0-block-sda-sda1.device loaded active plugged   SanDisk_SDSSDA2
sys-devices-pci0000:00-0000:00:1f.2-ata1-host0-target0:0:0-0:0:0:0-block-sda-sda2.device loaded active plugged   SanDisk_SDSSDA2
sys-devices-pci0000:00-0000:00:1f.2-ata1-host0-target0:0:0-0:0:0:0-block-sda-sda3.device loaded active plugged   SanDisk_SDSSDA2
sys-devices-pci0000:00-0000:00:1f.2-ata1-host0-target0:0:0-0:0:0:0-block-sda-sda4.device loaded active plugged   SanDisk_SDSSDA2
sys-devices-pci0000:00-0000:00:1f.2-ata1-host0-target0:0:0-0:0:0:0-block-sda.device loaded active plugged   SanDisk_SDSSDA240G
sys-devices-pci0000:00-0000:00:1f.2-ata2-host1-target1:0:0-1:0:0:0-block-sr0.device loaded active plugged   HL-DT-STDVDRAM_GT33N
sys-devices-platform-serial8250-tty-ttyS0.device                                        loaded active plugged   /sys/devices/platform/seri
sys-devices-platform-serial8250-tty-ttyS1.device                                        loaded active plugged   /sys/devices/platform/seri
```

Figure 11-5. *Output from systemctl*

This lists everything and it can be hard to read through. If you want to look at specifically unit file services that are running, you can use

```
systemctl list-units --type service
```

Another useful thing about this is that you can see services which are set to be running but have failed for some reason, as is the case with `postfix@-.service` in Figure 11-6.

```
networking.service                      loaded active exited  Raise network interfaces
NetworkManager-wait-online.service      loaded active exited  Network Manager Wait Online
NetworkManager.service                  loaded active running Network Manager
nordvpnd.service                        loaded active running NordVPN Daemon
openvpn.service                         loaded active exited  OpenVPN service
packagekit.service                      loaded active running PackageKit Daemon
polkit.service                          loaded active running Authorization Manager
postfix@-.service                       loaded failed failed  Postfix Mail Transport Agent (instance -)
postgresql.service                      loaded active exited  PostgreSQL RDBMS
postgresql@10-main.service              loaded active running PostgreSQL Cluster 10-main
rsyslog.service                         loaded active running System Logging Service
rtkit-daemon.service                    loaded active running RealtimeKit Scheduling Policy Service
setvtrgb.service                        loaded active exited  Set console scheme
snapd.seeded.service                    loaded active exited  Wait until snapd is fully seeded
lines 1-44
```

Figure 11-6. *Listing services only with systemctl*

If we wanted to look at only failed services, we could add the --state failed flag to our previous command.

Also, take note of the services that are active but have exited, meaning technically they are working but not running. To see only programs which are currently running, you can use the command:

```
systemctl list-units --type service --state failed
```

Another useful command will allow you to see all the unit files and their current status:

```
systemctl list-unit-files --type service
```

This will output all the unit files and their current status, example shown in Figure 11-7.

```
philip@philip-ThinkPad-T420:~$ systemctl list-unit-files --type service
UNIT FILE                          STATE
accounts-daemon.service            enabled
acpid.service                      disabled
alsa-restore.service               static
alsa-state.service                 static
alsa-utils.service                 masked
anacron.service                    enabled
apache-htcacheclean.service        disabled
apache-htcacheclean@.service       disabled
apache2.service                    enabled
apache2@.service                   disabled
apparmor.service                   enabled
apport-autoreport.service          static
apport-forward@.service            static
apport.service                     generated
apt-daily-upgrade.service          static
apt-daily.service                  static
atop.service                       enabled
atopacct.service                   enabled
autovt@.service                    enabled
avahi-daemon.service               enabled
```

Figure 11-7. *Listing unit files with systemctl*

There are several possible states, which are listed in Table 11-1. The most popular are enabled, disabled, and static.

Table 11-1. *Possible service states with systemd*

State	Description
enabled	Service is turned on
disabled	Service is turned off
static	Service can't be turned on/off, dependency or single run script
masked	Locked so it can't be turned on even manually
linked	Made available through a system link
indirect	Indirectly enabled
generated	Dynamically generated via generator tool
transient	Dynamically generated via runtime API
bad	Invalid unit file

For more details on these states, you can run

```
man systemctl list-unit-files
```

journalctl

systemd doesn't just handle scheduling tasks. It also plays a part in directing the logs that are generated from running services. That's where journalctl comes in, short for journal control. As with systemctl, the simplest command you can run is journalctl by itself.

```
journalctl
```

This will return a list of all logs created through systemd. We can watch a live version of this file as it updates by using the -f flag:

```
journalctl -f
```

This will display any logs as they happen; to exit, you can press ctrl+c.

journalctl has many options which spare you from having to come up with complex parsers yourself; Table 11-2 contains a list of several useful options.

Table 11-2. *List of options for journalctl*

Option	Description
-f	Get live stream of logs
-k	Show kernel logs
-u <service>	Show service for specific service
-b	Show boot messages
-r	Sort in reverse order
-p	Sort by process priority
_PID=<number>	Get logs from specific process ID
_UID=<number>	Get logs from specific user ID
_GID=<number>	Get logs from specific group ID

journalctl – Parsing by Time

In addition to the preceding flags, it is also possible to parse logs between specific times using the --since and --until flags, for example:

```
journalctl --since yesterday
```

up until a time using basic hour notation

```
journalctl --until 13:00
```

or using a combination of the two

```
journalctl --since "2 days ago" --until yesterday
```

Traditional timestamps are also supported:

```
journalctl --since "2019-12-24 23:15:00" --until "2019-12-25"
```

Other Init Systems

While systemd has become widely used, there are still several places where you'll find other init systems – just to name a few examples:

- Minimal Linux versions like Alpine Linux

- Older versions of Linux

- Less used operating systems

- Highly customized operating systems

SysV Init

Before systemd became the standard, classic Linux systems used SysV init. The word "init" refers to the first process started during boot. You can still see it by running

```
ps -up 1
```

However, the script itself will likely be a systemd version of init. systemd was purposefully designed to be SysV init compatible. With SysV init, the kernel starts the init process, which handles changing the systems state for booting, rebooting, and shutting down. With SysV, there are eight different runlevels defined in Table 11-3.

Table 11-3. *Runlevels on SysV*

Runlevel	Directory	Use
N	--	System boot
0	/etc/rc0.d/	Halt system
1	/etc/rc1.d/	Single-user mode
2	/etc/rc2.d/	Multiuser mode
3	/etc/rc3.d/	Multiuser with networking
4	/etc/rc4.d/	Reserved for custom runlevels
5	/etc/rc5.d/	Graphic user interface started (*X11*)
6	/etc/rc6.d/	Reboot

As the system starts, it moves between runlevels, not always sequentially, for example, going into single-user mode (runlevel 1) is a special state. When your OS becomes broken during initiation, for example, a script in /etc like /etc/fstab is broken, you will only be able to log in to single-user mode with user root. Other levels are more sequential, for example, normally one would pass through runlevels 2 and 3 before arriving at level 5.

The folder associated with each of the levels contained bash scripts associated with the programs that need to be started at that level.

Note   While runlevels are crucial to SysV-style init, they still exist in systemd init with the same levels N, 0, and 1 - 6. On most systems, you can see your current runlevel by running who -r.

Upstart

Another previously popular init system is Upstart (*last release was in 2014*). Upstart was used on Ubuntu before they switched to systemd as of Debian 8. Despite this, you'll still find Upstart in use today.

Upstart is made to look like other init systems and does not include a command called "upstart". If you're unsure your OS is running Upstart, you can check for the binary with

```
ps -eaf | grep '[u]pstart'
```

If you see some processes other than the grep call itself, your system has Upstart installed. You can use it to check what services are running with

```
service --status-all
```

This will return a list of services and their status. You can interact with the services by interacting with their init scripts directly, for example:

```
sudo /etc/init.d/ssh status
```

Or to restart a service, run

```
sudo /etc/init.d/ssh restart
```

This method of interaction isn't actually specific to Upstart. Even on systemd systems, you'll find many programs have a /etc/init.d file which can be interacted with directly like shown earlier.

Summary

In this chapter, we looked at the systemd system and how it is used to control what programs are running on your system. We looked at how systemctl can be used to work with these services by stopping, starting, enabling, and disabling. To look at services running and their logs, we explored the use of journald. We even created our own unit file to make a systemd service from scratch.

CHAPTER 12

Vim

Sooner or later, you're going to want to start using a terminal-based text editor, if not full time, then at least when you're remotely logged in to a server or device.

Many system admins end up relying on nano, a simple text editor that is preinstalled on many systems. The main advantage of nano is that it's easily understood and usable by new users. In the long run, using nano will slow you down significantly. With nano, you end up having to hold down the arrow keys or delete for long periods as you try to navigate a text document.

Vim creates a solution to this by creating a keyboard-based syntax for navigating around a document and making changes quickly without the need for a mouse. In one keystroke, you can go from the top of a document to the bottom G and back again with two gg. Vim has all kinds of keystroke-based commands like this that help you move quickly and edit.

Modes

As mentioned in the previous chapter, many keys are bound to special movements or command, for example, G to go to the bottom of the document. So what about when you actually want to type "G" into the document? This is where modes come in. There are two main modes in Vim and a third less used but still important mode:

- Normal mode – For running commands like G

- Insert mode – For writing text like you would in other editors

- Visual mode – For selecting text, similar to highlighting text with a mouse

© Philip Kirkbride 2020
P. Kirkbride, *Basic Linux Terminal Tips and Tricks*, https://doi.org/10.1007/978-1-4842-6035-7_12

Common Commands

When you open a document in Vim, you'll be in normal mode by default. Normal mode is where Vim-specific commands are run. Some of the most common you'll want to be familiar with are shown in Table 12-1.

Table 12-1. *Vim commands*

Command	Description
:q	Quit Vim
:w	Save the document
:x	Save and exit
i	Enter insert mode
:u	Undo
ctrl+r	Redo
<Esc>	Return to normal mode from insert mode
:e <filename>	Open a file with Vim already open
:h	Help screen

Take note of how to exit Vim; it's a common issue and joke that newcomers to the program have extreme difficulty with exiting the program.

Note   Often people have trouble exiting Vim. When in normal mode, you can press :q. If you've changed the file, you'll get a prompt above an unsaved file. You can save a file with :w and combine the two actions as :wq. Save and quit can also be done with a slightly shorter command :x.

Using Help Command

If ever you find yourself forgetting the Vim basics, you can open up the help page by running :h. This will bring you to a general help page. If you need information on a specific command, you can follow the :h with the command, for example:

:h G

This will bring up the specific help text for the G command, as shown in Figure 12-1.

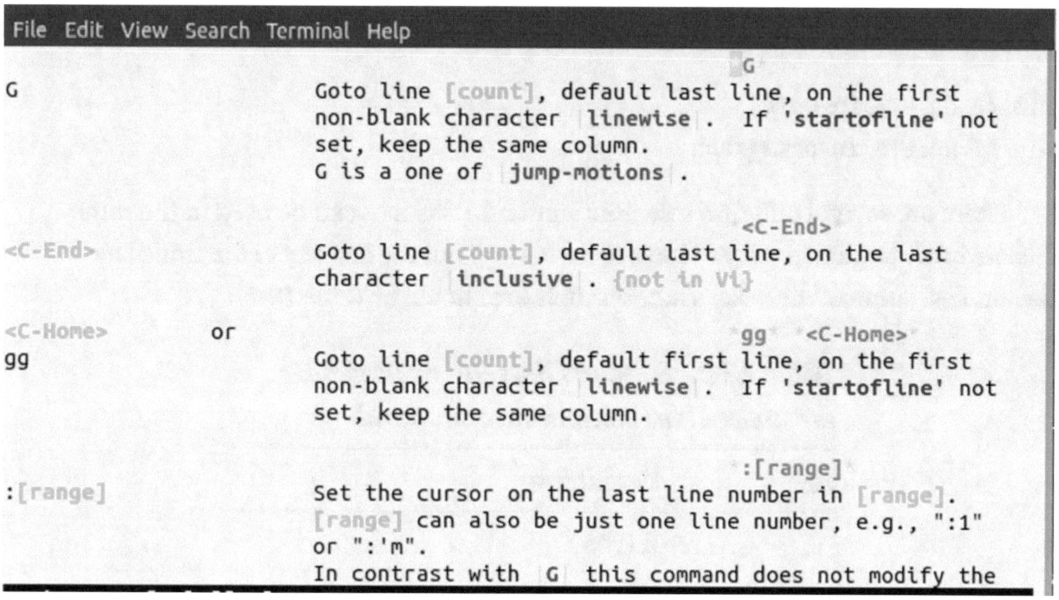

```
 File  Edit  View  Search  Terminal  Help
                                                  G
G                            Goto line [count], default last line, on the first
                             non-blank character  linewise .  If 'startofline' not
                             set, keep the same column.
                             G is a one of  jump-motions .

                                                  <C-End>
<C-End>                      Goto line [count], default last line, on the last
                             character  inclusive . {not in Vi}

<C-Home>           or                            gg  <C-Home>
gg                           Goto line [count], default first line, on the first
                             non-blank character  linewise .  If 'startofline' not
                             set, keep the same column.

                                                 :[range]
:[range]                     Set the cursor on the last line number in [range].
                             [range] can also be just one line number, e.g., ":1"
                             or ":'m".
                             In contrast with  G  this command does not modify the
```

Figure 12-1. *Help screen for G command*

Compound Commands

One of the great things about Vim is that commands can be combined in a way that it has a very simple language for combining commands. Certain power commands can be strung together to create new commands. Doing things like "delete inside quotes" can be accomplished in three keystrokes; simply press

di" // delete in quotes

The preceding command represents three smaller components strung together:

```
d = delete
i = in
" = quotes
```

Now that you know how to delete in quotes, how do you think you delete inside brackets?

```
di) // delete in brackets
```

Delete the current word? Delete in paragraph?

```
diw // delete in word
dip // delete in paragraph
```

There are several different selectors similar to this that can be used in the same "delete in X" sequence. All you have to do is swap out the last key in the three key sequences. Some of these keys and symbols are shown in Table 12-2.

Table 12-2. *Selectors that can be used with the "deleted in" compound command*

Key	Description
"	Quotes
(, {, [, <	Various bracket types
t	HTML tag
p	Paragraph
w	Word

Note   For any of the brackets like (, {, and [listed earlier, you can also use the closing version of said bracket for the same effect.

We can also take all these statements and swap out the first letter to change the meaning. Some example compound commands are shown in Table 12-3. In rare cases the adjective might not be needed at all. For example 'diw' can be further simplified to 'dw'.

Table 12-3. *Examples of compound commands*

Verb	(Number)	Adjective	Noun	Description
c	--	i	t	Create - in - HTML tag
d	4	--	l	Delete four letters
c	--	a	<	Delete - around - < bracket
d	2	--	w	Delete two words

Selecting with Visual Mode

Vim has a third mode which provides functionality which is similar to that provided by highlighting a block of text with your mouse in other programs. For example, open up /etc/passwd with Vim (make sure not to use sudo or root as we don't want to save any changes to this file, better yet copy /etc/passwd into your /tmp folder and practice editing the copy).

With the file open, press v; this will cause you to enter visual mode. Now that you're in visual mode, press the down arrow on the keyboard or j; as you move down the text, your highlighting will change. See Figure 12-2 for an example of what you should see.

Figure 12-2. *Selecting text in visual mode*

Now with the text highlighted, we can perform operations on it. If we press d, all of our highlighted text will be deleted.

Notice that we have the hanging selected character in the previous image for the word "games". A nice way to avoid this is to enter visual line select mode, which is the same as visual select mode but only highlights full lines. To use visual line select, use shift+v instead of just v.

While this might look similar to what you're used to using your mouse in a normal text editor, Vim visual mode is actually much more powerful. Instead of selecting lines of text, we can instead select a vertical chunk of code. To do this, first make sure you're in normal mode by pressing esc. Now press ctrl+v and scroll down using j or the down arrow.

After scrolling down four lines, press l a few times or the right arrow key. Notice we're doing the same thing we did above with visual mode but selecting a vertical chunk of code, which will be highlighted as shown in Figure 12-3.

Figure 12-3. *Selecting vertically in visual mode*

From this point, we can perform an operation on the selected code like d for delete or press esc to switch unselect and go back to normal mode. Another common use for visual mode is to prepend all your lines with some common text. For example, say we want to comment out the first four lines of code. Return to the top left-hand corner and press ctrl+v. Next, scroll down four lines and press ctrl+I (must be capital I); this enters into insert mode but we'll actually be typing on all four lines at once.

Now if we type # , the change will be repeated on each line, like in Figure 12-4. When you're happy with the inserted text, press esc to finish the operation. If we want to uncomment the lines, we can use the technique of selecting a vertical chunk of code and pressing d to delete what we've just added.

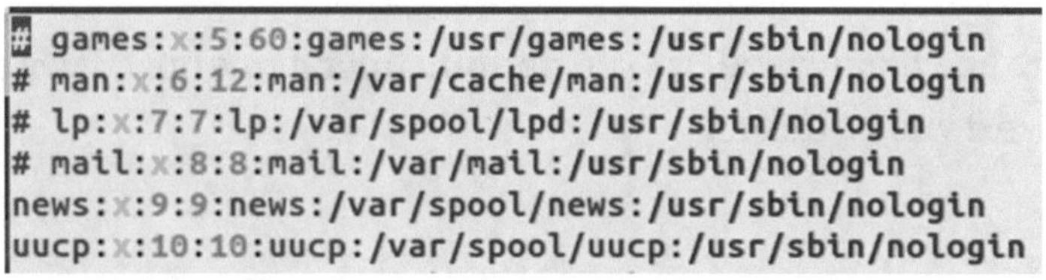

Figure 12-4. *Adding a hash sign to the start of several lines at once*

Make sure not to save any of these changes. To exit Vim without saving, you can press
:q! in normal mode.

Vim Tutor

When you install Vim, it also comes with another executable called vimtutor. When you
run it, a tutorial will open that walks you through using Vim. The first lesson from Vim
tutor is shown in Figure 12-5.

```
~~~~~~~~~~~~~~~~~~~~~~~~~~~~~~~~~~~~~~~~~~~~~~~~~~~~~~~~~~~~~~~~~~~~~~~~~~~~~~~~~~~
                      Lesson 1.1:  MOVING THE CURSOR


   ** To move the cursor, press the h,j,k,l keys as indicated. **
          ^
          k               Hint:  The h key is at the left and moves left.
    < h       l >                The l key is at the right and moves right.
          j                      The j key looks like a down arrow.
          v
  1. Move the cursor around the screen until you are comfortable.

  2. Hold down the down key (j) until it repeats.
     Now you know how to move to the next lesson.

  3. Using the down key, move to Lesson 1.2.

NOTE: If you are ever unsure about something you typed, press <ESC> to place
      you in Normal mode.  Then retype the command you wanted.

NOTE: The cursor keys should also work.  But using hjkl you will be able to
      move around much faster, once you get used to it.  Really!

~~~~~~~~~~~~~~~~~~~~~~~~~~~~~~~~~~~~~~~~~~~~~~~~~~~~~~~~~~~~~~~~~~~~~~~~~~~~~~~~~~~
                      Lesson 1.2: EXITING VIM
```

Figure 12-5. *Vim tutor*

It contains detailed lessons doing simple things like moving the cursor, editing,
deleting, and creating text. It's recommended you work your way through Vim tutor to
get the hang of doing common things in Vim.

Find Text

Another common thing you'll want to do when navigating text is finding some specific string of text. This can be done in normal mode using the / key. First press / and then type in the string you're searching for. You'll see your input in the bottom-left corner of the screen. After inputting your search phrase press enter and your cursor will go to the next instance of the string based on your cursors starting location.

With your cursor on the first instance, you can press n to go to the next instance or N to go to the previous instance.

Searching can be a powerful way to navigate a document and is often followed by a combination command like cw for "create word."

Find and Replace

Sometimes when you're searching, what you really want to do is find all instances of a variable or word and replace it with another name or word. This is also fairly easy in Vim once you memorize the command.

```
:%s/old/new/g
```

The %s here stands for substitute; then we have the old word, followed by what we'll replace it with. The g in this case stands for global, meaning we want to replace all instances of "old" with "new." Running the same command without the g will replace only the first instance found.

Another useful option that can be used with substitute is i for case insensitive (*same as with regex*), for example:

```
:%s/old/new/gi
```

This will replace any match of the word regardless of whether it uses a capital or lowercase for any of the letters.

Run a Command

It's also possible to run a Unix command from within Vim. As an example, let's create a file called "vim" in the /tmp folder:

```
:!touch /tmp/vim
```

On pressing enter, you'll go into a shell instance where the results of the command are shown. Then pressing enter again, you'll return to Vim. This can be handy for quick commands without leaving Vim or changing windows.

In addition to running one-off commands, it's also possible to run a full window terminal within Vim. You can open a mini-terminal in Vim by running :terminal or :term for short. It will open a new terminal session in the top half of the window like in Figure 12-6.

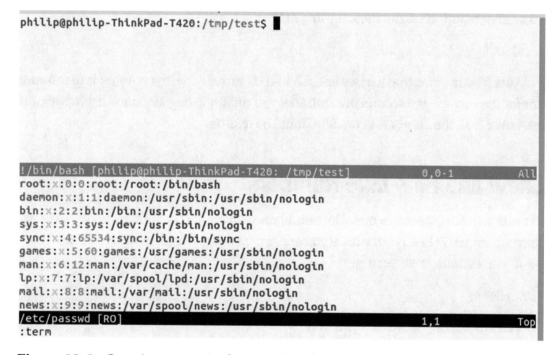

Figure 12-6. *Opening a terminal session inside Vim*

The terminal window shows on top, and you can quickly move back and forth between the in-app terminal and the text you're editing. To switch between the two windows, press ctrl+w followed by w.

To close the terminal window, first press ctrl+w and then press :q! followed by enter in the same way you would to force close a normal window.

Vim Sort Command

Another handy built-in command is Vim's sort, which is similar to the command-line sort utility we looked at in a previous chapter. To demonstrate sort, go into the /tmp folder and create a file with ten random numbers between 1 and 99:

```
for i in `seq 10`;
  do echo ${RANDOM:0:2};
done > /tmp/numbers.txt
```

Now if we open up /tmp/numbers.txt, you should have ten unsorted numbers, each on a different line. Next run the following in Vim:

```
:1,5!sort
```

After hitting enter, the first five lines should be sorted. The first number is the starting line for the sort and the second the end. So if you run the same command again with a 10 instead of 5, all the numbers in the file should be in order.

Show and Hide Line Numbers

In the last section, we made use of line numbers with the sort command, and it was easy since we started at line 1, but what if you are in the middle of a long file? If you need to see the line numbers, you can run

```
:set number
```

Then to remove numbers again, run

```
:set nonumber
```

Swap Files

As you use Vim, you may notice the creation of files with the extension .swp. These are backup files automatically created and deleted when you properly close Vim. If for some reason your SSH connection is disrupted or Vim closes unexpectedly, you'll have a chance to recover your changes. Just reopen the file which has an associated .swp file, and you'll see a screen like in Figure 12-7.

```
E325: ATTENTION
Found a swap file by the name ".vim.swp"
          owned by: philip    dated: Sat Jan 11 15:00:04 2020
         file name: /tmp/vim
          modified: YES
         user name: philip    host name: philip-ThinkPad-T420
        process ID: 7187
While opening file "vim"
              dated: Sat Jan 11 14:58:47 2020

(1) Another program may be editing the same file.  If this is the case,
    be careful not to end up with two different instances of the same
    file when making changes.  Quit, or continue with caution.
(2) An edit session for this file crashed.
    If this is the case, use ":recover" or "vim -r vim"
    to recover the changes (see ":help recovery").
    If you did this already, delete the swap file ".vim.swp"
    to avoid this message.

Swap file ".vim.swp" already exists!
[O]pen Read-Only, (E)dit anyway, (R)ecover, (D)elete it, (Q)uit, (A)bort: ▮
```

Figure 12-7. *Vim when opening a file that has a swap file*

Notice the options displayed at the bottom of the page. To recover the changes, press R. If you don't want to recover the changes, you should press D; otherwise, you'll see this message every time you open that file until the .swp file is removed.

Summary

In this chapter, we looked at how we can use the Vim text editor to increase productivity. It allows you to quickly manipulate text without the use of a mouse which can cause you to lose context. We looked at some of the three main modes Vim has – normal mode, insert mode, and visual mode. We also saw how Vim has its own language that can be used to create compound commands such as ciw which stands for "create in word." While this chapter only showed a small section of what is possible with Vim, hopefully it serves as a starting point that allows you to make use of the editor and increase the speed at which you can edit files.

CHAPTER 13

Emacs

In this chapter, we're going to talk about a very popular editor in the Linux world. Emacs is one of the oldest and most liked editors. While Vim is quite compact and focuses simply on the task of editing files, Emacs is more of a platform which "modes" can be created for. Different modes in Emacs interpret commands and text in different ways.

Modes can be related to the type of text file being edited, for example, a mode specific to programming Python, JavaScript, C++, and so on. However, modes can also be like programs, for example, org-agenda which provides a fully functional agenda, to-do lists, and calendar or EWW which provides a functional web browser without ever leaving Emacs. There are even community-made modes which tie into external APIs, for example, `telega` mode which provides a fully functional Telegram chat application embedded into Emacs.

We won't look at every mode or even all the features which come standard in Emacs as that would take a whole book in itself. Instead, we'll survey a few of the interesting ones which are useful from the terminal and can provide a starting point if you wish to delve deeper into the Emacs world.

Note When discussing Emacs, I'll use their standard syntax for describing commands. When you see something like

`M-x run-command`

the "M-x" stands for press "x" while holding the modifier key, which on most machines will be the ALT key.

The second thing you'll see is RET; this simply stands for press the enter key.

247

© Philip Kirkbride 2020
P. Kirkbride, *Basic Linux Terminal Tips and Tricks*, https://doi.org/10.1007/978-1-4842-6035-7_13

Installing Emacs

A relatively up-to-date version of Emacs can be found on most package managers. To install Emacs on a Debian-based system, run

```
sudo apt-get install emacs
```

At the time of writing, we found the GPG key that ships with the program to verify packages on ELPA (Emacs Lisp Package Archive) was out of date. You can manually update the key with the following command:

```
gpg --homedir ~/.emacs.d/elpa/gnupg \
  --receive-keys 066DAFCB81E42C40
```

Depending on the time of reading, the key above 066DAFCB81E42C40 may need to be changed. Check the GNU website link, https://elpa.gnu.org/packages/gnu-elpa-keyring-update.html, where you can find the most up-to-date key to be used with the command in the body of the "Full description."

In order to tell Emacs to make use of the MELPA package archive, you'll have to create a file in your home folder called .emacs. It should contain the following code:

```
(require 'package)
(add-to-list 'package-archives '("melpa" . "https://melpa.org/packages/"))
(package-initialize)
```

Vim Bindings aka Emacs Evil Mode

I love Vim because you can find it almost anywhere, if not in full, then at least the limited version vi. What makes Vim great for me is that the keybindings allow me to modify and enter data extremely quickly. Yet when it comes to interesting modes, modules, and extensions, I prefer Emacs for a lot of things.

Examples of interesting modules we'll look at include artist-mode, org-mode, presentations, and tramp. Before we take a look at those modules, we'll enable Vim keybindings so we can use the best features of Vim we've looked at while running Emacs. It's worth noting that several other programs and IDEs offer optional Vim keybindings (with various levels of quality in implementation), for example, VS Code and Qt Creator. Some terminal programs like Ranger even use them by default, while others like bash allow you to set them with an option.

To enable Vim keybindings on Emacs, we first need to install the module "evil-mode"; the name is half a joke about the Emacs vs. Vim rivalry and half word play based on e (Emacs) + vi (Vim).

Before installing any package, you should update the local package list. This is similar to updating your OS package manager, for example, on Debian `apt-get update`. To update the Emacs package manager, run the following command:

```
M-x package-refresh-contents
```

To install evil-mode, you can use the built-in package manager MELPA. Run the following:

```
M-x package-list-packages
```

This will show a list of all available packages on MELPA. Next we'll install evil-mode using

```
M-x package-install RET evil
```

This will install the package, and in the bottom left of the screen, you should see "Done." With the package installed, you should be able to run the following command to enable the keybindings for your current session:

```
M-x evil-mode
```

However, after closing Emacs and reopening, the bindings will no longer be enabled. To ensure that the bindings are enabled by default on opening Emacs, we'll modify our `~/.emacs` file. Add the following two lines to the bottom of the file:

```
(require 'evil)
(evil-mode 1)
```

Note   One of the major concepts in Emacs is that of modes. Changing modes can change the way input keys react. The mode to make Emacs use Vim bindings is itself a mode called `evil-mode`. There are two subcategories of modes in Emacs: minor modes and major modes. Major modes are exclusive, while multiple minor modes can be enabled at once, and each adds some features.

A community extension for using Vim bindings in other modes exists and is actively being maintained/developed. You can read more about it at

`www.github.com/emacs-evil/evil-collection`

Built-in Tutorial

Like Vim, Emacs has a built-in tutorial which can be accessed by pressing

C-h t

This should open up a page of text like shown in Figure 13-1.

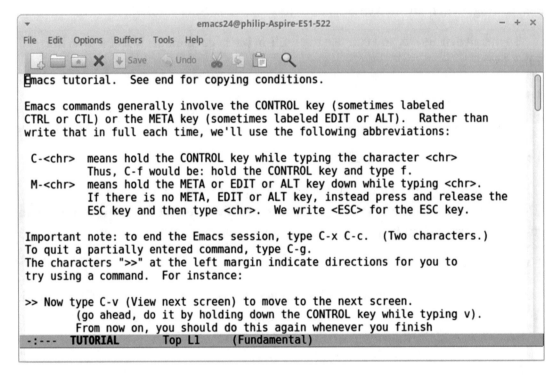

Figure 13-1. *Emacs built-in tutorial in GUI mode*

Before switching to the terminal mode as we'll do in the next section, it's worth exploring the default start page for options like "Open Home Directory" and the linked documentation. In many ways, Emacs is built to be used from the GUI rather than in the terminal. If you prefer the GUI version and it works for your setup, feel free to use it.

For the most part, not much is gained by using Emacs from terminal instead of the GUI. It does make it easier to go from terminal into a file and may feel comfortable for those coming from Vim, but many Emacs power users swear by the GUI version and keep it running at all times with multiple files opened and backgrounded in a single instance.

Run Emacs in Terminal

By default, Emacs is a desktop GUI program. Of course if you're reading this book, you're here for terminal-specific programs and workflow. You'll be happy to hear that Emacs can be run in the terminal too just like Vim. To do so, you'll want to open the program using the --no-window-system option, like this:

```
emacs --no-window-system
```

The same thing can be done using the short way -nw:

```
emacs -nw
```

Of course, you probably don't want to write this every time you launch Emacs from the terminal. What you can do instead is add an alias to your .bashrc file so that emacs instead calls emacs --nw. In my case, I decided to use e, as typing five keys seems like a lot of work. The .bashrc alias looks as follows:

```
alias e='emacs -nw'
```

Hints with which-key-mode

A great mode to install for if you're new to Emacs or even a veteran user is which-key-mode. This mode causes a mini-buffer to pop up and display the possible keyboard shortcuts that can be used from your current state. An example of the which-key dialogue is shown in Figure 13-2.

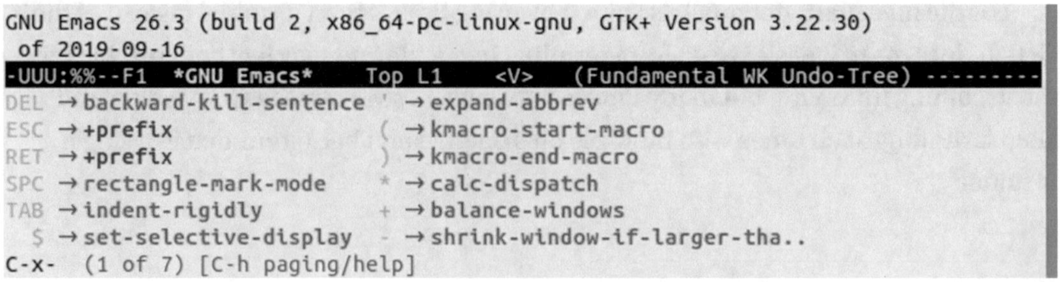

```
GNU Emacs 26.3 (build 2, x86_64-pc-linux-gnu, GTK+ Version 3.22.30)
 of 2019-09-16
-UUU:%%--F1  *GNU Emacs*    Top L1    <V>   (Fundamental WK Undo-Tree) --------
DEL → backward-kill-sentence ' → expand-abbrev
ESC → +prefix                ( → kmacro-start-macro
RET → +prefix                ) → kmacro-end-macro
SPC → rectangle-mark-mode    * → calc-dispatch
TAB → indent-rigidly         + → balance-windows
  $ → set-selective-display  - → shrink-window-if-larger-tha..
C-x- (1 of 7) [C-h paging/help]
```

Figure 13-2. *which-key-mode suggestions*

Installing which-key-mode from MELPA is similar to the process for evil-mode.

```
M-x package-list-packages
M-x package-install RET which-key
```

Once which-key-mode is installed, you'll want to modify your ~/.emacs file to tell which-mode to show suggestions in the mini-buffer as you type commands. We'll be making use of the use-package command so we first need to import it. Under the code chunk ending in (package-initialize) that we wrote in the last section, add

```
(unless (package-installed-p 'use-package)  (package-refresh-contents)

  (package-install 'use-package))
(require 'use-package)
```

This will allow us to make use of use-package in our command. Now at the bottom of the file, add

```
(use-package which-key
  :ensure t
  :config
  (which-key-mode))
```

This ensures which-key-mode is turned on when Emacs opens.

With this done, close and reopen Emacs. Now if you type

```
C-x
```

you should see a mini-buffer showing all the keys that can be used to complete after C-x and what they do, example shown in Figure 13-3.

```
-UU-:----F1  .emacs         Top L1    <N>   (Emacs-Lisp WK Undo-Tree ElDoc) --------------
DEL  → backward-kill-sentence  )  → kmacro-end-macro          3  → split-window-right
ESC  → +prefix                 *  → calc-dispatch             4  → +ctl-x-4-prefix
RET  → +prefix                 +  → balance-windows           5  → +ctl-x-5-prefix
SPC  → rectangle-mark-mode     -  → shrink-window-if-larger-tha..  6  → +2C-command
TAB  → indent-rigidly          .  → set-fill-prefix           8  → +prefix
  $  → set-selective-display   0  → delete-window             ;  → comment-set-column
  '  → expand-abbrev           1  → delete-other-windows      <  → scroll-left
  (  → kmacro-start-macro      2  → split-window-below        =  → what-cursor-position
C-x-  (1 of 4) [C-h paging/help]
```

Figure 13-3. *which-key-mode suggestions for C-x*

If there are too many possibilities to be listed, the mini-buffer will be split into sections. To switch between them, press

C-h

This will allow using n to go forward or p to go back a section.

which-key has some other built-in commands that can be run. For example, if you want a general overview of commands available in your current major mode, run

M-x which-key-show-top-level

If you're in evil-mode, for example, you'll see the options available for evil-mode.

Being able to see all possible commands is especially useful when you're new to Emacs so this mode is highly recommended.

Emacs Artist Mode

While I prefer to use Vim for text editing, I appreciate the uniqueness and interesting modes which come with Vim's rival text editor Emacs. Some of these modes are built-in, while others have to be installed using the built-in package manager MELPA.

One of these interesting modes is Emacs artist-mode. artist-mode provides a set of tools for creating text-based art or diagrams. Figure 13-4 shows a diagram of a server architecture which I included in both a presentation and README document.

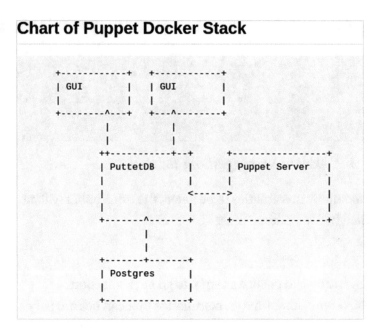

Figure 13-4. *Example of a chart made in artist-mode*

The real strength of these types of diagrams is the ability to both make and view them on a terminal. When logging in to a server over SSH and coming across a README, normal images cannot be displayed. However, the diagrams created with Emacs artist-mode can be changed easily.

These kinds of images are particularly useful in nongraphical READMEs or manuals. As an example, I used this kind of art in a presentation about a system for delivering updates to IoT devices, in conjunction with Emacs presentation mode, another module that we will look at next.

Note   We'll show you how to use artist-mode via the terminal version of Emacs here, but this is one mode which is much easier to use in the GUI version. This is due to the fact that with the GUI, you can draw text using the mouse and drag and drop shapes, whereas in the terminal you need to use the keyboard for everything. If your setup allows it, you may want to start Emacs in GUI mode and give drawing text with your mouse in artist-mode a try.

Create a blank file with Emacs and then switch into artist-mode. Before switching to artist-mode, you'll want to create a "canvas" of blank space (literal space characters) where you'll draw your image. An easy way to do this with Vim bindings is to press i to go into insert mode and hold down the space bar until your cursor goes as far right as you want the canvas width to be. Then press esc to exit insert mode. Press y twice to copy the blank line; next hold p until your cursor goes as far down as you want your canvas to be. Your cursor should end up in a bottom-right location like in Figure 13-5.

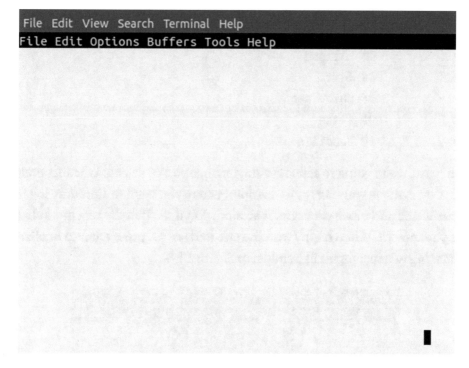

Figure 13-5. *Creating a canvas of white space in Emacs to use with artist-mode*

The space from the cursor to the top left is now all white space, which we will operate while using artist-mode.

Next switch to artist-mode using the following command:

```
M-x artist-mode
```

You'll also want to turn off Vim bindings if you have them enabled as they don't play nicely with artist-mode. You can do that by running the same command which turns them on:

```
M-x evil-mode
```

Once in artist-mode, we have a large variety of shape tools we can select from to draw with. When using Emacs in terminal mode, all the shapes can be switched between by first pressing ctrl+c, followed by ctrl+a, after that you but in the letter corresponding to the specific shape (*case insensitive, I have copied the shortcuts as they appear in Emacs GUI*).

```
C-c C-a L          ## Line
C-c C-a r          ## Rectangle
C-c C-a s          ## Square
C-c C-a P          ## Poly-line
C-c C-a C          ## Ellipse
C-c C-a T          ## Text
C-c C-a z          ## Spray-can
C-c C-a E          ## Erase
C-c C-a V          ## Vaporize
```

In our case, we're going to select rectangle; once you've selected the rectangle shape with C-c C-a r, move your cursor to the point where you want to start drawing from. Then press enter and move your cursor around; you'll see that the rectangle changes shape as you move it. When happy with the size and shape, press enter to finalize it.

Try making two rectangles like shown in Figure 13-6.

Figure 13-6. *Two rectangles created in artist-mode*

Next switch to the line tool using

```
C-c C-a l
```

Move your cursor to the bottom middle of the top rectangle, then press enter to start your line. Move it down to the top of the second rectangle so they're connected like in Figure 13-7.

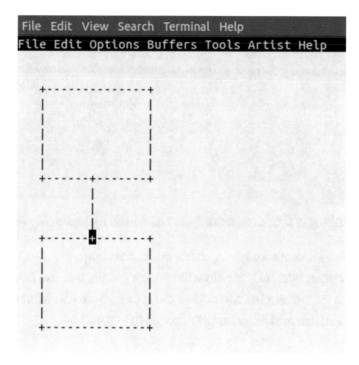

Figure 13-7. *Artist-mode connecting two rectangles with a line*

To make it look more like an arrow going from the top rectangle to the bottom one, we'll replace the + with a v. To do so, simply press v while your cursor is in the place shown in the preceding picture. You should end up with something like Figure 13-8.

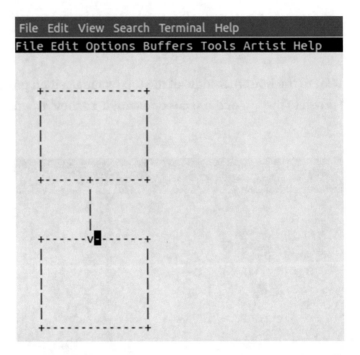

Figure 13-8. *Making a line an arrow in artist-mode by replacing + with v*

When not using a specific shape in artist-mode, pressing a key simply replaces the text of where the cursor currently is with what you press. We can use this same effect to add some labels to the rectangles. Move your cursor to where you want to add the labels and simply type. You can add label text like shown in Figure 13-9.

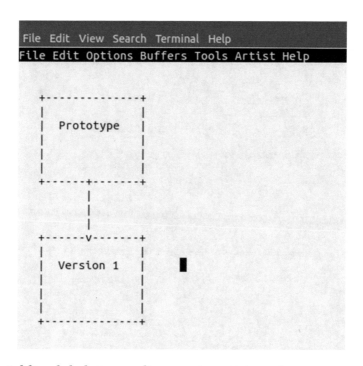

Figure 13-9. *Adding labels to our diagram in artist-mode*

If you accidentally write it noncentered, you can simply put your cursor to the start of the word and press the spacebar to overwrite the text with white space. The same goes for if you accidentally mess up your shape while writing; simply add the missing text of the shape manually this way.

With those two simple shapes and techniques, you can create relatively complex graphics of architecture like the puppet pop machine one shown at the top of this section. However, if you explore the other tools and have the time, there's no limit to the text art you can create. I'll leave you with some inspiration, a pop machine text art graphic I found and used in the same presentation, shown in Figure 13-10. You can find text art like this on sites like www.asciiworld.com and www.asciiart.eu.

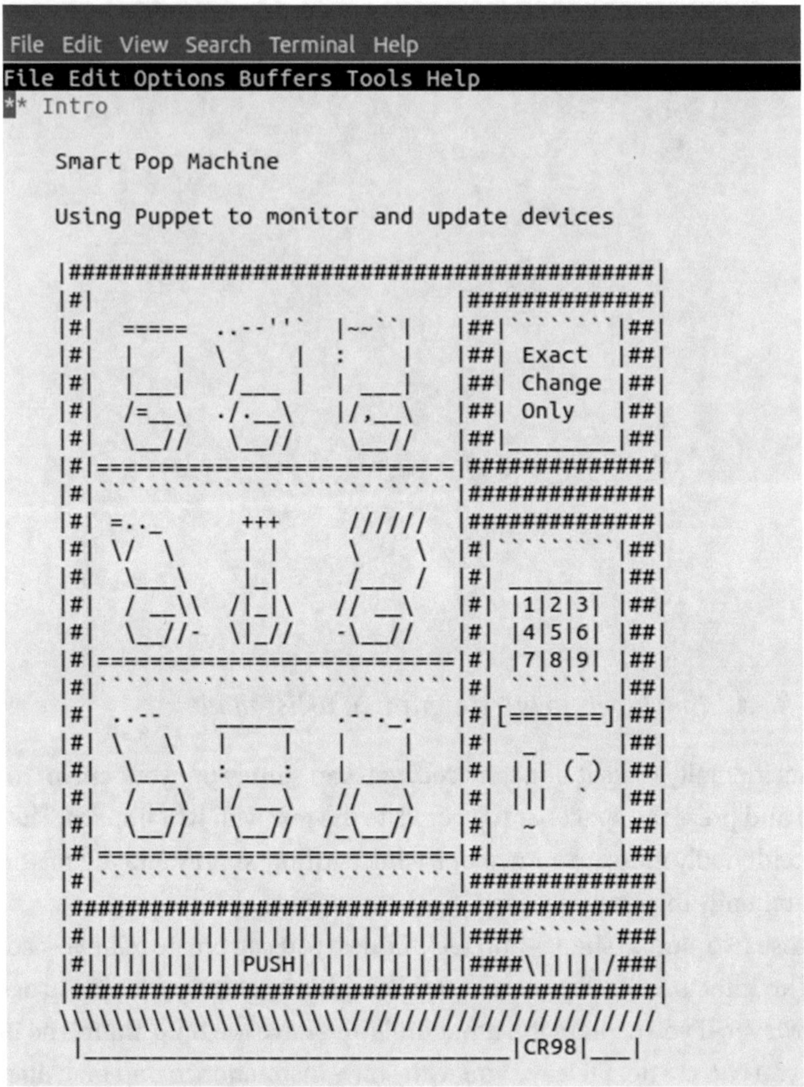

Figure 13-10. *Pop machine text art*

Org-Mode

Another useful mode to keep notes efficiently in raw text and even give presentations (*more on that in the next section*) is Emacs org-mode. Emacs org-mode, short for organization mode, provides the ability to write text under hierarchical headings with the ability to easily expand and compress sections, for example, given the format shown in Figure 13-11 (headings specified by *).

```
* Linux

An open-source opperating system

** Emacs

An extensible text-editor with several modes for editting

*** Evil-Mode

Vim bindings for Emacs

*** Org-Mode

A mode for organizing notes in hierarchical format
█
```

Figure 13-11. *Org-mode with expanded sections*

To collapse a section, you simply put the cursor on the heading to collapse and press tab. The level is defined by the number of stars in front of the heading like shown in Figure 13-12.

```
* Linux

An open-source opperating system

** Emacs

An extensible text-editor with several modes for editting

*** Evil-Mode...
*** Org-Mode...
█
```

Figure 13-12. *Org-mode with condensed subsections*

Collapsing a higher heading will hide all of its children, as shown in Figure 13-13.

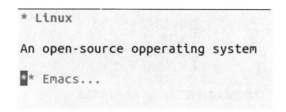

```
* Linux

An open-source opperating system

█* Emacs...
```

Figure 13-13. *Org-mode collapsing a section*

As with `artist-mode`, it does not play well with Vim bindings. If you want to use both Vim bindings and `org-mode`, there are some packages which try to add patches to `org-mode` to make it work with Vim bindings, but I found it wasn't worth the effort. Packages include `evil-org`, `org-evil`, and `syndicate`. My recommendation is to simply not use both modes at the same time. If you have `evil-mode` enabled on startup, you will have to manually turn it off by running `evil-mode` before running `org-mode`.

There is no need to install any additional packages to use `org-mode` as it ships standard with Emacs.

Tables in Org-Mode

Org-mode also has a built-in mode for making and working with tables. A table in org-mode is specified by the | character. To generate a table, start by pressing

`C-c |`

This will open a dialog in the footer asking what size you'd like for the table, like in Figure 13-14.

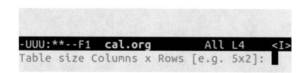

Figure 13-14. *Dialog at the bottom of the screen asking for dimensions of the new table*

For our example, we'll use 2x3. After entering the size, an empty table like that shown in Figure 13-15 will be generated.

Figure 13-15. *Empty 2x3 table created in org-mode*

Next fill out the form with some sample data. After doing so, the table will likely be misaligned like in Figure 13-16.

```
| mode | description |
|---+---|
| org-mode | Create structrured documents |
| artist-mode | Create text art ▊
```

Figure 13-16. *Unformatted table in org-mode*

To reformat the table, make sure you have your cursor somewhere on the table and press ctrl+c twice.

```
C-c
C-c
```

After pressing a second time, org-mode will realign the table, resulting in a nicely laid out table like shown in Figure 13-17.

```
| mode          | description                   |
|---------------+-------------------------------|
| org-mode      | Create structrured documents  |
| artist-mode   | Create text art               |
```

Figure 13-17. *Formatted table in org-mode*

You should now have a nicely formatted text-based table.

You can find additional features for working with tables such as converting CSV format to a table and rearranging rows in The Org Manual page for tables: `https://orgmode.org/worg/org-tutorials/tables.html`.

Export from Org-Mode

One of the handy things you can do with `org-mode` is export to several other file formats using a simple command. Possible formats include

- PDF
- HTML
- LaTeX

- OpenDocument Text (ODT) file

- Plain text

- iCalendar

To get started, press

C-c C-e

This will open up an export menu which shows possible export options, as shown in Figure 13-18.

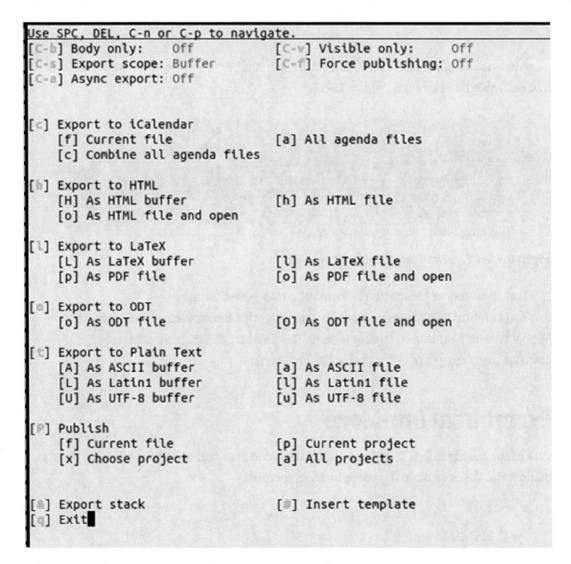

```
Use SPC, DEL, C-n or C-p to navigate.
[C-b] Body only:    Off          [C-v] Visible only:     Off
[C-s] Export scope: Buffer       [C-f] Force publishing: Off
[C-a] Async export: Off


[c] Export to iCalendar
    [f] Current file             [a] All agenda files
    [c] Combine all agenda files

[h] Export to HTML
    [H] As HTML buffer           [h] As HTML file
    [o] As HTML file and open

[l] Export to LaTeX
    [L] As LaTeX buffer          [l] As LaTeX file
    [p] As PDF file              [o] As PDF file and open

[o] Export to ODT
    [o] As ODT file              [O] As ODT file and open

[t] Export to Plain Text
    [A] As ASCII buffer          [a] As ASCII file
    [L] As Latin1 buffer         [l] As Latin1 file
    [U] As UTF-8 buffer          [u] As UTF-8 file

[P] Publish
    [f] Current file             [p] Current project
    [x] Choose project           [a] All projects


[&] Export stack                 [#] Insert template
[q] Exit
```

Figure 13-18. *Export type selection in org-mode*

If we want to export to PDF, for example, press l and that subsection will be highlighted. See Figure 13-19 for an example of the PDF subsection.

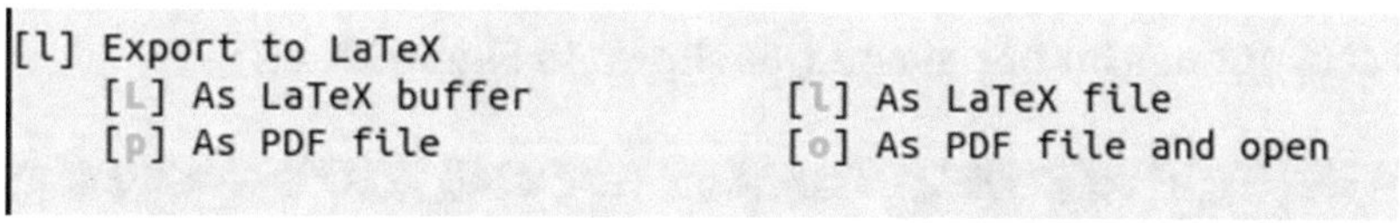

```
[l] Export to LaTeX
    [L] As LaTeX buffer          [l] As LaTeX file
    [p] As PDF file              [o] As PDF file and open
```

Figure 13-19. *LaTeX subsection highlighted in org-mode export menu*

We can now press p to export as a PDF. Upon doing so, a PDF in the same directory as your org file will be created.

Org-Agenda

When working with org files, it's possible to use a special TODO indicator to mark text as an agenda item. You can also tell org-agenda to keep track of certain files as part of a globally accessible agenda, which includes things like a daily planner and calendar.

To demonstrate, create a file called /cal.org. Then, create sections for different priority tasks (high priority, low priority like in Figure 13-20). Once you've created the file, press

C-c [

This will add the file to Emacs list of files to be queried by org-agenda. You can remove a file by running

C-c]

Once a file is added, any TODO instance will be included in org-agenda. The TODO has to be preceded by an * as shown in Figure 13-20.

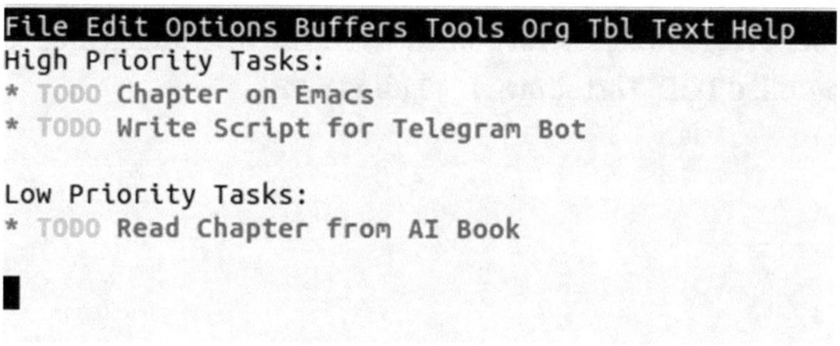

```
File Edit Options Buffers Tools Org Tbl Text Help
High Priority Tasks:
* TODO Chapter on Emacs
* TODO Write Script for Telegram Bot

Low Priority Tasks:
* TODO Read Chapter from AI Book

█
```

Figure 13-20. *TODO list in org-mode*

Now if we press alt+x, enter org-agenda, and press enter:

`M-x org-agenda RET`

we'll get a list of options for org-agenda, as shown in Figure 13-21.

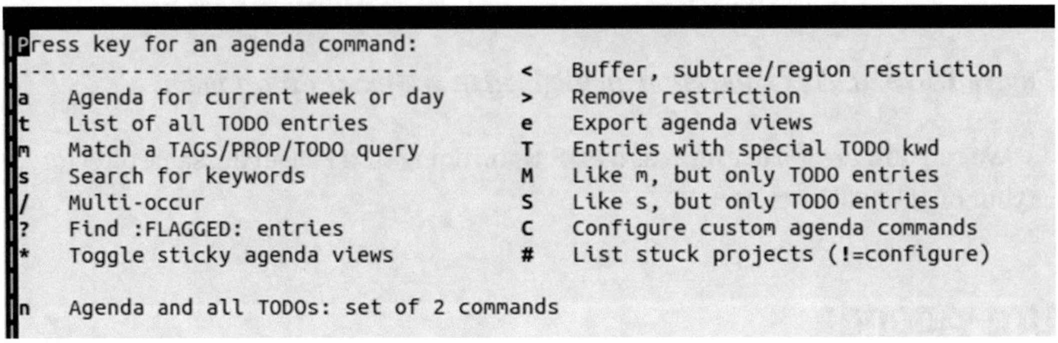

```
Press key for an agenda command:
--------------------------------        <    Buffer, subtree/region restriction
a    Agenda for current week or day     >    Remove restriction
t    List of all TODO entries           e    Export agenda views
m    Match a TAGS/PROP/TODO query       T    Entries with special TODO kwd
s    Search for keywords                M    Like m, but only TODO entries
/    Multi-occur                        S    Like s, but only TODO entries
?    Find :FLAGGED: entries             C    Configure custom agenda commands
*    Toggle sticky agenda views         #    List stuck projects (!=configure)

n    Agenda and all TODOs: set of 2 commands
```

Figure 13-21. *Org-agenda menu*

Press t to see a list of all TODO items, as shown in Figure 13-22.

```
Global list of TODO items of type: ALL
Available with 'N r': (0)[ALL] (1)TODO (2)DONE
   cal:        TODO Chapter on Emacs
   cal:        TODO Write Script for Telegram Bot
   cal:        TODO Read Chapter from AI Book
```

Figure 13-22. *All TODO items listed in org-agenda*

In this agenda tab, we can now press n for next line and p for previous line. Go down to one of your list items and press t. This will mark the task as done both in your agenda and inline in the file where it was originally written. Keep in mind you can have as many different files tracked by the agenda as you'd like. So if you want to have different files to list different types of tasks, you can do that and have them all pulled into your agenda (example of compiled TODO list shown in Figure 13-23).

```
Global list of TODO items of type: ALL
Available with 'N r': (0)[ALL]
  cal:          TODO Chapter on Emacs
  cal:          DONE Write Script for Telegram BotLow Priority Task
  cal:          TODO Read Chapter from AI Book
```

Figure 13-23. *Marking a TODO item as done in org-agenda*

To exit the agenda, press q.

Org-agenda also has support for task deadlines. To add a deadline to a TODO item, put your cursor over the TODO task and then press

```
C-c C-s
```

This will open up a prompt where you can input a date, as shown in Figure 13-24.

```
-UU-:----F1  cal.org            All L2     <N>    (Org Undo-Tree) -----------------
        December 2019              January 2020            February 2020
     Su Mo Tu We Th Fr Sa      Su Mo Tu We Th Fr Sa     Su Mo Tu We Th Fr Sa
      1  2  3  4  5  6  7                1  2  3  4                           1
      8  9 10 11 12 13 14       5  6  7     9 10 11      2  3  4  5  6  7  8
     15 16 17 18 19 20 21      12 13 14 15 16 17 18      9 10 11 12 13 14 15
     22 23 24 25 26 27 28      19 20 21 22 23 24 25     16 17 18 19 20 21 22
     29 30 31                  26 27 28 29 30 31        23 24 25 26 27 28 29
     <     Calendar      ? info / o other / . today    Wed, Jan 8, 2020       >
Date+time [2020-01-08]: 2020-01-10  => <2020-01-10 Fri>
```

Figure 13-24. *Adding a date to a TODO item in org-mode*

After entering a date/time and pressing enter, you'll have an associated date placed under the task, shown in Figure 13-25.

```
High Priority Tasks:
* TODO Chapter on Emacs
  SCHEDULED: <2020-01-10 Fri>
* DONE Write Script for Telegram BotLow Priority Task
* TODO Read Chapter from AI Book
```

Figure 13-25. *Example of a TODO item with a scheduled date in org-mode*

Now if you return to the org-agenda options by entering

```
M-x org-agenda RET
```

then pressing a to go to agenda weekly view, you'll see your tasks for the week displayed by day, example shown in Figure 13-26.

```
Week-agenda (W02):
Monday        6 January 2020 W02
Tuesday       7 January 2020
Wednesday     8 January 2020
Thursday      9 January 2020
Friday       10 January 2020
   cal:          Scheduled:  TODO Chapter on Emacs
Saturday     11 January 2020
Sunday       12 January 2020
```

Figure 13-26. *Weekly agenda view in org-agenda mode*

A scheduled item will remain on your agenda until completed. Org-agenda also offers the ability to create an entry that shows on the calendar but will pass whether or not it is marked as DONE; to use this alternative timestamp, press C-c . instead of C-c s on an item. There is also a high-priority timestamp deadline which can be used by pressing C-c d while on a TODO item.

Sync Org-Agenda with Google Calendar

Org-agenda is a great tool, but it doesn't provide seamless integration between devices like mobile phones or even other computers. There is a community package on MELPA called org-calendar that makes pulling, pushing, and two-way sync between org-agenda and Google Calendar easy.

After installing from MELPA, you'll have to set up a project on Google Developer Console to make use of their calendar API. You can find the most up-to-date instructions on setting up org-calendar on their GitHub page. Keep in mind the last commit was in April 2017, so updates and support may be limited.

www.github.com/myuhe/org-gcal.el

Outline Presentation Mode

Another great mode that can be used in conjunction with Emacs artist-mode is Emacs presentation mode. Outline presentation mode allows you to take an org-mode outline and turn it into a presentation where each section acts as a slide. Unfortunately, this mode isn't distributed in the MELPA package manager. In order to install outline presentation mode, you'll need to manually download the script and then add it to your ~/.emacs. I found difficulty finding the original code online so I've uploaded the script to GitHub. You should download it using GitHub:

```
cd /tmp
git clone https://github.com/kirkins/outline-presentation-mode
```

Then go into the downloaded folder and move the script to your ~/.emacs.d/extra/ folder (*create the folder if it doesn't exist*).

```
cd /outline-presentation-mode
mv outline-presentation-mode.el ~/.emacs.d/extra/
```

Now with the Emacs script saved in your ~/.emacs.d/extra/ folder, you'll have to modify your ~/.emacs file to load the script when Emacs starts. At the bottom of the file, add the following:

```
(load-file (expand-file-name "~/.emacs.d/extra/outline-presentation-mode.el"))
```

Now when you open Emacs, you'll have the ability to open a file in outline presentation mode. You likely don't have an org-outline file presentation to test with; I've made one available on a repository, you can download it with

```
git clone https://github.com/kirkins/puppet-pop-machine
cd puppet-pop-machine
```

Next, open the file called presentation.org in Emacs. With the file open, switch to presentation-outline-mode:

```
M-x presentation-outline-mode
```

This will open the presentation file and show the outline of the presentation as shown in Figure 13-27.

```
File Edit Options Buffers Tools Help
* Puppt for IoT Updates and Monitoring

** Intro...
** Scenario:...
** Puppet is f(x) = f(f(x))...
** Puppet allows for custom facts...
** Puppt has built in diagnostics...
** External node classifier...
** R10K - What is it...
** R10K - for QA...
** R10K - for development...
** R10K - for release...
** Puppet on Docker...
** Webhooks...
```

Figure 13-27. *presentation-outline-mode in Emacs*

You can now hold down the alt key and tap n to go to the next slide; to go back, tap p. A list of commands that can be used is shown in Table 13-1 (*M signifies the modifier key which is alt by default*).

Table 13-1. *Emacs outline mode commands*

Command	Description
M-n	Next slide
M-p	Previous slide
M-f	First slide of next section
M-b	Back to previous section slide
M-a	First slide
M-y	Expanded table of contents
M-s	Show the slide cursor is on in table of contents
M-r	Return to the slide you went to table of contents from
M-q	Quit presentation mode and return to org-mode

An example of what can be done for slides in plain text is shown in Figure 13-28.

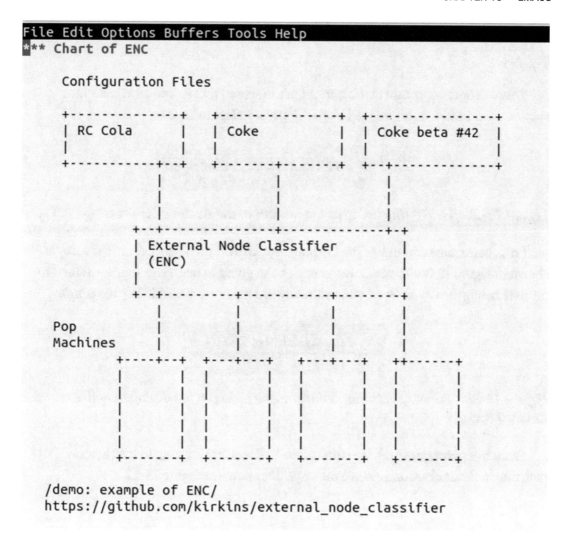

Figure 13-28. *A chart made in artist-mode embedded in an outline presentation slide*

Emacs TRAMP

Emacs TRAMP stands for Emacs Transparent Remote Access, Multiple Protocols. It allows you to access remote filesystems as if they're part of your local system by using rlogin, telnet, or ssh in the background.

Emacs TRAMP is included with Emacs by default as of version 22.1 so you won't have to do anything extra to install it.

To use ssh TRAMP, you'll first want to press

C-x C-f

This will open a prompt at the bottom of the screen that lets you navigate your system to find a file. It should look something like in Figure 13-29.

```
-UUU:----F1  presentation.org   All L260
Find file: /tmp/puppet-pop-machine/
```

Figure 13-29. *Find a file dialog at the bottom of the screen after pressing C-x C-f*

Press backspace and delete the file path and instead put /ssh:<your server>, as shown in Figure 13-30. To make things easier, I'm going to use a shortname defined in my SSH config file called "aws" which already has my username and key file setup.

```
-UUU:----F1  presentation.org
Find file: /ssh:aws
```

Figure 13-30. *Entering /ssh:remotehostname in find a file dialog to activate Emacs TRAMP*

From this point, press tab and the system will start connecting to the remote machine in the background, with a message like shown in Figure 13-31.

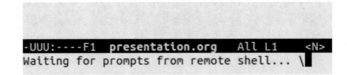

```
-UUU:----F1  presentation.org   All L1    <N>
Waiting for prompts from remote shell... \
```

Figure 13-31. *Dialog showing Emacs TRAMP connecting to remote server*

Once connected, you'll be able to press tab and get a list of all the remote files as if it were a folder on your local machine. An example of this is shown in Figure 13-32.

```
-UUU:----F1  presentation.org  All L1   <N>  Git-master  (Org Undo-Tree) --------------
In this buffer, type RET to select the completion near point.

Possible completions are:
../                                      ./
.Xauthority                              .aws/
.bash_logout                             .bashrc
.cache/                                  .config/
.deeppavlov/                             .electron/
.electrum/                               .gem/
.gnupg/                                  .irssi/
.local/                                  .mozilla/
.mysql_history                           .node-gyp/
.nvm/                                    .pki/
.putty/                                  .python_history
.rnd                                     .selected_editor
.sudo_as_admin_successful                .thumbnails/
.vim/                                    .viminfo
.wajig/                                  .wget-hsts
.xsession-x2go-ip-172-31-58-133-errors   .xsession x2go-ip-172-31-58-133-errors.old
.yarnc                                   Desktop/
Downloads/                               Music/
Public/                                  Templates/
authorized_keys                          backup/
nltk_data/                               packt/
-UUU:%*@-F1  *Completions*  All L1   <E>  (Completion List Undo-Tree) ---------------
Find file: /ssh:aws:
```

Figure 13-32. *Autocomplete showing files on remote server via Emacs TRAMP*

What's handy about this is you can edit a file on the remote machine, then switch to a file on the local machine, and then go back to a file on the remote machine, and the connection will stay open.

You could even have simultaneous connections with several remote machines and switch between files seamlessly, all while keeping your local Emacs editor settings – as opposed to if you SSH into those machines and have to use the config file for the editor that's on each local machine. For this reason, Emacs TRAMP is particularly useful for anyone who has to switch between editing files on several machines regularly.

Other Modes

We've only looked at a few Emacs modes here, but there are lots out there. If you're interested, here is a small list to get you started. Keep in mind I'm focusing on application-like modes here, but there are also modes for almost every programming language and config file type. See Table 13-2 for a list of other popular modes.

Table 13-2. *Emacs modes*

Name	Description
shell	Command-line shell in Emacs
dired	Mode for navigating directories
eww	Web browser in Emacs
magit	Advanced git interface for doing things like merging
ivy	Interactive interface for autocomplete
gnus	Read email, RSS, Usenet groups, and more
rainbow-mode	Set background for hex color codes
company	Text completion
ediff	Tool for comparing files and patches
flyspell-mode	Spell-check highlights wrong words in red

If you have the mode installed, you can simply press alt+x and enter the name. If you want to get a complete list of modes installed, press

C-h a

Then enter "mode"; this will list all the modes installed with a very short description.

Summary

In this chapter, we looked at the Emacs text editor and some of the many capabilities it has via modes and embedded applications – from creating text art–style diagrams and text tables to managing task lists and your personal calendar. As we've seen, Emacs can be much more than a text editor and is more akin to a platform on which text-based applications can build on top of.

CHAPTER 14

Configure Bash

In this chapter, we'll look at various configurations that can be made to bash. Often this is done by using configuration scripts that run when bash starts as well as other configuration files that control installed utilities or lower-level libraries like `.inputrc`.

Configuration Scripts

We'll start with the three configuration files that are used for customizing bash directly. These include `.bashrc_profile`, `.bashrc`, and `.profile`.

.bashrc_profile or .profile

The `.bashrc_profile` configuration script is similar to `.bashrc`, but it only runs once when the user first logs in. On some systems, this file may be specified as `.profile` instead, though if both `.profile` and `.bash_profile` exist, then `.bash_profile` will be used.

`.bashrc_profile` is the entry point which defines the location of `.bashrc`. Here is an example:

```
if [ -n "$BASH_VERSION" ]; then
    # include .bashrc if it exists
    if [ -f "$HOME/.bashrc" ]; then
        . "$HOME/.bashrc"
    fi
fi
```

The preceding code checks the language executing the script. If the language is bash, it then checks that a `.bashrc` file is present in the home folder. If a `.bashrc` file exists, it is executed.

© Philip Kirkbride 2020
P. Kirkbride, *Basic Linux Terminal Tips and Tricks*, https://doi.org/10.1007/978-1-4842-6035-7_14

A more simple implementation might just include the following which says if `.bashrc` exists, then load it:

```
test -r ~/.bashrc && . ~/.bashrc
```

While normally `.bashrc_profile` simply loads `.bashrc`, it is possible to include anything that would be done in `.bashrc` directly in `.bashrc_profile`.

Note   The "." in `. ~/.bashrc` earlier is shorthand for built-in bash command `source` which allows you to load an external script into the script being run.

.bashrc

The `~/.bashrc` file contains bash configurations. It can be used to define variables or functions which will be available in all your sessions. Every time you open a new bash terminal, the script is run.

As an experiment, try opening your `.bashrc` which should be accessible at `~/.bashrc`. Add a line with the following to the bottom of the file (though it should work when added anywhere in the file):

```
export HELLO=world
```

Next reload the `~/.bashrc` file by running (*or close the terminal and reopen*)

```
source ~/.bashrc
```

Now you should be able to use the variable `$HELLO` in bash and have it return a value of "world," for example, with `echo`:

```
echo $HELLO
```

.bash_logout

While the `.profile` script runs once on login, the `.bash_logout` is just the opposite. It runs a single time when you log out. This can be useful if you want to do things like remove temporary files. As an example, the default `.bash_logout` on my Ubuntu system includes the following:

```
# when leaving console clear the screen to increase privacy

if [ "$SHLVL" = 1 ]; then
    [ -x /usr/bin/clear_console ] && /usr/bin/clear_console -q
fi
```

The preceding code says if the shell being logged out from is the base level, and the file /usr/bin/clear_console exists, then run that file with -q flag.

The $SHLVL here is an environment variable which exists automatically. To get an idea of how it works, try echo $SHLVL; this should return a value of 1. Then try

```
bash
echo $SHLVL
```

After running a bash session within your bash, the number will be 2. If you were in turn to run another bash session in that session, the number would go to 3.

Note   Depending on your distro and user, the file may or may not exist. For example, we found that when using the root user, there was no .bash_logout by default. When using Fedora instead of Ubuntu, we found the file did exist, but the code contained was different.

Global Versions

In addition to the .bashrc in your home directory, you will have a global version at /etc/bash.bashrc if you're on Debian-based systems and /etc/bashrc on Red Hat based. In addition, you should have a /etc/profile which acts as the global version of .profile. These files are used to set the initial state of bash for all users and are run before the local profile, and .bashrc files are run for each user.

During the startup process when /etc/profile is running, there is also a folder which executes several scripts called /etc/profile.d/. If you place an executable script in this directory, it will be run at startup, as long as it has the extension .sh. Unlike normal executables, the extension is required for these files to be executed.

Useful Configs for .bashrc

There are several useful things you can do with a .bashrc file. Some of the most common include creating aliases for commonly used tasks or adding simple functions to be accessed system wide.

Defining Aliases

An alias is a short command which translates into a longer command. This makes it more convenient to write the command. For example, many Ubuntu systems come by default with the alias ll as a short way of doing ls -alF, which shows a more detailed view of your current directory. When I open up my .bashrc, I see ll defined along with some other aliases that came by default:

```
alias ll='ls -alF'
alias la='ls -A'
alias l='ls -CF'
```

One I add on my own machine is aliasing vi to vim. This allows me to run the same command whether I'm running on a machine that has full Vim or just vi. If you're on Fedora, you may find this alias exists by default.

```
alias vi="vim"
```

In the same spirit, you might want to upgrade diff to instead use colordiff (note that colordiff may not be installed by default):

```
alias diff="colordiff"
```

Custom Functions

In some cases where you want to create a quick shortcut, you'll find you need to create a short function rather than use an example. One common thing people like to do is create a single function to create a folder with mkdir and then immediately move into that directory with cd. Let's create a command that does just that by adding the following function to .bashrc:

```
mkcd() { mkdir -p "$1" && cd "$1"; }
```

After saving, close your terminal and reopen it, since the `.bashrc` file is run when a new terminal opens up. Alternatively, you can run `source .bashrc` to reload the configuration without restarting your terminal. Now if you run `mkcd hello`, you'll create a folder called hello and move into it right away.

In some cases, you might just want to wrap an existing command that is somewhat difficult to remember. For example, many systems make use of `amixer` for sound. It's possible to change the volume with `amixer`; we can wrap the existing command to make it a bit easier:

```
volume() { amixer sset 'Master' $1%; }
```

This allows you to pass in any value between 0 and 100 to set the volume from the terminal.

Adding to PATH

Another common change made in `.bashrc` is adding to the $PATH variables. This variable keeps track of a list of folders on your system where executables are stored. When you run an executable without specifying the full path, for example, `nmap`, the system will check all the folders specified in your path. When a match is found, it is used.

If you install programming languages on your system, often they'll automatically modify your `.bashrc` file and add the folder where they keep executables to your path. By doing this, they make all their modules available to you as part of your path. The following is an example of a line created when installing the Rust programming language.

```
export PATH="$HOME/.cargo/bin:$PATH"
```

Notice the `:$PATH` at the end. This specifies that we're using our old $PATH and prepending everything that appears before the `:`. Always make use of the existing $PATH variable when appending or prepending to it. Otherwise, you might remove a folder which was added in another file or location.

Changing PS1 Prompt

Another common customization in `.bashrc` is to change the color or content of the prompt text. The prompt shown to the left of our cursor is controlled by the environment variable PS1. If you run `echo  $PS1`, you'll see an encoded version of the one on your system.

It can be changed by updating the PS1 variable, for example, let's turn the text red (to experiment, run in the terminal directly rather than modifying .bashrc):

```
export PS1="\e[0;31m[\u@\h \W]\$ \e[m "
```

Running the preceding command should cause the prompt to change red. Next try running the same command again but incrementing the 31, and observe how each number results in a different color. An example of expected result is shown in Figure 14-1.

```
philip@philip-ThinkPad-T420:~$ export PS1="\e[0;31m[\u@\h \W]\$ \e[m "
[philip@philip-ThinkPad-T420 ~]$  export PS1="\e[0;32m[\u@\h \W]\$ \e[m "
[philip@philip-ThinkPad-T420 ~]$  export PS1="\e[0;33m[\u@\h \W]\$ \e[m "
[philip@philip-ThinkPad-T420 ~]$  export PS1="\e[0;34m[\u@\h \W]\$ \e[m "
[philip@philip-ThinkPad-T420 ~]$  export PS1="\e[0;35m[\u@\h \W]\$ \e[m "
[philip@philip-ThinkPad-T420 ~]$  export PS1="\e[0;36m[\u@\h \W]\$ \e[m "
[philip@philip-ThinkPad-T420 ~]$  export PS1="\e[0;37m[\u@\h \W]\$ \e[m "
[philip@philip-ThinkPad-T420 ~]$  █
```

Figure 14-1. *Changing the color of bash prompt text*

This code content is a bit hard to understand as it first starts with an escape character which isn't seen at all `\e[o;`. The presence of the escape character causes the title bar for the window to include the working directory, like shown in Figure 14-2.

```
philip@philip-ThinkPad-T420: /etc/profile.d
minal  Help
T420:/etc/profile.d$ █
```

Figure 14-2. *File path in the title bar due to* `\e[o;` *in PS1*

After that we have `31m[` to set the color. This is an ANSI escape sequence which dates back to the 1970s; they were used as a way to embedded text which should be interpreted as a command instead of text. At the very end of the line, we have \e[m which resets the color; if not included, the text you type into the terminal would end up being the same color as the alias. A list of different ANSI color codes is shown in Table 14-1.

Table 14-1. *ANSI escape sequences for color*

Sequence	Description
30m[	Black
31m[	Red
32m[	Green
33m[	Yellow
34m[	Blue
35m[	Magenta
36m[	Cyan
37m[	White

The \u translates to the username, the \h stands in for hostname, and the \W stands in for the base of the working directory. If we instead wanted minimal prompt text, we could replace it all with just

```
export PS1="-> "
```

or if we only wanted the working directory base:

```
export PS1="\W -> "
```

This results in a more minimal look, showing only the base of the working directory. If you prefer the default way of displaying the full working directory rather than just the base, you just need to replace the \W with the lowercase version \w. A list of PS1 symbols is shown in Table 14-2.

Table 14-2. *PS1 prompt commands*

Characther	Description
h	Hostname to first "."
H	Full hostname
s	Shell name, e.g., "bash"
t	Current time in 24-hour format
@	Current time in 12-hour format
u	Username
w	Complete path of working directory
W	Current folder name

Another way to modify the color of your prompt is to use `tput`. This method is actually a bit more flexible as it allows you to use 256 colors. However, you'll have to have 256 colors enabled in your terminal; to quickly see how many are supported, run

```
tput colors
```

If you get back a number less than 256, you'll need to make sure you have `xterm-256color` enabled. You can do that by adding the following line to your `.bashrc`:

```
export TERM=xterm-256color
```

Make sure to run `source ~/.bashrc` after the update.

With 256 colors enabled, you can now use `tput setaf` with 1 of 256 color codes. You can find a complete list by searching "256 color codes." However, we can actually make our own list that includes all the colors by running the following in bash:

```
for c in {0..255}
do
    :
    if ! (( $c % 16 )) ; then
      printf '\n'
    fi
    printf '\e[48;5;%dm'"%5s" $c $c; printf '\e[0m'
done
```

This script will go through each number from 0 to 255 and print the number with a background color based on that code. Running it should produce a result like in Figure 14-3.

```
~ -> for c in {0..255}
> do
>     :
>     if ! (( $c % 16 )) ; then
>         printf '\n'
>     fi
>     printf '\e[48;5;%dm'"%5s" $c $c; printf '\e[0m'
> done
```

Figure 14-3. *Creating a table with all 256 color codes*

We'll take our previous minimal PS1 and then wrap it with a tput command to set the color and another to reset the color:

```
export PS1="$(tput setaf 166)\W -> $(tput sgr0)"
```

After experimenting directly in your terminal, if you find something you want to make permanent, simply add it to the bottom of your .bashrc file. Then if you decide you don't want it anymore, you can remove the line in question.

PS2, PS3, and PS4

In addition to the PS1 environment variable, there is also a PS2. To see your PS2, run the following:

```
echo $PS2
echo "hi
```

On the second line, be sure not to include the close ". This will cause the PS2 prompt to show, indicating you need to finish the previous command. Notice how these two symbols are the same like in Figure 14-4.

```
philip@philip-ThinkPad-T420:~$ echo $PS2
>
philip@philip-ThinkPad-T420:~$ echo "hi
> █
```

Figure 14-4. *Comparing PS2 to interactive shell text prompt*

Notice that the two commands earlier display the same ">".

Besides PS1 and PS2, there are also PS3 and PS4, but they are not commonly used. PS3 is used when a select prompt is used in bash, for example:

```
PS3=">"
select i in red blue green exit
do
  case $i in
    red) echo "Red";;
    blue) echo "Blue";;
    green) echo "Green";;
    exit) exit;;
  esac
done
```

When run we'll see a select menu using our PS3 value beside where the user is prompted to enter text, as shown in Figure 14-5.

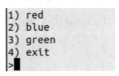

Figure 14-5. *Example of PS3 in a script using* `select`

If no value is specified with PS3, the default will be #?.

Finally, PS4 is specific to debugging bash with the -x flag. This flag is used for debugging; if we take our script that asks the user to pick a color and put it in a file, we can run it with the -x flag:

```
bash -x ./choice.sh
```

When we do this, we'll see the lines shown as they're run and to the left will be the value of PS4, in this case, a "+" sign. See Figure 14-6 for an example.

```
philip@philip-ThinkPad-T420:/tmp$ bash -x ./choice.sh
+ select i in red blue green exit
1) red
2) blue
3) green
4) exit
#? 1
+ case $i in
+ echo Red
Red
#?
```

Figure 14-6. *Example of PS4 when using -x flag for debug mode*

Themes

You can go through and change all aspects of visual display manually, or install a community project that make pre-created terminal color themes available.

Some popular projects include "Bash-it" and "Oh My Bash"; however, these two projects both come bundled with a large amount of functions and configurations. Other projects such as Gogh are more minimal and provide just the themes.

- Bash-it – https://github.com/Bash-it/bash-it

- Oh My Bash – https://github.com/ohmybash/oh-my-bash

- Gogh – https://github.com/Mayccoll/Gogh

These all require running external bash scripts so make sure to do your own research to check that the projects are still in good standing at the time of reading. It's also worth scanning through some of the scripts yourself and checking the public issue tracker just to make sure the projects are still in good health before experimenting. This can be done by viewing the last commit or release for a project. Also you can check the issues tab on a project's GitHub page to see recent feedback from users.

Live Clock in Terminal

Another neat trick which demonstrates the many possibilities of spicing up your terminal is adding a live clock. This can be done by running the following code snippet (or placing it in your `.bashrc` to make permanent):

```
while sleep 1;
do
  tput sc;
  tput cup 0 $(($(tput cols)-11));
  echo -e "\e[31m`date +%r`\e[39m";
  tput rc;
done &
```

This creates a loop which runs once a second. It gets the width of your terminal and moves the cursor 11 spaces to the left of the top right. Then it outputs the current time using `date` and finally returns the cursor to the normal location with `tput rc`. An example of the live clock effect is shown in Figure 14-7.

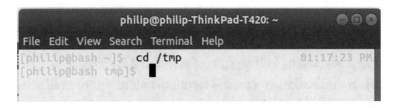

Figure 14-7. *Live clock in the upper right of the terminal*

Alternatively, we can put the time in the prompt text if we don't mind that it only updates after each command. To do that, you can just take one of the commands we used previously to update the prompt color and add \t which specifies the current time, for example:

```
export PS1="\e[0;32m\t \W \$ \e[m "
```

After running the preceding command, you'll instead see the time in the prompt text. If you want to use the 12-hour clock format instead, switch the t to T:

```
export PS1="\e[0;32m\T \W \$ \e[m "
```

Alternatively you can use the @ charachter for a complete 12-hour format with AM/PM indicator:

```
export PS1="\e[0;32m\@ \W \$ \e[m "
```

Examples of the three prompt time formats are shown in Figure 14-8.

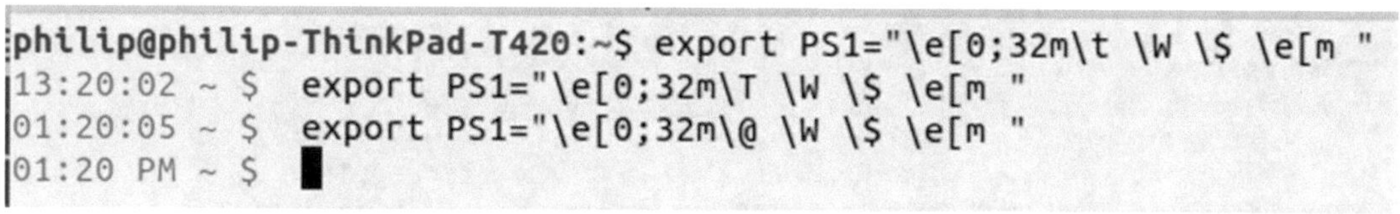

```
philip@philip-ThinkPad-T420:~$ export PS1="\e[0;32m\t \W \$ \e[m "
13:20:02 ~ $  export PS1="\e[0;32m\T \W \$ \e[m "
01:20:05 ~ $  export PS1="\e[0;32m\@ \W \$ \e[m "
01:20 PM ~ $ ■
```

Figure 14-8. *Time formats in bash prompt text*

Run a Program on Open

Sometimes people will run programs on terminal start using .bashrc for the added aesthetic. This can include things like fortune or perhaps echoing out a text file containing some TODO items.

Another common thing to run is the neofetch command. This isn't installed by default but can be found on most package managers. It's a highly customizable system information script. It's used as a way of sharing their chosen setup with the world in a screenshot while at the same time showing off the terminal theme they've chosen. An example of the output of Neofetch on my machine is shown in Figure 14-9.

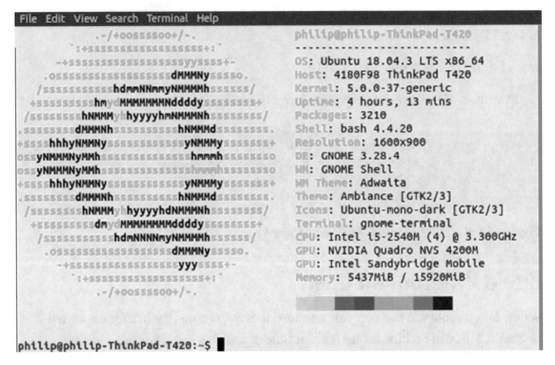

Figure 14-9. *Output from Neofetch*

Figure 14-9 is an example of running neofetch on my machine.

To run this command or any command on terminal open for that matter is as simple as adding a line at the bottom of your .bashrc with the command. Any programs you run from .bashrc will run when opening a new bash terminal.

Note   The program screenfetch provides a similar alternative to neofetch with a slightly different rendering for logos. It may also be slightly faster than neofetch.

Importing a File

If your .bashrc file becomes large, you may want to separate it into multiple files. This allows you to share and reuse parts and pieces without having to deal with one long file.

For example, you may want to separate all your aliases into a single file called `.bash_aliases`. Simply move the alias lines into a new file and import the new file using `source`:

```
source ~/.bash_aliases
```

The preceding code placed in `.bashrc` would cause `.bash_aliases` to be loaded and run every time a new terminal is opened.

.inputrc

We mentioned `.inputrc` in an earlier chapter as a way to change bash (*and several other programs*) keyboard shortcuts to Vim-based ones instead of the default Emacs-like ones.

The `.inputrc` file affects all programs that make use of the GNU readline library which includes several popular programs including bash as well as the REPLs for programming languages like Ruby, Python, and MySQL.

As was mentioned earlier, one of the options in `.inputrc` is to switch to Vim keyboard shortcuts by adding the lines

```
set editing-mode vi
set keymap vi
```

We can see all the default values for `.inputrc` by opening up the global file /etc/inputrc, which provides starting values for all users. This file likely contains some configurations as well as comments explaining what the configurations do.

One possible modification is turning off the sound which is output when you double tap tab to activate autocomplete. You may not have even noticed but on many systems when you press tab to activate autocomplete, an audio sound is made. This can be turned off by adding

```
set bell-style none
```

Another option which is possible but rarely used is making autocomplete case insensitive, so that if you write the name of a folder with or without a capital, it will complete regardless of what case is used by the matched folder.

```
set completion-ignore-case On
```

You may have noticed you often have to tap the tab key twice to show all the completions. If you'd prefer to see all the possible completions immediately instead, you can add the following line:

```
set show-all-if-unmodified On
```

Sometimes pressing tab will cause a file to partially complete, but then you'll hit a point where there are two or more possible ways to complete the file name. Normally, it will complete up to the difference, and then you have to press tab again to see the possible completions. If you'd rather it automatically complete what is possible and show all endings in a single ending, enable show-all-if-ambiguous:

```
set show-all-if-ambiguous On
```

When you run a command like ls, you may receive color-coded results depending on your system. If you want to also enable this for autocomplete, you can add the following line:

```
set colored-stats On
```

If you instead want a visual symbol to indicate file type similar to that shown when running ls -F, you can add the line

```
set visible-stats On
```

While it isn't common to modify .inputrc, it does provide a few different options which can't be done elsewhere.

Aside from changing the notification sound and switching between Vim- and Emacs-style keyboard shortcuts, you'll likely never need to modify your .inputrc though it is also possible to modify the functionality of keyboard shortcuts or add new ones. To get a complete list of all the possible options for .inputrc, run

```
man 3 readline
```

Other Dotfiles

The term dotfiles refers to hidden files starting with a dot that are used to configure programs. While .bashrc is one of the most popular dotfiles, it's far from the only one.

There are all kinds of dotfiles for both default programs and extras installed. Some other examples that can be used to customize programs include

- .wgetrc
- .curlrc
- .gitconfig
- .vimrc
- .tmux.conf

Summary

In this chapter, we looked at `.bashrc` and `.inputrc`, two dotfiles which can be used to customize the bash terminal. We saw some common modifications like adding to the path, defining functions, and making aliases. We also looked at some less used configuration files like `.bash_logout` and configuration options like terminal prompt and colors.

CHAPTER 15

Tmux Workflow

In this chapter, we'll be looking at Tmux, short for terminal multiplexer – a utility which is primarily used for managing backgrounded processes, but also has many other uses. In addition to keeping processes running, Tmux can also be used for dividing your terminal into smaller screens, creating a customized layout where you can monitor several panes at once.

Background Scripts

Tmux is one of my most used programs. It's primarily used for managing running shell scripts, ssh sessions, and any type of bash shell process. In the past years, Tmux has become so popular that it is shipping preinstalled on some Linux distributions like the latest Ubuntu Desktop.

If Tmux isn't installed on your machine, it should be available via your package manager:

```
sudo apt-get install tmux
```

Once you start using terminal-based applications and processes, you will quickly find you may want to run a process and keep it running without having to keep a dedicated terminal window open on your user interface. Traditionally, this could be done with a combination of built-in commands.

To demonstrate, let's create an ongoing process that will update a file with the current time every 3 seconds:

```
(while sleep 3; do date > /tmp/time; done)
```

With the preceding command running in your active terminal, press ctrl+z to pause the process. Then run

```
bg
```

© Philip Kirkbride 2020
P. Kirkbride, *Basic Linux Terminal Tips and Tricks*, https://doi.org/10.1007/978-1-4842-6035-7_15

Running bg will start the process again, but in the background. However, the process will still be associated with the terminal session. Next let's get a list of jobs running in the current terminal session.

```
jobs
```

You'll get back a list of jobs running in the current terminal, each with an associated number. You can use the job number to disassociate it with the terminal session by running the following command:

```
disown %1
```

You'll need to replace the 1 with the number associated with the process you want to disown. Once you've run that command, you can safely close the terminal window, and the process will continue to run. You can confirm this by going into the /tmp folder and ensuring that the time file is updating every 3 seconds.

Background Scripts with Tmux

The problem with the manual method is that there is no easy way to reattach a disowned process or program. Instead it is recommended that you use Tmux to manage and switch between virtual terminal windows. To create a new terminal session, simply run

```
tmux
```

You should see a small green bar at the bottom of the page which indicates your window is a Tmux session. Now as an example program, run the following:

```
top
```

You should now see top running and listing all the running processes on your machine. Now we will detach from the Tmux session and keep the window running in the background on the operating system, so we can easily reattach later. To do this, press ctrl+b (at the same time) followed by d.

Note   It's important to not press the d button at the same time here. With all Tmux commands, you first press ctrl+b, then release, and then press the command-specific key.

You will now be back at your default terminal window, which can be closed without affecting the Tmux session running in the background.

If you want to see all the Tmux sessions running on your computer, run

```
tmux ls
```

This will return a list of Tmux sessions and their associated IDs. To reconnect to one of these sessions, run the following (replacing 1 with the ID of the session you want to attach to):

```
tmux a -t 0
```

This can be useful in several situations including but not limited to

- You want to connect to multiple servers or IoT devices at once to run commands which may take some time to complete.

- You want to background a command but keep the ability to return to debug.

- You're using a terminal-based editor like Vim and want to switch between multiple files without closing them.

Tmux with SSH

One of the most useful situations that you'll want to use Tmux in is working with remote servers or devices over SSH. Often when connecting to a server, you'll need to perform a long-running task. Without the ability to background and reattach to a session easily, some resort to leaving the SSH session running on their desktop waiting for the job to finish.

Not only does this restrict the user by forcing them to keep their computer on for the duration of the command, it also introduces the risk of the connection breaking. When a normal SSH session breaks, often the running script will be killed; thus after reconnecting, you need to start back at square one.

Tmux gives you the freedom to start a command, disconnect from the session, and then close SSH. When you return to the server and attach to the session, it will be as if you never left. If you're actively in the Tmux session and your SSH connection gets disrupted, no need to worry, as it will continue running and be available when you reconnect.

This makes Tmux ideal not only for long-running commands but also scripts you intend to keep running permanently such as a web server or script. In the case that something goes wrong, it becomes easy to connect to the session in question by name, see the error in the program's output, make necessary changes, and restart the script.

Named Sessions

When we made our first Tmux session, we saw that it was automatically named 0 and we reattached using `tmux a -t 0`. When creating a new session, it's also possible to give the session a nickname to help you what's running in it. Let's create a session called "top":

```
tmux new -s top
```

Now if we detach from our session and use `tmux ls`, we'll "top" in the place of where we previously saw "0". If you've already created a session and you want to change the name, you can run

```
tmux rename-session -t top new-name
```

Just switch out "top" for the name of your target session and "new-name" with your desired new name.

Switching Tmux Sessions

`tmux` is highly customizable and has many quick keyboard shortcuts. Most of the keyboard shortcuts will use ctrl+b followed by a letter. One of my most used keyboard shortcuts is ctrl+b followed by s. In this case, s stands for switch and allows you to quickly switch between open Tmux sessions without detaching.

For example, say you have a few ssh sessions open and want to switch from one to another while waiting for a process to complete. Simply run `ctrl+b s`, and use the down arrow to select the session you want to open. Then run whatever command you want in another session and quickly press `ctrl+b s` again to switch back.

Killing Sessions

There are a few ways you can kill an existing session. If you're already actively attached to the session, simply press ctrl+d and the session will close in the same way your normal terminal would.

Alternatively, you can kill a session without being attached to it with the kill-session command. As with attach and renaming, you'll provide the name of the terminal in question with the -t flag:

```
tmux kill-session -t new-name
```

The preceding command will kill the session with name "new-name". It's also possible to close all sessions at once by killing the whole server. To do this, run

```
tmux kill-server
```

Be careful with this command as it stops any scripts you have running in Tmux sessions immediately without warning.

Windows in Sessions

It's possible to create multiple windows within a single Tmux session, each running their own bash session. Before we talk about creating and navigating between windows, we should clarify the three levels of hierarchy that exist in Tmux and the technical definition of a Tmux window, as it differs slightly from what we normally consider to be a window. The hierarchy that terminal sessions exist within on Tmux is described in Table 15-1.

Table 15-1. *Tmux levels of hierarchy*

Term	Description
Session	A group of windows. Is the highest level of hierarchy in Tmux
Window	A bash session contained within a Tmux session. A session can contain multiple windows
Pane	A pane is contained within a window. A window can be split up into multiple panes so that more than one pane can be viewed at one time

When we create a Tmux session, it automatically has a single window by default. To create a second window, make sure you're inside a tmux session, and then run `ctrl+b` followed by `c`. This will cause you to go into a new window.

Often windows are compared to tabs as they are workspaces that can be easily switched between while in a session. Furthermore, in the bottom-left corner of the screen, all the windows in a session are displayed, with the active window having a "*" at the end. An example of the text indicating running Tmux windows is shown in Figure 15-1.

Figure 15-1. *List of windows in Tmux status bar*

To get a better view of how the windows relate to our session, press `ctrl+b` followed by `w`. This will open up a list of all sessions and windows; it's an easy way to move between either. An example of the Tmux session list is shown in Figure 15-2.

```
File  Edit  View  Search  Terminal  Help
(0)   - 0: 2 windows (attached)
(1)   |-> 0: bash- (1 panes) "philip-ThinkPad-T420"
(2)   |-> 1: bash* (1 panes) "philip-ThinkPad-T420"




1 (sort: index)
ilip@philip-ThinkPad-T420:~$ █
```

Figure 15-2. *List of active sessions and windows in Tmux*

Notice how the two windows are listed as children of the session with label 0. You can press the up and down arrow keys to move between the windows and press enter to focus on one. To emphasize how windows are children of sessions, let's detach from Tmux completely by pressing ctrl+b followed by d.

Next create a new session by running tmux, and when the session opens, create a new window with ctrl+b followed by c. Now if we again press ctrl+b followed by w, we will see something like the session list shown in Figure 15-3.

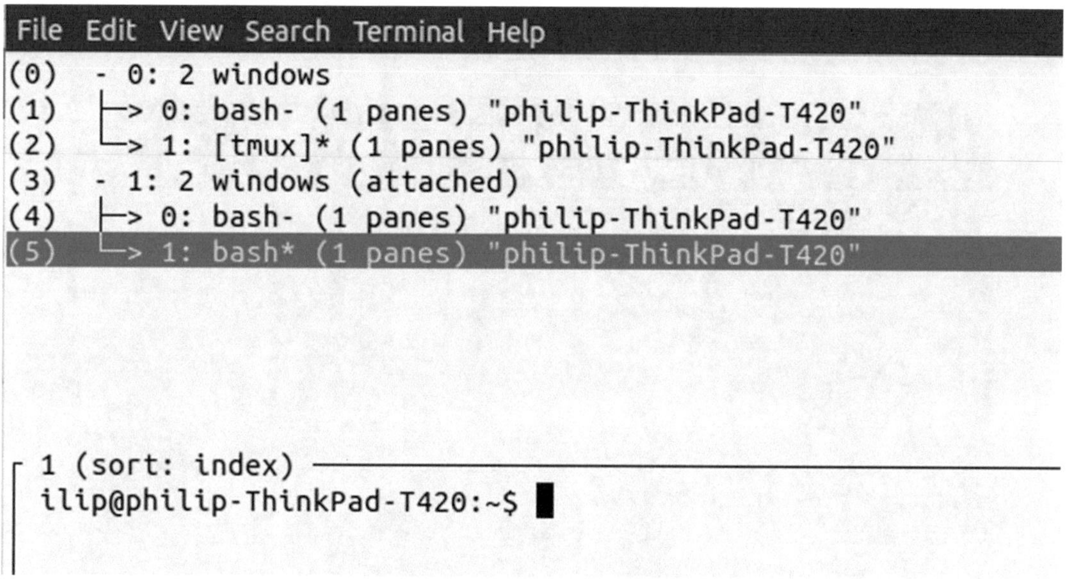

```
File  Edit  View  Search  Terminal  Help
(0)   - 0: 2 windows
(1)    ├─> 0: bash- (1 panes) "philip-ThinkPad-T420"
(2)    └─> 1: [tmux]* (1 panes) "philip-ThinkPad-T420"
(3)   - 1: 2 windows (attached)
(4)    ├─> 0: bash- (1 panes) "philip-ThinkPad-T420"
(5)    └─> 1: bash* (1 panes) "philip-ThinkPad-T420"




 1 (sort: index) ───────────────────────────────
 ilip@philip-ThinkPad-T420:~$ █
```

Figure 15-3. *Two sessions each with two child windows*

We have two sessions which each have two children windows. Let's go into the third window labeled "(4)". Now if from here we want to go back to "(5)", we could reopen the window list, but a shorter way would actually be ctrl+b followed by p for previous. To go back to "(4)" again, you can press ctrl+b followed by n for next. Alternatively, we can use the window number in place of p or n if we want to specify the specific window.

This can be useful for sorting windows in sessions based on their use, for example, having all windows for SSH sessions in a single session.

Pane Splitting

Tmux also provides a powerful secondary functionality that allows you to split a window up into separate sections, known as panes, each running its own bash instance. This can be extremely useful when needing to run multiple terminal applications simultaneously or when monitoring multiple full-screen terminal applications.

To get started, first make sure you have a Tmux session open, and then press ctrl+b followed by ". This will split your window horizontally. An example of a window split horizontally is shown in Figure 15-4.

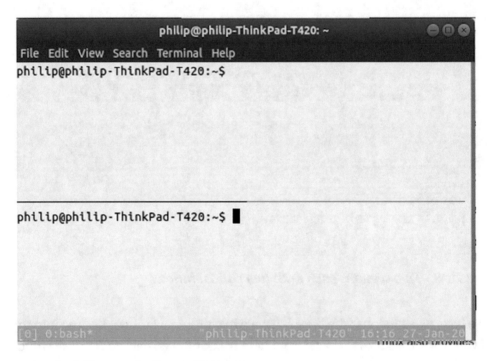

Figure 15-4. *A Tmux window split into two panes*

Or if you instead want to split the session horizontally, press ctrl+b followed by %. An example of a vertically split window is shown in Figure 15-5.

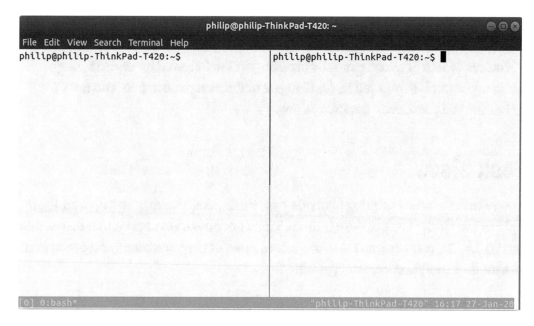

Figure 15-5. *Vertically split window in Tmux*

It's also possible to split an already split subsection to create as many windows as you'd like per session. To do so, simply run the command to split horizontally or vertically a second time. See Figure 15-6 for an example of a window split into three bash terminals.

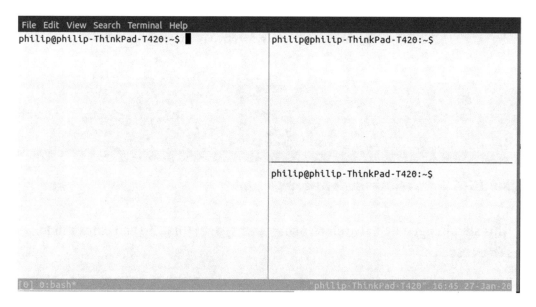

Figure 15-6. *Combination of vertical and horizontal panes in Tmux*

Your pane setup will be saved if you decide to detach from Tmux or switch between windows and sessions.

You can switch between panes by pressing ctrl+b followed by any arrow key. Alternatively, ctrl+b followed by o will toggle to the next pane in line, and once it reaches the last pane, cycle back to the first.

Clock Mode

If you're using window splitting to divide your workspace, you may end up wanting to display a live clock in one of the windows. Tmux provides a small extra that makes this easy. With a Tmux session active in a window, press ctrl+b and then t. An example of a clock mode display is shown in Figure 15-7.

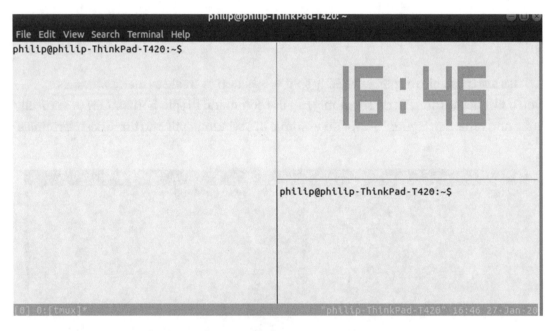

Figure 15-7. *Tmux clock mode in a single pane*

This should open up a live clock using your system time. To exit clock mode, press q or esc.

Help Page

Tmux also comes with a built-in help page which contains a list containing every keyboard shortcut; there are several so it is multiple pages long. To activate it, press

`ctrl+b, ?`

You should get a scrollable page like shown in Figure 15-8; it can be exited with esc or q.

```
 File  Edit  View  Search  Terminal  Help
bind-key      -T copy-mode    C-Space        send-keys -X begin-selection          [242/242]
bind-key      -T copy-mode    C-a            send-keys -X start-of-line
bind-key      -T copy-mode    C-b            send-keys -X cursor-left
bind-key      -T copy-mode    C-c            send-keys -X cancel
bind-key      -T copy-mode    C-e            send-keys -X end-of-line
bind-key      -T copy-mode    C-f            send-keys -X cursor-right
bind-key      -T copy-mode    C-g            send-keys -X clear-selection
bind-key      -T copy-mode    C-k            send-keys -X copy-end-of-line
bind-key      -T copy-mode    C-n            send-keys -X cursor-down
bind-key      -T copy-mode    C-p            send-keys -X cursor-up
bind-key      -T copy-mode    C-r            command-prompt -i -I "#{pane_search_string}" -
p "(search up)" "send -X search-backward-incremental \"%%%\""
bind-key      -T copy-mode    C-s            command-prompt -i -I "#{pane_search_string}" -
p "(search down)" "send -X search-forward-incremental \"%%%\""
bind-key      -T copy-mode    C-v            send-keys -X page-down
bind-key      -T copy-mode    C-w            send-keys -X copy-selection-and-cancel
bind-key      -T copy-mode    Escape         send-keys -X cancel
bind-key      -T copy-mode    Space          send-keys -X page-down
bind-key      -T copy-mode    ,              send-keys -X jump-reverse
bind-key      -T copy-mode    ;              send-keys -X jump-again
bind-key      -T copy-mode    F              command-prompt -1 -p "(jump backward)" "send -
X jump-backward \"%%%\""
[0] 0:[tmux]*                                  "philip-ThinkPad-T420" 19:06 27-Jan-20
```

Figure 15-8. *Tmux help page*

Customize with .tmux.conf

Tmux can be customized to change the key combinations used to trigger actions as well as modifying the look and layout. All customization of Tmux is done by editing ~/.tmux. conf; if that file doesn't exist on your system, simply create it and tmux will make use of it. This configuration file can be used for creating new keyboard shortcuts, as well as changing the visual appearance of tmux.

Tmux first looks in /etc/tmux.conf for a global configuration that applies to all users and then looks in the home directory for the file .tmux.conf. So if you'd like to apply settings across multiple users, you can make use of the global version. If you don't have a ~/.tmux.conf file, start this section by creating one.

```
touch ~/.tmux.conf
```

Configure Color and Style

Similar to changing colors in .bashrc, we can only use as many colors as are enabled. To check what colors are enabled on your terminal, run

```
tput colors
```

If you get a number less than 256, you'll want to enable 256 by adding the following to your .bashrc file:

```
export TERM=xterm-256color
```

The 256 colors available are the same as in the previous chapter. Besides using color codes directly, we also have keywords for common colors including *black, blue, cyan, green, magenta, red, white,* and *yellow*.

If we want to make the Tmux bar at the bottom of our terminal blue, for example, we can add the following to our .tmux.conf:

```
set-option -g status-bg blue
```

This will change the background color to blue. If we want to change the text for the Tmux bar, we can add

```
set-option -g status-fg white
```

This will result in a bottom bar styled like Figure 15-9.

Figure 15-9. Tmux status bar with modified colors

Note   When updating the colors and style of tmux, you'll need to make sure all tmux windows have been terminated before the new style takes effect. If you have even a single tmux window open in the background, change the style, and then open a new window, the old values will still be active.

If we want to use one of the 256 color codes directly instead, we would do so with `color` followed by the color code like the following:

```
set-option -g status-bg color14
```

We can also change the color used for our windows open and have it display a color different from the rest of the status bar.

```
set-option -g window-status-bg blue
set-option -g window-status-fg black
```

This becomes even more useful when you set the active window name to be a different color:

```
set-option -g window-status-current-bg white
```

This creates the feeling of windows really being like tabs, as you get some visual feedback when switching between windows. An example of the status bar with this style enabled is shown in Figure 15-10.

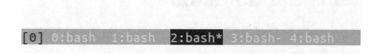

Figure 15-10. *Current window highlighting in Tmux status bar*

In addition to the status bar, you can also change the colors used for pane borders.

```
set-option -g pane-border-bg green
set-option -g pane-border-fg yellow
```

As with windows, there is a separate selector for the pane.

```
set-option -g pane-active-border-bg blue
set-option -g pane-active-border-fg yellow
```

An example of these styles applied is shown in Figure 15-11.

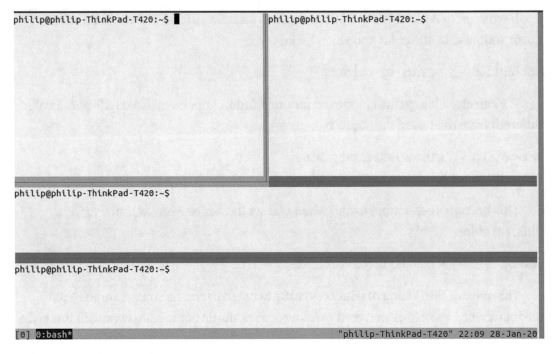

Figure 15-11. *Modified pane border colors in Tmux*

Change Status Bar Contents

Similar to how text prompt in bash can be changed, the text in the Tmux status bar can be changed. The left side and right side are controlled by two different variables. As an example, let's use some simple static text to update both the left and right sides. Like with the last section, the following lines can be added to .tmux.conf file:

```
set -g status-left "Hello"
set -g status-right "World"
```

This results in replacing the default left and right status bar text as shown in Figure 15-12.

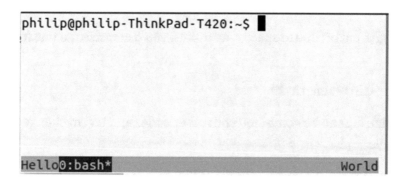

Figure 15-12. *Modifying status bar text in Tmux*

Of course, in most cases, you'll want some interactive aspects like time, hostname, and number of windows open. Like .bashrc special codes are reserved for these elements. A list of codes that can be used in the status bar is shown in Table 15-2.

Table 15-2. *Status bar codes*

Code	Description
#I	Index of current window
#P	Index of current pane
#S	Session name
#T	Title of current window
##	Used for a literal #
#H	Hostname up to first
#h	Full hostname
#(command)	Runs a command and shows first line of output
#[attribute]	Modifies color or attribute of text by wrapping

So if we wanted hostname followed by index of current window on the left side, for example, run

```
set -g status-left "#h #I"
```

If the text gets cut off due to space constraints, you can resize the maximum space available with

```
set -g status-left-length 200
```

The attribute tag can be combined with other codes and text to change the color of text, for example:

```
set -g status-left "#[bg=red, fg=white]#h #I"
```

Remap Commands

If you find a key combination you use often is uncomfortable, you can modify it. For example, people who use GNU Screen before switching to Tmux often find themselves wanting to use ctrl+a in place of ctrl+b for the prefix used before tmux keyboard shortcuts. To bind the prefix command to ctrl+a, the following line should be added to the config file:

```
set -g prefix C-a
```

This will cause ctrl+a to be used for the prefix for commands like detaching, creating a new window, and so on. By default, your ctrl+b will also still be connected to the prefix command. If you want to detach a combination from a command, you have to do it manually as another step.

```
unbind C-b
```

If you're running tmux while editing the .tmux.conf file, you'll have to manually source the config for it to take effect.

```
tmux source-file ~/.tmux.conf
```

If you're using Vim, you may want to add keybindings to make navigation possible with h, j, k, and l, each mapped to a direction similar to that used in Vim.

```
# Vim Movement
bind h select-pane -L # left
bind j select-pane -D # down
bind k select-pane -U # up
bind l select-pane -R # right
```

This will allow you to use ctrl+b followed by h to switch to the pane to your left as well as the associated direction for the other keys.

Screen Sharing with Tmux

Another interesting use case that Tmux makes possible is screen sharing terminal windows. If you have two people logged in to a server or device using the same user, they'll both have full access to all the Tmux sessions of that user. This includes the ability to have both people connected to the same Tmux session at once and both seeing live updates as either person interacts with the terminal.

This is a great way to do pair programming or work with another person to debug a system. Unlike other methods of screen sharing, Tmux over SSH takes hardly any bandwidth, and it provides the ability for both users to interact rather than simply having one person watch the other.

Theme Packs

As with styling .bashrc, some projects exist which specialize in the customization and theming of Tmux. One of the most popular is "Oh My Tmux" which in addition to providing a pleasing theme adds some additional functionality like a battery indicator. The default style that comes out of the box with "Oh My Tmux" is shown in Figure 15-13.

```
philip@philip-ThinkPad-T420:/tmp$ git clone https://github.com/gpakosz/.tmux.
git
Cloning into '.tmux'...
remote: Enumerating objects: 644, done.
remote: Total 644 (delta 0), reused 0 (delta 0), pack-reused 644
Receiving objects: 100% (644/644), 272.97 KiB | 731.00 KiB/s, done.
Resolving deltas: 100% (312/312), done.
philip@philip-ThinkPad-T420:/tmp$ cd .tmux/
philip@philip-ThinkPad-T420:/tmp/.tmux$ cp .tm
.tmux.conf          .tmux.conf.local
philip@philip-ThinkPad-T420:/tmp/.tmux$ cp .tmux.conf ~/█
```

```
 0   1 bash      ↑ ▮▮▮▮ 100% | 11:59 | 29 Jan   philip  philip-ThinkPad-T420
```

Figure 15-13. *Oh My Tmux theme*

Another piece of functionality added by "Oh My Tmux" is a keyboard indicator which indicates when the prefix ctrl+b has been pressed and Tmux is waiting for the command key. This keyboard symbol is shown in Figure 15-14; when shown, it means the prefix has been pressed and Tmux is waiting for the command key.

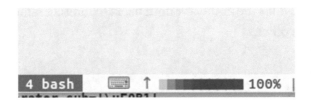

Figure 15-14. *Oh My Tmux prefix pressed indicator in status bar*

To install Oh My Tmux, simply clone the project and move .tmux.conf and .tmux. conf.local to your home folder. Make sure to back up your original .tmux.conf if you want to save anything.

```
git clone https://github.com/gpakosz/.tmux
cd .tmux
cp .tmux.conf* ~
```

Then all you have to do is open and/or restart Tmux.

In addition to the style change, you'll also have some additional keybindings such as the Vim keybindings that we configured manually – extra bindings for creating windows with `ctrl+b` followed by - for a horizontal pane or _ for a vertical one.

As well as a new binding for `ctrl+b` followed by + to move a pane within a window to a new window displaying only that pane using the full screen. For a complete list of features and bindings, see the included README on the Oh My Tmux GitHub.

Tmuxinator

As you start using Tmux and creating custom workspaces by splitting your windows up into panes, you may find you have certain setups you want to create often. For example, say we want to run a window split up into `systemctl`, `htop`, and `nmon` like shown in Figure 15-15.

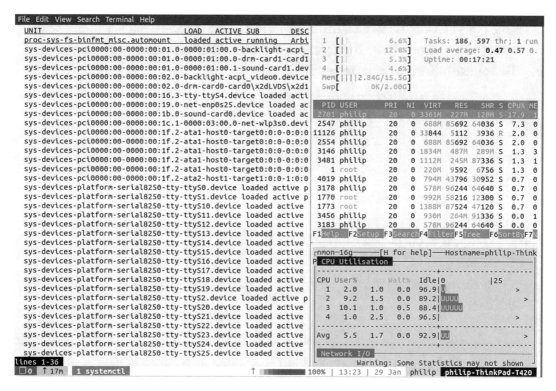

Figure 15-15. *System monitoring workspace in Tmux*

Tmuxinator is a Tmux launcher which allows you to make predefined layouts so that you can easily open specific workspaces without manually doing it on each open. You'll need to have the Ruby programming language installed to make use of Tmuxinator.

```
sudo apt-get install ruby
gem install tmuxinator
```

Tmuxinator also requires the environment variable EDITOR to be set; if you run echo $EDITOR and it's empty, you'll need to set it in your .bashrc file. Swap out the value for whatever your preferred editor is:

```
export EDITOR='vim'
```

With Tmuxinator installed, you can create a new layout by running

```
tmuxinator new system-monitor
```

A template for a YAML file will be opened in your chosen editor, including comments to help guide you with the syntax. An example layout that opens a single window with three panes is as follows (it uses htop and nmon so you'll need to make sure they're installed or use other programs instead):

```
name: system-monitor
root: ~/

windows:
  - monitor:
      layout: main-vertical
      panes:
        - systemctl
        - htop
        - nmon
  - editor: vim
```

Note   When you create a new layout in Tmuxinator, make sure to delete all the boilerplate code that is there by default. Below the many comments in the boilerplate is an example layout which will overwrite your code if not removed or edited.

The preceding example creates a window called "monitor" which contains three panes with the programs listed as well as a second window that has Vim running. Tmuxinator also provides other configuration variables such as `root` that defines what directory the windows or panes start in or attach which specifies if the session should be opened on creation.

For a full list of features and options, see the README included on the Tmuxinator GitHub page.

Summary

In this chapter, we looked at how Tmux can improve your workflow when working with long-running terminal sessions both locally and remotely. In addition to the basics, we saw how Tmux also allows splitting our screen up between multiple bash sessions to make custom layouts for any purpose. We further automated the creation of layouts using tmuxinator, which allows layouts to be saved as YAML config files and quickly opened in a single command.

We also saw how Tmux has a configuration file `~/.tmux.conf` similar to the bash configuration file, where we can override any keybindings and change the colors and style of Tmux. Using even a small subsection of the techniques described here should allow you to improve your terminal workflow significantly.

## CHAPTER 16

Terminal Tools for Working with Images and Videos

While the command line is primarily text based, there are surprisingly some great tools for working with images and videos which rival or in some cases are the basis for their GUI equivalents. For example, if you've used any type of website that modifies or generates images, it's likely it was using ImageMagick on the back end. In the same way, if you've used any Linux-based video editor, there is a good chance it was built on top of ffmpeg.

Given that many of these visual-based programs are simply calling the command-line equivalents, you can save yourself some time by learning to use the command-line versions for simple tasks like modifying images or videos. We'll also look at some less used programs like gnuplot and how to modify the animation which is displayed during startup.

ImageMagick

One of the most powerful utilities for manipulating images is actually native to the command line. ImageMagick is widely used not only on the command line but also in server-side code using languages like PHP, Python, and Node.js. These languages essentially just provide a wrapper to the feature-rich command-line utility.

Some of the things you can do with ImageMagick include

- Convert images
- Draw shapes
- Draw text and manipulate it
- Paint an image

© Philip Kirkbride 2020
P. Kirkbride, *Basic Linux Terminal Tips and Tricks*, https://doi.org/10.1007/978-1-4842-6035-7_16

- Deform an image

- Crop an image

- Image filters

Creating an Image with Text

To get started, make sure you have ImageMagick installed; it can be found in most package repositories. Unlike many programs, it isn't called with the same name that it is installed from. Instead ImageMagick makes other commands such as `convert` available. As a starting point, let's create a blank canvas with a size of 400 x 400 pixels:

```
convert -size 400x400 xc:white white.png
```

You should now have a blank white image that is 400 x 400 pixels.

Next let's add some text to our image:

```
convert white.png -gravity North \
  -pointsize 30 -annotate +0+100 \
  'Basic Linux Terminal' white.png
```

The `-gravity North` option used here tells ImageMagick to place the text at the top of the image; alternatively, we could use South, West, or East. Let's create another section of text at the bottom of the image using South; this one saying "Tips and Tricks":

```
convert white.png -gravity South \
  -pointsize 30 -annotate +0+100 \
  'Tips and Tricks' white.png
```

Then `pointsize` specifies the font size, followed by `annotate` which adds space around the text so it isn't placed right against the top of the image.

After checking that the text rendered as expected, try rotating the text:

```
convert white.png  -distort ScaleRotateTranslate 30 white.png
```

You should now have a result that looks something like Figure 16-1.

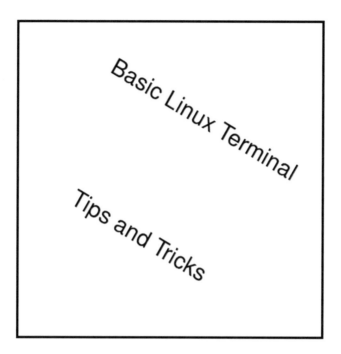

Figure 16-1. *Image generated by ImageMagick*

To make the preceding preview easier to see, I actually added a 3 pixel black border, making it easier to see where it starts and ends. This can be done with the command

```
convert -bordercolor Black -border 3x3 white.png white.png
```

Getting Image Information

Early on in the book, we saw that we can use the `file` command to get information on file types. However, when it comes to images, there's actually a lot more metadata that you might want to see. ImageMagick provides another utility for examining image details called `identify`. The simplest use is just running it with a file as input:

```
identify white.png
```

This returns basic information about the image including type, dimensions, color spectrum, and size. You can get even more detailed information by adding the `-verbose` flag; see Figure 16-2 for some example output from the `identify -verbose` command.

```
philip@philip-ThinkPad-T420:/tmp$ identify -verbose white.png
Image: white.png
  Format: PNG (Portable Network Graphics)
  Mime type: image/png
  Class: PseudoClass
  Geometry: 406x406+0+0
  Units: Undefined
  Type: Grayscale
  Base type: Grayscale
  Endianess: Undefined
  Colorspace: Gray
  Depth: 8-bit
  Channel depth:
    gray: 8-bit
  Channel statistics:
    Pixels: 164836
    Gray:
      min: 0 (0)
      max: 255 (1)
      mean: 243.049 (0.953132)
      standard deviation: 51.7609 (0.202984)
      kurtosis: 16.6457
      skewness: -4.27824
      entropy: 0.0726504
  Colors: 256
```

Figure 16-2. *Image data using ImageMagick* `identify` *command*

You may find that the -verbose flag actually returns too much data. If you want to pick and choose what specific attributes to show, you can specify them directly, for example:

```
identify -format '%f - %m - %w \n' white.png
```

The preceding example specifies the file name, file type, and width followed by a newline. You can find a full list of letters and the attribute they represent at https://imagemagick.org/script/escape.php.

Label an Image

Another common task you might want to perform is adding a small label to a photo; this can be handy when you plan to display the images online and want people to know you're the original source if the image is saved and displayed somewhere else.

To do this, we can simply use the built-in `composite label` which will add some text to the top left of our photo in a single step:

```
composite label:'github.com/kirkins' white.png labeled.png
```

The result will look like the input image with the addition of our small but persistent label in the top left, as shown in Figure 16-3.

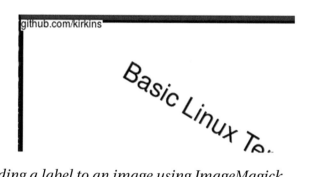

Figure 16-3. *Adding a label to an image using ImageMagick*

ffmpeg

This is similar to ImageMagick but for videos instead of still images. `ffmpeg` can be used for all kinds of common video editing tasks, and it is actually used in the code of many popular video and audio editing GUI software suites including Audacity and VLC media player.

Some of the things you can do with ffmpeg include

- Convert video file type

- Compress a video

- Speed up/slow down a video

- Trim a clip

- Increase/decrease sound

Convert File Types

One of the simplest and most common commands offered by ffmpeg is the simple conversion of file types. In many cases, converting a video is very simple – just use the -i flag for input and specify the output type by using the desired file type extension for your output. For example, if we want to convert an mp4 to a webm, simply run the following:

```
ffmpeg -i video.mp4 video.webm
```

This same technique can be applied to audio files as well, for example, mp3 to ogg:

```
ffmpeg -i audio.mp3 audio.ogg
```

It's even possible to take a video and output it as a gif, though you'll likely want to stick to converting only short videos:

```
ffmpeg -i video.mp4 picture.gif
```

Another common conversion which is slightly more complicated is going from a video file type to an audio-only file type. In this case, you'll need to add the -vn flag which stands for "video no," for example:

```
ffmpeg -i video.mp4 -vn song.mp3
```

Compress a Video

After recording a video locally and wanting to upload it to the Web, you may find the size is too large for practical use. Instead of loading up some clunky video editing software, you can run a one-liner with ffmpeg to compress it:

```
ffmpeg -i input.mp4 -b 1000000 output.mp4
```

In the preceding example, we're taking a video called input.mp4 and outputting it as output.mp4 with a reduced bitrate of 1,000,000 bits or 1 megabit per second. To put that in perspective, a DVD is generally 4–8 megabits per second, and Blu-ray is 24–40. The size depends on both the dimensions of the video and the quality.

Slow Down a Video

If you've ever wanted to watch something in slow motion but didn't want to do the hard work of opening up a full-fledged video editor, ffmpeg has a solution for you. Any video (or sound file for that matter) can easily be sped up or slowed down with ffmpeg. This can be done with the command:

```
ffmpeg -i video.webm -filter:v "setpts=2.0*PTS" slow.webm
```

In the preceding command, the 2.0 means that our video is spread out over two times the original length. If we instead used setpts=0.5*PTS, we'd have the opposite effect, speeding up the video by compressing it into half the length.

The same can be applied to audio such as an mp3 by using a different filter:

```
ffmpeg -i audio.mp3 -filter:a "atempo=2.0" slow.mp3
```

The preceding example will only affect the video, but the sound will play at normal speed. If you want to change both, you'll need to add a second filter. For example, to slow the sound at the same rate as the video add -filter:a "atempo=0.5":

```
ffmpeg -i video.webm \
  -filter:v "setpts=2.0*PTS" \
  -filter:a "atempo=0.5" slow.webm
```

Or to speed both video and sound to 2x, use

```
ffmpeg -i video.webm \
  -filter:v "setpts=0.5*PTS" \
  -filter:a "atempo=2" slow.webm
```

Trim a Video

Another common task you might want to use ffmpeg for is trimming a video so you can create a new video from some subsection of the original video. If we wanted to cut the contents starting at 3 seconds into the video with a duration of 8 seconds, we could run

```
ffmpeg -i vid.webm -ss 00:00:03 -t 00:00:08 -async 1 cut.webm
```

This will result in a new video file called `cut.webm` which is 8 seconds in length going from the 3-second mark to the 11-second mark. This same command can also be applied to audio files like mp3.

Increase Volume in a Video

If you've ever come across a video where it was hard to hear the audio even on max volume, this next command is for you. With `ffmpeg` we can actually upscale the audio of a file so that it plays at a louder volume.

Volume is measured using "dB" which stands for decibels. If we want to increase the audio on our video by 5 decibels, we would run the following:

```
ffmpeg -i in.mp4 -vcodec copy -af "volume=5dB" out.mp4
```

In the same way, we can lower the volume by using a negative value for the volume, for example, `-5dB` which would turn down the volume by 5 decibels:

```
ffmpeg -i in.mp4 -vcodec copy -af "volume=-5dB" out.mp4
```

Download Videos with youtube-dl

Now that you're a little familiar with how you can modify, trim, and process videos with ffmpeg, you may find yourself wanting to work with videos from around the Web, for example, downloading a commonly listened song from YouTube and converting it to an mp3 or cutting a clip from a funny video to turn into a gif to share with your friends.

`youtube-dl` is a very actively developed command-line tool for downloading YouTube videos as well as over 1000 different websites including

- Vimeo

- SoundCloud

- Facebook

- Twitter

- News sites like Fox and CBC

That's just a few out of the over 1000 supported sites. The full list can be found at `https://github.com/ytdl-org/youtube-dl/blob/master/docs/supportedsites.md`.

The most common way to install `youtube-dl` is via Python's package manager `pip`:

```
sudo -H pip install --upgrade youtube-dl
```

However, it's also possible to download an executable from the official site with `curl` in a single step if you prefer not to use `pip`. To get the most up-to-date options for installing, check out the projects on GitHub at `https://github.com/ytdl-org/youtube-dl`.

The simplest command and likely your most used one is to simply use the utility passing in the URL of the video you want to download:

```
youtube-dl https://www.youtube.com/watch?v=DfK83xEtJ_k
```

Be aware that by default the highest quality available will be downloaded, which with the preceding video is over 1GB. If you want to download another format, you can see the available formats for a video by using the `-F` flag. An example of returned available formats is shown in Figure 16-4.

```
philip@philip-ThinkPad-T420:/tmp$ youtube-dl -F https://www.youtube.com/watch?v=DfK83xEtJ_k
[youtube] DfK83xEtJ_k: Downloading webpage
[youtube] DfK83xEtJ_k: Downloading video info webpage
[info] Available formats for DfK83xEtJ_k:
format code  extension  resolution note
599          m4a        audio only tiny    32k , mp4a.40.5 (22050Hz), 2.05MiB
600          webm       audio only tiny    35k , opus  (48000Hz), 2.31MiB
249          webm       audio only tiny    52k , opus @ 50k (48000Hz), 3.37MiB
250          webm       audio only tiny    65k , opus @ 70k (48000Hz), 4.06MiB
251          webm       audio only tiny   118k , opus @160k (48000Hz), 7.39MiB
140          m4a        audio only tiny   130k , m4a_dash container, mp4a.40.2@128k (44100Hz), 8.64MiB
598          webm       256x144    144p    29k , vp9, 13fps, video only, 1.66MiB
597          mp4        256x144    144p    40k , avc1.4d400b, 13fps, video only, 2.25MiB
160          mp4        256x144    144p    84k , avc1.4d400c, 25fps, video only, 2.55MiB
278          webm       256x144    144p    96k , webm container, vp9, 25fps, video only, 5.40MiB
133          mp4        426x240    240p   150k , avc1.4d4015, 25fps, video only, 4.82MiB
242          webm       426x240    240p   191k , vp9, 25fps, video only, 8.20MiB
134          mp4        640x360    360p   355k , avc1.4d401e, 25fps, video only, 13.96MiB
243          webm       640x360    360p   377k , vp9, 25fps, video only, 16.84MiB
244          webm       854x480    480p   695k , vp9, 25fps, video only, 30.07MiB
135          mp4        854x480    480p   758k , avc1.4d401e, 25fps, video only, 30.08MiB
247          webm       1280x720   720p  1398k , vp9, 25fps, video only, 61.96MiB
136          mp4        1280x720   720p  1514k , avc1.4d401f, 25fps, video only, 60.61MiB
248          webm       1920x1080  1080p 2598k , vp9, 25fps, video only, 125.16MiB
137          mp4        1920x1080  1080p 2821k , avc1.640028, 25fps, video only, 116.06MiB
271          webm       2560x1440  1440p 8264k , vp9, 25fps, video only, 383.81MiB
313          webm       3840x2160  2160p 17842k , vp9, 25fps, video only, 1.05GiB
18           mp4        640x360    360p   443k , avc1.42001E, mp4a.40.2@ 96k (44100Hz), 29.57MiB
22           mp4        1280x720   720p 1037k , avc1.64001F, mp4a.40.2@192k (44100Hz) (best)
philip@philip-ThinkPad-T420:/tmp$ █
```

Figure 16-4. *Viewing available formats with youtube-dl*

Take note of the first column "format code" for the video you want. The format code can be specified with the -f flag allowing you to download a much smaller version, thus speeding up the download and saving you date (*or downloading audio only if you just want to list*). Given the preceding list, if we want to download the smallest video possible, we could pick format code 598, which downloads almost instantly:

```
youtube-dl -f 598 https://www.youtube.com/watch?v=DfK83xEtJ_k
```

As mentioned, youtube-dl is a very active project with lots of options and features. It's definitely worth checking out some of those extra features on their GitHub README, but for most situations, what we've seen here will get the job done.

Creating Charts with gnuplot

Another visual-based task which is possible from the command line is visualizing data as graphs – either by viewing that data in the terminal itself or converting data into image files for later use.

One program that makes this easy is gnuplot which is widely available in package managers.

To demonstrate plotting a simple bar chart, let's create a data file called days.dat containing the following:

```
0 Monday 100
1 Tuesday 220
2 Wednesday 75
```

Next open gnuplot, which is done by simply entering the command with no inputs or options.

With gnuplot open, first change the mode to dumb which causes the generated chart to be displayed in the terminal as text art. By default, charts are generated in a qt-based GUI which pops up after each command; despite not being completely terminal based, the qt version of charts does look better. So if you prefer to use qt, simply skip this first command:

```
set terminal dumb
```

Next we'll set the boxwidth for our chart and fillstyle:

```
set boxwidth 0.5
set style fill solid
```

Finally, tell gnuplot to plot the days.dat file using

```
plot "days.dat" using 1:3:xtic(2) with boxes
```

The 1:3 here specifies that we're using column 1 of the data for the x-coordinates and column 3 for the y-coordinates. Then xtic(2) says that we apply column 2 as the label for each x value. If we instead use xtic(1), our day name labels would be replaced with the index numbers. Finally, with boxes simply specifies the chart type. An example of the visualization output is shown in Figure 16-5.

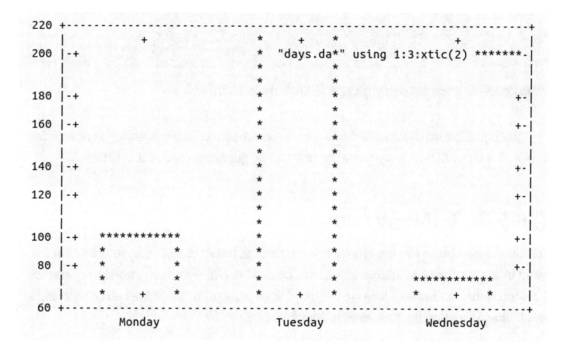

Figure 16-5. *gnuplot displaying a bar chart in terminal*

gnuplot can also be used to graph mathematical equations, for example, running plot sin(x) generates the chart shown in Figure 16-6.

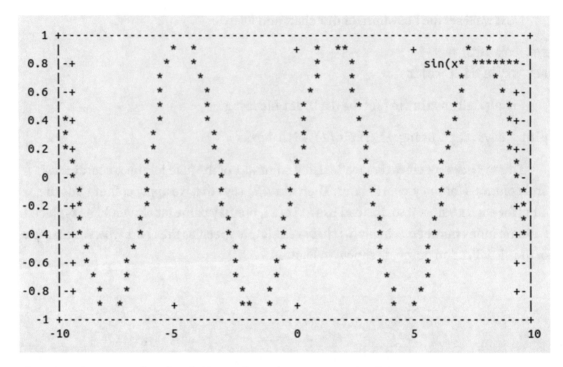

Figure 16-6. *gnuplot displaying a line chart in terminal*

Any equation can be graphed this way, for example, a simple equation representing a line with a slope of 5 with a y-intercept of 3 can be generated with plot 5*x + 3.

gnuplot to Image File

It's neat being able to display charts in the terminal, but in most cases, you're going to want to export charts as images which can be used to convey information in reports or presentations. In the same way we set gnuplot to use dumb mode, we can set it to export as an image file. Run the following to switch to png mode:

```
set terminal png
```

Next, you'll have to tell gnuplot where you want to output the image file; otherwise, you'll see the raw unprocessed png data on your screen, which isn't useful at all.

```
set output "graph.png"
```

Now, if we follow the exact same steps used to make our first bar chart, we'll end up with a "graph.png" file in our working directory. Each time you plot a graph to a file, you'll need to respecify the output file using the preceding command.

As we're no longer working in the terminal, you'll likely want to add some color to your charts. To do this, we'll modify our original plot command to

```
plot "days.dat" using 1:3:0:xtic(2) with boxes lc var
```

We're adding a new value in `1:3:0` which creates a new variable using the index; this variable is then used with `lc var` and incremented for each bar. The preceding command should produce something like in Figure 16-7.

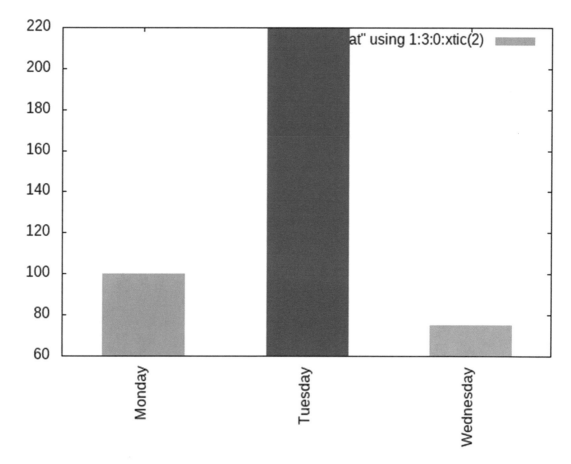

Figure 16-7. *gnuplot bar chart exported to an image file*

There are a variety of built-in color schemes including podo, `classic`, and `default`. To change the scheme, run the following replacing podo with the scheme you want:

```
set colorsequence podo
```

Advanced Examples/Demo Folder

We've looked at some basic examples of plotting data with `gnuplot` of plotting lines and bar charts. However, this is only a fraction of what `gnuplot` is capable of. The program can be used to create in-depth infographics. Doing this is out of the scope of this book, but we'll share a few examples from the `gnuplot` official demos folder: `https://github.com/gnuplot/gnuplot/tree/master/demo`. See Figures 16-8, 16-9, and 16-10 for examples of the demos contained. The code for these demos can be used as a starting point for plotting your own data.

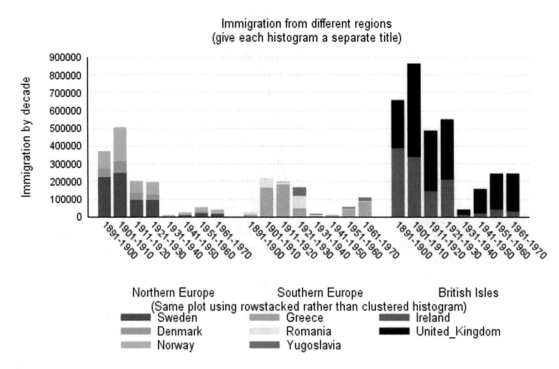

Figure 16-8. *gnuplot example chart histograms.8.gnu*

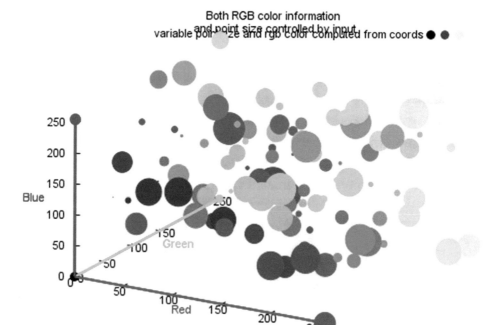

Figure 16-9. *gnuplot example chart rgb_variable.5.gnu*

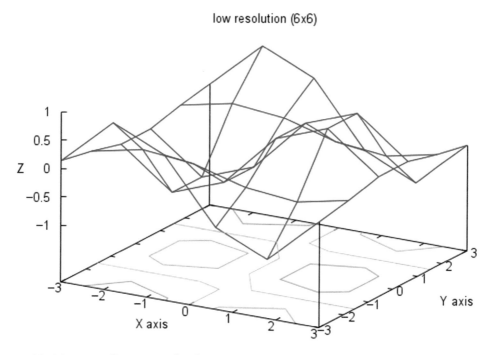

Figure 16-10. *gnuplot example chart contours.11.gnu*

Startup Animation

Another interesting modification we can make to our operating system is changing the default animation screen at startup time. In some cases, this can actually be useful to know, for example, if you're working on a custom embedded device or perhaps even a gaming unit and want to have a themed startup screen.

A good example is the open source theme PlymouthTheme-Cat (`https://github.com/krishnan793/PlymouthTheme-Cat`), which when installed and enabled will replace your default startup screen with an animated cat, shown in Figure 16-11.

Figure 16-11. *Custom startup animation*

Making use of this theme requires that your OS is using Plymouth. Plymouth is a package which provides a flicker-free graphical boot process and is installed by default on Debian- and Fedora-based distros.

First install the theme in your /usr/share/plymouth/themes; this can be done by cloning directly into the folder:

```
sudo git clone \ https://github.com/krishnan793/PlymouthTheme-Cat.git \
/usr/share/plymouth/themes/PlymouthTheme-Cat
```

With the theme successfully downloaded to your theme folder, you'll next want to install the theme:

```
sudo update-alternatives --install \ /usr/share/plymouth/themes/default.
plymouth default.plymouth \ /usr/share/plymouth/themes/PlymouthTheme-Cat/
PlymouthTheme-Cat.plymouth 100
```

Once installed, set it to your default by running

```
sudo update-alternatives --config default.plymouth
```

This should bring up a selection menu; enter the number for the option listing PlymouthTheme-Cat, as shown in Figure 16-12.

```
philip@philip-ThinkPad-T420:~$ sudo update-alternatives --config default.plymouth
There are 2 choices for the alternative default.plymouth (providing /usr/share/plymouth/themes/default.plymouth).

  Selection    Path                                                                      Priority   Status
------------------------------------------------------------
* 0            /usr/share/plymouth/themes/ubuntu-logo/ubuntu-logo.plymouth                 100       auto mode
  1            /usr/share/plymouth/themes/PlymouthTheme-Cat/PlymouthTheme-Cat.plymouth     100       manual mode
  2            /usr/share/plymouth/themes/ubuntu-logo/ubuntu-logo.plymouth                 100       manual mode

Press <enter> to keep the current choice[*], or type selection number: 1
```

Figure 16-12. *Selecting Plymouth theme to use*

Finally, you'll need to update the initramfs image. This is the image which runs on boot with the purpose of mounting the filesystem.

```
sudo update-initramfs -u
```

With this done, you can now restart your computer and enjoy the custom cat animation during the boot process.

Make a Custom Boot Animation

While the cat animation is definitely well done, you may want to make your own custom animation. The easiest way to experiment with making your own is to look at the source of Plymouth Cat. Notice that the source contains 111 sequential PNG files starting at `progress-0.png` and ending at `progress-111.png`. Sequentially viewed, these images create the animation.

If you'd like to create your own, the best place to start is by replacing these images with your own PNG files of the same dimensions and rerunning the steps used to install Plymouth Cat. This will result in an animation based on the images you provided.

Once you're happy with the results, you can update the values in `PlymouthTheme-Cat.plymouth` and rename the folder.

We won't go into the details of how to produce the image files, but applications like GIMP and Photoshop both support exporting an animation as several PNG files.

Summary

In this chapter, we looked at utilities that make it possible to work with images and videos without ever opening a bulky editor. This is great for common quick tasks like converting file types, adding watermarks, or trimming video and audio content. In some cases, as with gnuplot, we created new images using data, again without having to open an image editor.

Finally, we saw how the splash screen shown during the startup process is actually controlled by a program called Plymouth. We downloaded a simple animation and set it as our startup animation. This is a fun modification that can be useful when setting up custom-purpose hardware. For example, a Linux system that automatically boots into a video game emulator or multimedia box hooked up to your TV can be made to seem like a unique creation by adding a custom animation.

CHAPTER 17

Extras

We've looked at all kinds of commands and utilities throughout this book. Yet there are several handy commands which defy any category. In this final chapter, we'll look at fun or useful commands and utilities that don't necessarily fit into a category.

Cal

Another simple but useful command-line program is `cal` which provides a simple calendar via the command line. One of the great things about `cal` is that it comes installed standard on nearly all Linux distributions as it was present in the first edition of Unix and is part of POSIX standard. The simplest use of `cal` is running it without any flags or arguments, which just produces a visual of the month with the current day highlighted, as shown in Figure 17-1.

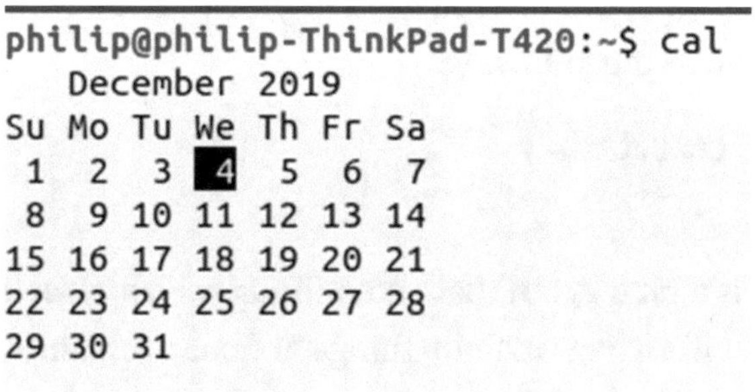

```
philip@philip-ThinkPad-T420:~$ cal
     December 2019
Su Mo Tu We Th Fr Sa
 1  2  3  4  5  6  7
 8  9 10 11 12 13 14
15 16 17 18 19 20 21
22 23 24 25 26 27 28
29 30 31
```

Figure 17-1. *Output of* `cal` *command*

To visualize the whole year, you can add the `-y` flag, which will produce a similar graphic but will show all the months in the current year formatted in month chunks like in the figure.

© Philip Kirkbride 2020

P. Kirkbride, *Basic Linux Terminal Tips and Tricks*, https://doi.org/10.1007/978-1-4842-6035-7_17

For the most part, that is the extent of my use of `cal`, a small program that I use surprisingly often. It does however also offer the ability to look at specific years or months, for example:

```
cal 2000      # display the year of 2000
cal june 2009 # display June of 2009
```

Looking back to the section on `.bashrc`, you might also consider adding a line which simply has `cal` to show a calendar highlighting the current day when you open your terminal – though personally I dislike the clutter that this adds.

espeak

If you're someone who likes to listen to text rather than read it, you'll really want to know about espeak. espeak takes text input and reads it as audio or outputs that audio to an audio file. The package can be found on the Ubuntu package manager.

```
sudo apt-get install espeak
```

After installing, the simplest thing you can do is pipe some text into `espeak` and listen to the audio directly on your machine.

```
echo Hello World | espeak
```

If instead of using a pipe, you instead want to provide a file containing text, you can use the `-f` flag as shown in the following:

```
echo Hello World > text.txt
espeak -f text.txt
```

The default voice is a bit flat, but that's something we'll look at improving in the next section. Some of the built-in flags include things like changing the speed. The speed is controlled by the `-s` flag which takes a value representing "words per minute" (*default 175*) and the `-g` flag which sets the gap between words in milliseconds (*default 10*). Below are examples of slow at 100 wpm and fast at 250 wpm:

```
echo hello world | espeak -s 100 -g 20 # slow
echo hello world | espeak -s 250 -g 5 # fast
```

Improve Sound of espeak Voice

The voice used by espeak can be drastically improved by installing voices from the open source speech engine MBROLA. Unfortunately, the website for MBROLA is no longer online; however, it can still be accessed along with the voice files using the Wayback Machine. To view information on the very outdated site, check out the following link:

https://web.archive.org/web/20180625050250/http://www.tcts.fpms.ac.be/ synthesis/mbrola/

To download and install MBROLA, run the following commands:

```
cd /tmp
wget \
https://web.archive.org/web/20180627172600/http://www.tcts.fpms.ac.be/
synthesis/mbrola/bin/pclinux/mbr301h.zip
unzip mbr301h.zip
sudo cp mbrola-linux-i386 /usr/bin/mbrola
```

Next we'll download the English voice files. If you want another language, you'll have to find the appropriate file using the archived MBROLA website. To install the English voices, run the following commands:

```
cd /tmp
wget \
https://web.archive.org/web/20160706052143/http://www.tcts.fpms.ac.be/
synthesis/mbrola/dba/en1/en1-980910.zip
unzip en1-980910.zip
sudo cp en1/en1 /usr/share/mbrola/en1
```

With MBROLA and the English voice installed, you can now select the voice using the -v flag as shown in the following (*slowing the speed to 120 words per minute is recommended*):

```
echo Hello World | espeak -v mb-en1 -s 120
```

Output espeak to Audio File

If you end up using espeak to convert large amounts of text, you'll likely want to output it as an audio file rather than having it play directly. This gives you the freedom to pause, play, and rewind as you wish – not to mention moving the file to other devices or sharing. An example of how this can be done is as follows (*we assume you have text in a file called* text.txt *in the same directory; if not, copy and paste some text from a web page into a text file*):

```
espeak -f text.txt -w audio.wav
```

Unfortunately, espeak only has the option to output as a wav file, so if you want mp3 or some other type, you'll need to run an additional command to convert using ffmpeg.

```
ffmpeg -i audio.wav -vn -ar 44100 -ac 2 -b:a 192k audio.mp3
```

Math on the Command Line

We've made use of bc in a few past chapters, but it's worth mentioning because it is often overlooked. The initials stand for basic calculator. It comes installed on most Unix-like operating systems, as it is a POSIX standard. It provides the ability to do math on the command line or write bc-specific scripts.

From the command line, bc is used by piping output from another command, for example:

```
echo 1 + 1 | bc
```

Running the preceding script will return an output of 2. There is support for the basic operations you'd expect on any calculator for addition, subtraction, multiplication, and division. In addition, you have some special commands, for example, to get the square root of a number:

```
echo "sqrt(169)" |  bc
```

Notice that when using any bc notation with a bracket, we need to surround it in quotes; this is to avoid bash interpreting it as a subshell. Another special command available in bc is length which returns the number of digits in a number:

```
echo "length(169)" |  bc
```

The preceding script returns 3. Similarly, there is a function scale which counts the digits to the right of a decimal place, for example, the following which returns 3:

```
echo "scale(169.777)" |  bc
```

Rather than using a pipe, it's also possible to start bc in an interactive mode. To do so, run it with the -l flag:

```
bc -l
```

In addition to being a command-line utility, bc can actually be used as a full scripting language which has support for C syntax for number manipulation and the creation of functions for code reuse.

Another command expr can also be found on many systems which evaluates math statements without the pipe. However, using expr isn't recommended as it is outdated:

```
expr 1 + 1
```

In the same vein, you'll also find dc on many systems which is also a reverse polish notation calculator which predates the C language.

Tiling Window Managers

Another class of applications that power users should look into are tiling window managers. A tiling window manager replaces the GUI interface for your Linux operating system (*gnome, xfce, lxde, etc.*) and provides a way to split your workspace up into tiles.

Tiling window managers are touted for their aiding in making OS use a completely mouseless process. Anything that could be done with a mouse is better done with a keyboard when using a tiling window manager. For this reason, tiling window managers are often promoted as a way of improving efficiency of command-line interface use.

Personally, I find that the usefulness of tiling window managers depends on the task at hand. If my workflow involves around a dozen different terminal sessions running at once, I'll always almost opt for a tiling window manager. If however my workflow involves a web browser, word editor, and a few terminal sessions, I'll instead opt for a normal desktop experience with my terminal sessions in tmux.

In the past, there were several different competing tiling window managers, but at current i3wm seems to be the most popular. While looking for popular alternatives, I found that i3wm was the only tiling window manager for Linux with a stable release in the last 12 months. For this reason, we'll focus on i3wm as the best and most common tiling window manager. If you're interested in researching additional window managers, some alternatives include "Awesome window manager," xmonad, dwm, and ratpoison.

i3wm excels at being able to quickly switch between terminal sessions and groups of terminal sessions. For example, I might have a page of terminals which are monitoring a system with various tools, creating a sort of dashboard. Then in another window, I might have some SSH sessions to different devices being tested.

If you're new to tiling window managers, I recommend installing it alongside a traditional desktop rather than as your only installed desktop interface. This will make things easier if you forget how to do something or are having difficulty doing some particular thing within i3wm. If that's the case, you can always switch back to Ubuntu Desktop (*or your chosen interface*) and come back to i3wm later.

i3wm can be installed simply on most Linux distributions by running the equivalent of the following on your package manager:

```
sudo apt-get install i3
```

With i3wm installed, log out or restart your computer. If you're on Ubuntu or Fedora, on the login screen, you should see a settings icon, as shown in Figure 17-2. After clicking the settings icon, a list of possible desktop interfaces should appear. Select the one labeled i3.

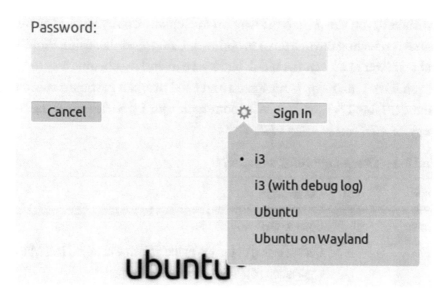

Figure 17-2. *Selecting i3 at the login screen*

On your first login with i3wm enabled, you'll be asked if you want to create a configuration file, as shown in Figure 17-3. We recommend using the defaults which will set the Windows key as the i3wm modifier key used for keyboard shortcuts. However, at the time of writing, we found that pressing <enter> and then choosing the default option while generating a config worked better than choosing <esc> which seems to be causing issues at this time.

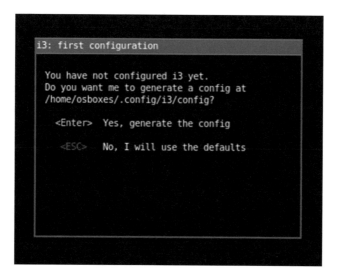

Figure 17-3. *i3 first configuration dialog box*

Once installed, you can switch to i3wm on most platforms by logging out and at the login screen selecting i3wm from a dropdown. Using i3wm like using Vim can be daunting at first. You're met with a blank black screen and no obvious way to open an application. Like Vim, i3wm is navigated and used through keyboard shortcuts and commands. Table 17-1 shows a list of commands for i3wm (*substitute the "win" or Windows key for alt if you've selected it*).

Table 17-1. *i3wm keyboard shortcuts*

Shortcut	Description
win+enter	Open a new terminal tile
win+d	Open a dialog at the top of the screen where you can type an application name and press enter to open it
win+j	Move focus one tile left
win+k	Move focus one tile down
win+l	Move focus one tile up
win+;	Move focus one tile right
win+shift+j	Move focused tile left
win+shift+k	Move focused tile down
win+shift+l	Move focused tile up
win+shift+;	Move focused tile right
win+f	Toggle between full-screen mode on focused tile
win+shift+q	Kill the focused tile
win+<number>	Switch to a workspace where <number> is any value between 0 and 9. Each number being a separate workspace with tiles
win+v	Next tile will split space vertically
win+h	Next tile will split space horizontally
win+r	Enter resize mode for tile. From here arrow keys can be used to expand or compact a tile either horizontally or vertically
win+shift+space	Toggle floating mode on a tile. Floating mode allows you to drag a window without concern for the grid
win+<mouse>	Drag a floating mode tile with your mouse

Creating Tiles

The most basic commands you'll want to learn first are for creating new tiles which is synonymous with opening applications, since all applications are contained in tiles on the window manager's grid. If you're opening a terminal, you can use win+enter. For all other applications, press win+d; this will open a small dialog in the top left, as shown in Figure 17-4.

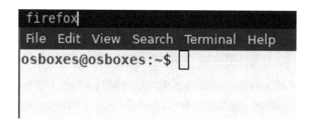

Figure 17-4. *i3 application search*

As you type the name of an application, the dialog will show the state of autocomplete, and if at any time it shows your target program, press open. This will open your application as a tile. An example of Firefox open as a tab along with two terminals is shown in Figure 17-5.

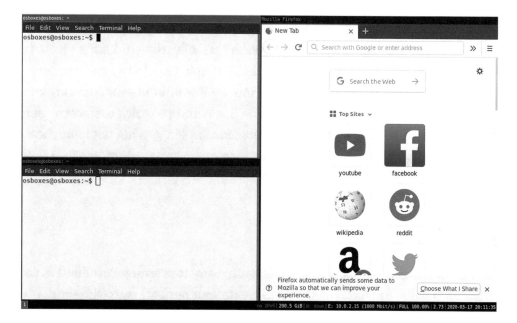

Figure 17-5. *i3 with multiple tiles open*

Opening additional applications will automatically create additional tiles in your workspace which will be distributed on the grid. As a consequence, program tiles will be resized as you add additional tiles. If your screen starts to get crowded and you need more space, you can make use of workspaces which we explain later. Or if you have tiles you no longer need, you can focus them and press win+shift+q.

Your workspaces will be numbered and displayed in the status bar at the bottom of the screen. In addition to your workspaces, the status bar shows basic information about the time, Internet connection, and free space.

By default, your tiles will split the current focused tab horizontally when adding a new one. To switch to vertical splitting, press win+v and your next created tiles will split vertically. To switch back to horizontal splitting, press win+h. Try experimenting by creating new tiles and switching between vertical and horizontal as well as deleting tiles with win+shift+q as needed.

Once you have a workspace, split into multiple tiles, you may want to resize a tile. If you press win+r, you'll go into resize mode for the highlighted tile where you can use the arrow keys to expand or shrink the tile. There is also an indicator in the status bar that will tell you when resize mode is active.

Change Tile in Focus

Now that you have multiple programs running as tiles in i3wm, you probably want to know how to switch between tiles. The tile you're currently using in i3wm is said to be in focus. If you want to change focus between tiles, just hold the win key and use the arrow keys to navigate your focus. You should see a thin outline around your currently focused window. Alternatively, you can use the letters – j, k, l, and ; – which each correspond to a direction. These keys are similar to the direction keys in Vim but not quite the same. If you want to modify these keys so that they're the same as Vim, see the section "Modifying i3wm Config File."

Move Tiles

In addition to changing your focus, you might also want to rearrange windows as you create additional tiles or resize those tiles to create your perfect setup. The shortcuts for moving tiles are nearly identical to that of moving focus except you need to hold both the

win and shift keys instead of just win. So to move right, you could do win+shift+right
arrow or win+shift+;. As mentioned, you can also resize a window. To enter resize
mode, press win+r while focused on the tile you want to resize. Once in resize mode, you
can use the arrow keys to expand or contract the tile.

Workspaces in i3wm

When you first open i3wm, you will see a small square in the bottom left which reads
"1". This number represents your current workspace. There are 10 workspaces on i3wm
numbered 1–9 and 0 as the tenth. You can switch between workspaces by pressing
win+<number> where <number> is any number between 0 and 9. Upon switching to a new
workspace, your screen will appear as a fresh i3wm instance with no tiles open.

So if you open four different tiles in workspace 1 and then switch to workspace 2,
you can create new tiles on a fresh layout and at any time switch back to workspace 1.
The programs within your workspaces will continue to run regardless of whether that
workspace is in focus.

Floating Tiles

While the tile grid system is essentially the core utility of i3wm, it is possible to create tiles
which exist outside of it and float overtop of everything else. To toggle a tile in and out of
float mode, put it in focus and press win+shift+space. Once the tile is in float mode, you
can hold win and drag it using your mouse. If you want to return the tile to the grid, press
win+shift+space again.

Full-Screen Mode

If you're working with a tile and you find it's too small, you can switch the tile into full-
screen mode temporarily and switch back when you're done. To switch to full-screen
mode on a tile, simply press win+f. To switch back out, press win+f while already in full
screen mode.

Modifying i3wm Config File

There are several settings and configurations that can be set by modifying the config file for i3wm. The default location for the configuration file is ~/.config/i3/config.

Bind Keys in i3wm Config

The most common thing you'll want to modify in i3wm is which keys are responsible for which functions. A common change people who are used to Vim keybindings like to make is remapping the keys for focusing tiles. This is done by using the bindsym keyword in your config file like in the following example:

```
bindsym $mod+h focus left
bindsym $mod+j focus down
bindsym $mod+k focus up
bindsym $mod+l focus right
```

If you decide to do this, you'll also need to remap the default use of $mod+h which is used to split windows horizontally. It's up to you as to what key you use for split horizontal, but in this example, we'll use "-", with the line as follows:

```
bindsym $mod+minus split h
```

Also search through the file for any existing bindings using the same key combinations, for example, "$mod+k"; if you find a duplicate, you'll need to remove one as each key combination can only be mapped to a single function.

After making a change to the i3 config file, you will need to reload it. To do that without restarting your system, run the following command:

```
i3-msg reload
```

In the preceding example, we mapped each of the Vim movement keys (*plus the modifier key "win" by default*). It's likely you'll also want to apply a similar change for moving the focused window as shown in the following:

```
bindsym $mod+Shift+h move left
bindsym $mod+Shift+j move down
bindsym $mod+Shift+k move up
bindsym $mod+Shift+l move right
```

You can also bind custom functionality to unused key combinations. For example, say we wanted a special key combination to open a new web browser window. We could add the line shown here:

```
bindsym $mod+shift+z exec "firefox"
```

Using the preceding pattern, you can map key combinations to any application or even your own custom scripts.

Change Colors in i3wm Config

As with other configuration files we've looked at in this book, the i3wm config file allows for modifying the theme and color of your interface. We won't look at every possible configuration, but the following configuration will help you get started; it's an example of modifying the status bar at the bottom of the screen by changing the color of various subelements (*make sure to replace your existing instance of bar in the config file or you'll end up with two status bars*).

```
bar {
        colors {
        background #2f343f
        statusline #2f343f
        separator #4b5262
        focused_workspace      #2f343f #bf616a #d8dee8
        active_workspace       #2f343f #2f343f #d8dee8
        inactive_workspace     #2f343f #2f343f #d8dee8
        urgent_workspacei      #2f343f #ebcb8b #2f343f
    }
    status_command i3status
}
```

Additionally, we can change the colors of the client itself (*the five-color hex codes should be contained on a single line*).

```
client.focused            #bf616a #2f343f #d8dee8 #bf616a #d8dee8
client.focused_inactive   #2f343f #2f343f #d8dee8 #2f343f #2f343f
client.unfocused          #2f343f #2f343f #d8dee8 #2f343f #2f343f
client.urgent             #2f343f #2f343f #d8dee8 #2f343f #2f343f
client.placeholder        #2f343f #2f343f #d8dee8 #2f343f #2f343f
client.background         #2f343f
```

i3status Config File

While most customizations to i3wm are made in the ~/.config/i3/config file, there is a second config file which deals exclusively with the status bar. The status bar–specific config file can be found at ~/.config/i3status/config. Not only does it allow you to change colors and style of the status bar, it also allows for changing which content is shown. *Note that this file doesn't exist by default.* For additional information on the status bar, you can run the following to see a status bar–specific man page:

```
man i3status
```

In this man page, you'll find an example config file which can be copied and used as the basis for a custom status bar. Notice that all the subcomponents of the status bar are first added to the variable called order which tracks what subcomponents to display and in what order.

```
order += "cpu_temperature 0"
order += "load"
order += "tztime local"
order += "tztime berlin"
```

Then further down, each of these subcomponents is described with curly brackets. For example, the "tztime berlin" component which displays Berlin time in addition to the system's local time is shown here:

```
tztime berlin {
        format = "%Y-%m-%d %H:%M:%S %Z"
        timezone = "Europe/Berlin"
}
```

In order to have a fully working config file, you'll also have to add the "tztime local" component which is defined here:

```
tztime local {
        format = "%Y-%m-%d %H:%M:%S %Z"
}
```

For the status bar changes to take effect, you'll need to fully restart i3 rather than simply running the reload command. You can restart i3 by running

```
i3-msg restart
```

You can find several components in the man page to get you started. If you're looking for additional resources for customizing i3wm and using as the basis for config files, I recommend searching "i3wm config github."

Alternative Shells

Before listing many of the alternative shells which are available, I want to note why I don't use any. Firstly, I like my default work environment to reflect that of what I might find in "the wild." That is, if I SSH into a machine or go to a company and use their server, I feel right at home assuming they're using standard bash. If I had gotten used to using an alternative shell, I would likely find myself trying to use shortcuts and commands which simply don't exist by default.

The second major reason is that many alternative shells are not POSIX compliant, meaning that scripts written specifically for one of these shells cannot be shared with the wider community. I prefer to use standard POSIX-compliant bash, knowing that almost everyone will be able to use the scripts written on my computer in their local environment.

That said, many others do prefer alternative shells for the usability or other benefits they might provide. If you're interested in exploring alternative shells, here are some worth checking out:

- Z Shell
- Fish

Z Shell

The most popular alternative shell is Z Shell or "ZSH." Z Shell is an extension of bash which has a focus on improving user experience. Some of the features of Z Shell include

- Smarter autocomplete.
- Git integration (*git status hints*).

- Smart SSH autocomplete based on ~/.ssh/config & ~/.ssh/known_hosts.

- File name correction when making a typo.

- Wide variety of themes.

- All cd use is actually pushd; thus you can always use popd.

- Other smart autocomplete.

- Has a POSIX-compliant mode (though not compliant by default).

This is by no means a complete list of features.

Oh My ZSH

We looked at "Oh My Bash" in Chapter 14; "Oh My ZSH" is essentially the same thing but for Z Shell. It contains several premade themes and configuration files specific to Z Shell. More information can be found at https://github.com/ohmyzsh/ohmyzsh.

Fish

The second most popular alternative shell is Fish. As with ZSH, the focus of Fish is improved user experience in the terminal. Some of the features include

- Autocomplete as your type (*which considers your command history*)

- Improved default color themes

- More interactive autocomplete with tab

- GUI-based configuration menu that can be accessed in the web browser

One of the differences, which is highlighted, when comparing Fish and ZSH is that ZSH requires configuration to enable many of its key features, whereas Fish is a more out-of-the-box experience. This focus on "ease of use" can also be seen in the inclusion of a web browser–based configuration menu that allows you to interactively change things like color themes.

Remapping Keys

As you start customizing your Linux system more and more, you might get to the point where you actually want to change the behavior of certain keys. For example, it's quite common to remap the use of Caps Lock to some other use due to the fact that it is not often used.

The first step in doing any type of remapping is getting the keycode for the button in question. The best way to do this is by running xev which will start an interactive mode where you press a button and in return receive a keycode; an example is shown in Figure 17-6.

```
     root 0x5b7, subw 0x0, time 462602, (-183,-118), root:(411,201),
     state 0x0, keycode 9 (keysym 0xff1b, Escape), same_screen YES,
     XLookupString gives 1 bytes: (1b) "▓"
     XFilterEvent returns: False

KeyPress event, serial 37, synthetic NO, window 0x3800001,
     root 0x5b7, subw 0x0, time 465938, (-363,-85), root:(231,234),
     state 0x0, keycode 66 (keysym 0xffed, Hyper_L), same_screen YES,
     XLookupString gives 0 bytes:
     XmbLookupString gives 0 bytes:
     XFilterEvent returns: False

KeyRelease event, serial 37, synthetic NO, window 0x3800001,
     root 0x5b7, subw 0x0, time 466111, (-363,-85), root:(231,234),
     state 0x2, keycode 66 (keysym 0xffed, Hyper_L), same_screen YES,
     XLookupString gives 0 bytes:
     XFilterEvent returns: False

FocusOut event, serial 37, synthetic NO, window 0x3800001,
     mode NotifyNormal, detail NotifyNonlinear

PropertyNotify event, serial 37, synthetic NO, window 0x3800001,
     atom 0x168 (_NET_WM_STATE), time 467790, state PropertyNewValue
```

Figure 17-6. *Finding keycodes using* xev

In this example, we'll remap the Caps Lock key (*keycode 66*). To edit the mapping, open up ~/.Xmodmap. This configuration file is responsible for modifying keyboard bindings. Add the following lines to map the Caps Lock key to the hyperkey.

clear capslock

```
keycode 66 = Hyper_L
```

The preceding configuration removes the Caps Lock key's normal use, sets it to hyperkey using its keycode, and makes the hyperkey a modifier button.

The hyperkey is a key which existed on an old keyboard called the space-cadet keyboard, shown in Figure 17-7. The space-cadet keyboard allowed the user to type over 8000 distinct characters using key combinations, such as the "Greek" key. The keyboard was influential on the design of Lisp and Emacs, and the "hyperkey" is still referenced in many places today, despite not being present on most, if any, keyboards.

Figure 17-7. Special keys on the historic space-cadet keyboard. Courtesy of Dave Fischer, Retro-Computing Society of Rhode Island, Wikimedia Commons, Creative Commons Attribution-Share Alike 3.0 Unported License

On most systems, modifying the ~/.Xmodmap file will be sufficient for remapping the Caps Lock to the hyperkey. After making the change, you'll need to either restart your system or reload the configuration manually. To reload manually, run the following command:

```
xmodmap ~/.Xmodmap
```

Now if you run xmodmap stand-alone without an argument, you should get back information about the special keys on your system. The "lock" row should have nothing in the second column, and for the row labeled "mod4", you should see a list of keys including "Hyper_L" at the end.

The "mod" here stands for modifier key, meaning it can be used in conjunction with other keys to create an output, much the same as "alt" and "ctrl" keys. This is important for the next section as it allows us to associate Caps Lock plus some other keys with custom commands or scripts.

Custom Shortcuts with Xbindkeys

Now that you've mapped your Caps Lock to hyperkey, you're probably wondering what you can do with it. The main use of swapping the Caps Lock for hyperkey is to gain an additional modifier key, similar to alt or ctrl. We can associate key combinations with programs, tasks, and scripts.

In the section on i3, we created a custom command for opening Firefox with win+shift+z. This is essentially the same idea, except we're using caps and don't need to use i3.

To make keyboard shortcuts, we first need to install xbindkeys:

```
sudo apt-get install xbindkeys
```

Next create a xbindkeys config file based on the default by running the following command:

```
xbindkeys --defaults > ~/.xbindkeysrc
```

Next open up the ~/.xbindkeysrc file and add the following line at the end of the file:

```
"firefox"
    Mod4 + f
```

The Mod4 here represents our hyperkey, since we associated the hyperkey (via caps) with mod4 in the previous section. So we're binding caps+f to open the Firefox browser. We can replace firefox with any other program in our path. For example, try adding the following code to your ~/.xbindkeysrc; after running it, check your /tmp folder and you should see a file called hello. You can replace the quotes with any command and associate it with whatever keyboard shortcut you'd like below:

```
"touch /tmp/hello"
      Mod4 + t
```

With the Caps Lock key freed up for custom shortcuts, you have dozens of possible key combinations you can make use of, and that's not even making use of combining the Caps Lock key with other modifiers like shift or alt.

Additional Resources

Additional resources I have found useful in exploring Linux terminal include

- http://unix.stackexchange.com/
- https://askubuntu.com
- https://linuxjourney.com/
- www.tldp.org/
- http://explainshell.com/
- www.linuxquestions.org/
- https://training.linuxfoundation.org/resources/
- https://google.github.io/styleguide/shell.xml

Summary

In this chapter, we looked at programs that can be used to take your terminal use one step further. We looked at the built-in cal command which can be found on almost any Linux system and allows you to get a quick overview of the coming year. We saw how espeak can be used to convert text into an audio file.

After that, we looked at the tiling window manager i3wm, alternative shells, and how you can modify your keyboard input to create dozens of custom keyboard shortcuts which map to programs or custom scripts.

Index

A

Alpine Linux, 11
Arch Linux, 5, 10
arp-scan method, 120
Artist mode
    adding labels, 259
    built-in package manager MELPA, 253
    canvas creation, 255
    chart made, 254
    nongraphical READMEs or manuals, 254
    pop machine text art, 260
    replacing + with v, 258
    text-based art or diagrams, 253
    two rectangles creation, 256, 257
    Vim bindings, 255
ASCII garble glitch, 97
atop, 151

B

bash keyboard shortcuts, 51
.bash_logout script, 276
bash prompt text, 280
.bashrc file, 31, 275, 276
    alias, 278
    ANSI color codes, 281
    color codes, 283
    configs, 278
    custom functions, 278, 279
    global version, 277
    import file, 288
    live clock, 286, 287
    $PATH, 279
    PS1 prompt, 280, 282
    PS2/PS3/PS4, 284, 285
    run programs, 287
    themes, 285
.bashrc_profile configuration script, 275

C

cal command, 333
Chain commands with && and ||, 64, 65
    cowsay program, 66, 67
    exit codes, 65
Conditional expressions
    arithmetic operators, 75
    -d flag, 71
    double equal sign ==, 74
    -e flag, 72
    -eq flag, 76
    -f flag, 71
    -ge flag, 78
    -gt flag, 77
    -le flag, 77
    -lt flag, 76
    -ne flag, 76
    non-empty strings, 74
    options, 71

Printed in the United States
By Bookmasters